Authentic Learning

How Learning about the Brain Can Shape the Development of Students

Michael L. Slavkin

Rowman & Littlefield Education
Lanham • New York • Toronto • Oxford
2004

This title was originally published by ScarecrowEducation. First Rowman & Littlefield Education edition 2005.

Published in the United States of America
by Rowman & Littlefield Education
A Division of Rowman & Littlefield Publishers, Inc.
A wholly owned subsidiary of The Rowman & Littlefield Publishing Group, Inc.
4501 Forbes Boulevard, Suite 200, Lanham, Maryland 20706
www.rowmaneducation.com

PO Box 317
Oxford
OX2 9RU, UK

British Library Cataloguing in Publication Information Available

Library of Congress Cataloging-in-Publication Data

Slavkin, Michael L., 1971–
   Authentic learning : how learning about the brain can shape the development of students / Michael L. Slavkin.
      p. cm.
   Includes bibliographical references (p.   ) and index.
   ISBN 1-57886-094-6 (pbk. : alk. paper)
   1. Problem-based learning. 2. Motivation in education. 3. Brain—Research.
I. Title.
LB1027.42 .S52 2004
370.15'23—dc22

                                                                2003022279

∞™ The paper used in this publication meets the minimum requirements of American National Standard for Information Sciences—Permanence of Paper for Printed Library Materials, ANSI/NISO Z39.48-1992.
Manufactured in the United States of America.

Contents

Acknowledgments

There are a number of people I must thank as I finalize the process of writing this text. First, I offer special thanks to my wife Heidi, son Jacob, and daughter Emma for their support, encouragement, and especially their humor as I sat down to write. Special thanks also to my parents, students, and colleagues for their belief in my abilities.

Several people assisted in the development of this text. Although they are by no means the only support I have had in writing *Authentic Learning*, they have definitely been instrumental in nurturing the ideas and text found within this binding. Thank you to Melba Wilderman for taking the time as a principal to reflect on empowering teachers to reconsider what learning means. The chapter on integrated thematic units wouldn't be the same without your creativity and inspiration.

Thanks to the preservice teachers from Educational Assessment in the summer of 2003 at the University of Southern Indiana. Mandy Baker, Andrew Ball, Stacy Corn, Christina Freitag, Stephanie Geraci, Kristen Haas, Beth Hill, Lisa Hinton, Staci Kinman, Lucky Long, Crystal Loposser, Jason Lowe, Sarah Lueken, Abbi Mann, Ashley Mitchell, Amy Siebert, Erin Smith, Laura Thorne, and Candi Williams were instrumental in shaping the research and text involved in the chapters on problem-based learning, service learning, brain-based education, democratic classrooms, and standards-based practices. They helped to confirm that authentic methods have a place in all classrooms and demonstrated that the twenty-first century will be a powerful one for teachers in early childhood and elementary classrooms.

Thank you to Jonathan Plucker for his support and encouragement while I was a graduate student at Indiana University and for giving me the chance to begin this journey into authentic teaching through F401: "Enhancing Creativity and Debunking Myths." The experience has been one of the most rewarding of my academic career, and I am grateful for the opportunity to share some of our work on creativity here.

Finally, thank you also to LeeAnn McCarty of the Evansville Christian School and Tricia Anderson of the Evansville Vanderburgh School Corporation for allowing me to use portions of their thematic units. Readers will appreciate your innovation and determination in empowering students! Bravo to such expert educators!

Chapter One

Daniel Reconsidered

It would be simple to describe the premise of this book as the flight of a concerned educator, struggling to help parents, preservice teachers, and inservice teachers understand how knowledge of the brain can impact the development of a child. I could review how experience has shown that teachers and classrooms, principals and teachers, and parents and their children are apt to follow the paths taken by their own educators and parents: largely authoritarian, teacher/parent-centered, and with adults dominating children. I also could share how the 1990s, titled the "Decade of the Brain" by the U.S. Department of Education, were to be a decade where science and developmental information would challenge educators and parents alike to reconsider these methods and move into a new century and millennium with innovation and creative approaches to bettering ourselves and our children. Ah, it *would* be too simple.

Instead, in reality I am driven to write this book and continuously to share this information with my students, my preservice teachers, and the inservice teachers I work with because I am a father and a developmentalist. I, too, often have seen what occurs when children are not given the chance to explore their world. I have met families that question why their children have difficulty learning, only to hear these words spoken by people who were denied an education or lifestyle that provided literacy, questioning, and a dialogue of interesting subjects. If we recognize anything after studying how children develop and learn, it is that children's abilities are strengthened by their parents and significant caregivers, who hopefully interact and assist with providing them with unique experiences.

1

THINKING ABOUT DANIEL,
OR DANIEL RECONSIDERED

While working for a residential placement facility in Indiana during the 1990s, I had the opportunity to work with a child named Daniel. Daniel is a clear example of why educators need to recognize the role of authentic learning in the growth of a child. Daniel was a bright, inquisitive, and exceptionally interesting seven-year-old. His love of animals and of dinosaurs was infectious. He showed a clear determination and dedication to certain activities, but school and learning were not part of them. Despite Daniel's interest in his world and his intellectual potential, he demonstrated the reverse in school and at home. To anyone who had just met him, Daniel would be classified as a deviant who hated to learn.

Daniel arrived at the inpatient psychiatric program where I worked after he assaulted his second-grade teacher. His teacher shared that Daniel was precocious from the moment he walked into her classroom. Overwhelming, energized, challenging, and frustrating were the words she used to describe him. Daniel was a precocious student—always in trouble and not often on task. His teachers often complained about his behavior and rarely were interested in working with him (teachers tended to spend most of their time corralling his actions). In fact, I worked with Daniel after he had threatened his teacher with a pair of scissors when he had failed to get the attention he requested in class. Daniel was not an easy student.

Daniel couldn't read: it wasn't that he lacked the motivation; he was clearly desperate to learn the skills that would assist him in understanding the written word. In fact, it was essential—Daniel had been teased by peers throughout second grade because he was unable to read aloud whenever the teacher called on him (a cruel practice, and one that isn't recommended for any classroom). Though he was determined to learn to read, Daniel didn't have an environment at home that fostered literacy: his parents didn't enjoy reading and a limited supply of age-appropriate books was available to him and his siblings.

Daniel's learning challenges and his behavioral concerns were the least of his problems. Daniel acted much better at school than he did at home. Most of the time, Daniel was responsible for watching over his four younger siblings (remember, Daniel was seven years old when he was referred to us). His father was absent and hadn't been involved in his life for years. Daniel's mother worked two jobs to support her family on second and third shift, so she didn't often see them during the week. Daniel and his siblings stayed with a grandmother after school, three blocks away from his family's apartment, and only went home after his mother arrived home at 6:30 in the morning. Because of the poor health of his grandmother, Daniel and his siblings were allowed to have their run of the neighborhood, and few limitations were placed on the children.

Though the situation described above is one that may be unfamiliar to many of the parents reading this book, it is a common occurrence in the classrooms of today. Teachers are required to be both educators and parental figures, filling in for too many students who arrive in schools unprepared for learning or interacting with others. Oftentimes, these learning-challenged students lack parental support, have had limited experience with literacy or problem solving, and don't know how to socialize with other children their age. These students not only have had limited experience with learning, thinking about difficult situations, and solving problems, but also have limited experience in environments that require them to work through problems. Yet, teachers are expected to prepare all of their students for achieving at grade-appropriate levels, while working on basic skills that are required for standard learning to occur, skills that should have been taught years before they arrived at the schoolhouse doors.

LEARNING AND THINKING IN A TWENTY-FIRST-CENTURY WORLD

As the twenty-first century begins, many communities find themselves questioning the role of schools and the community's expectations of parents, students, and teachers. Increasingly, educators struggle to convince administrators, parents, students, and community members that the schools have strengthened teaching strategies and that students are doing better than in years past. Yet, teachers consistently share their concerns about the lack of parent and community involvement in education. Parents indicate their desire to improve the connections between the classroom and the surrounding environs, but are unsure how to go about initiating such relationships. If students are to meet their potentials and excel in to-day's classrooms, a number of things must occur prior to their entrance into elementary school. Parents and teachers should be working together to improve the ties between the community and their schools. This text reviews ways these two groups can work together to create meaningful learning experiences at home with schools that meet the needs of students, teachers, parents, and community members.

THE NEEDS OF STUDENTS: MOTIVATION AND FEELINGS OF EMPOWERMENT

Many students (as well as parents) today feel emotionally disconnected from learning. Students feel marginalized from the power and the culture of learning and, as such, are less likely to participate as school citizens or members of the school community. Educators and parents concerned with their school cultures need to ask themselves, When was the last time I listened to a student share his or her ideas, beliefs, and feelings? If used effectively, this form of communication can increase students' involvement within the school community, motivation, and feelings of empowerment. Further, such attention to motivation and empowerment helps to strengthen the learning of students and, as we will see, is a key factor in authentic learning.

The nature of cognition, the development of the brain, student motivation, and students' feelings of empowerment are inherently tied to one another. Teachers can help students to learn most effectively if they (1) create opportunities for students to relate material to their personal lives, (2) provide an environment that reveals the multiple meanings of material, and (3) allow students to see the dynamic nature of information. Throughout this text I may refer to this as authentic pedagogy, but in other forums it has simply been referred to as effective practice, "best practice," or developmentally appropriate practice (DAP). Regardless of the name, some key practices that can assist students in becoming empowered members of the school community include the following:

- Students, parents, and teachers share responsibility for learning.
- Teachers, parents, principals, administrators, and community members help students by guiding the practice of learning, not by instilling only one core of knowledge.

- Teachers and parents create assignments and activities that encourage their students to reflect upon the classroom and their school community, helping to foster reflective practice, as well as encouraging them to improve their citizenry.

Teachers and parents are likely to see the implications of authentic learning when it has been absent during the early years of a student's life. The child lacks the interest to learn, isn't curious about his or her world, and lacks the social and behavioral skills to pursue information building. If children are to be expected to learn, they must have adults who (1) model how important it is to learn and (2) develop an environment that exposes children to a variety of experiences and inquiries.

PURPOSE OF THIS TEXT

As a father, teacher, counselor, and developmentalist, I know that the goal of any adult who works with kids is to connect with all children. Parents want to create a home environment that is loving, supportive, nurturing, and provides whatever their kids need to maximize their potential. Teachers have the same goals for their classroom settings, based on my experience as a student and a professor who teaches teachers how to teach. Both groups want to help kids to recognize that what they learn now can have direct consequences on whom they become tomorrow. Educators strive to create environments that are meaningful and interesting to students (I will refer to parents, teachers, counselors, and administrators with this global term, *educators*, as all of them are involved in fields that challenge growth and development through education of some sort.

It is my hope that, in writing this book, I might synthesize several fields, bringing together what we know about the morphology of the brain and cognitive psychology, yet do so in a way that is accessible to those who work the front lines: teachers in the field and parents wanting what is best for their kids.

Authentic Learning provides laypeople and educational professionals the opportunity to understand that best practices, constructivism, student-centered practices, student choice, and democratic classrooms are effective because they result in a variety of environmental experiences. Such experiences have often been thought to be the environmental foundation that supports and nurtures a creative and challenged brain: guiding children to think in a variety of ways, providing the flexibility of thought that is critical in the twenty-first-century world.

The nature of cognition, the functioning of the human brain, and the construction of knowledge are tied to one another. Neural scientists and educators are identifying how an understanding of the ways students learn most effectively can improve pedagogy and increase the potential of students of all ages.

HOW LEARNING RELATES
TO AUTHENTIC PRACTICES

Students learn as the brain develops, which is a direct result of interactions with the environment (Sylwester, 1994). Information that is to be functional to the learner must be explored and interpreted a number of times before neural pathways can be hardwired for long-term use. As is similarly found in Howard Gardner's theory of multiple intelligences, information that is to be remembered by learners should be represented in multiple ways, so as to stimulate multiple neural networks and multiple areas of the brain simultaneously. Information also is better held over time if it is personalized in some way or if the information is closely connected with prior knowledge held by the learner. Information and the cognition that supports it now are being reinterpreted as reflexive, plastic, and dynamic, an interconnected and interdependent network, with a whole that is seen as being greater than the organized singularities (Donald, 1991; Wolfe and Brandt, 1998).

Thus, the step-like stages of Jean Piaget and the computer model of cognitive information processing are proving too simplistic in understanding the functions of human learning. In essence, there is a dynamic dance between the learner's brain and knowledge, each interacting to evolve and make sense within the contexts defined by the learning environment (Burke, 1997; Kosslyn and Koenig, 1992). If learning is a dynamic dance that moves in multiple steps, then the theories of Piaget and cognitive information processing are like dancing the two-step of country music: relatively simplistic, reductionist, and rote in functioning (not to malign either country music or the long-loved two-step). Constructivism and sociocultural theory, with their focus on dynamic and inductionist methods, serve as a creative mambo, ever evolving and including collaboration between individuals to grow into a more enriched product than would have been possible with only the dance steps of the individual (Burke, 1997; Caprio, 1994; Resnick, 1987).

A curriculum based on authentic learning could look much like the curriculum that already exists in many classrooms and schools, but with subtle variations. However, such pedagogy would provide the opportunity for children to show what they know, collaborate with each other on projects, incorporate thematic curriculums, provide opportunities for reflection, and create goal-based learning opportunities that build upon each other over the school year. Schooling could begin to take on the nature of an apprenticeship, providing experiences that will nurture well-rounded, functional professionals who can reflect on tasks and the reality of the professional environment—one that is ever changing and ever diversifying. Wouldn't children be better prepared for a technologically advanced society if they were given skills rather than information, goals rather than instructions, practical knowledge rather than organized information (also see Languis, 1998; Resnick, 1987)?

As will be identified in this text, the classroom environment, the curriculum, and the learner are interdependent. It would make sense that learners would function better in environments that are intriguing, provide multiple sensory experiences, and involve dynamic problems without singular answers. It seems relatively simple to suggest that teachers instruct in an environment that provides real-world problems that afford children the opportunity to collaborate and work with information in personal and individual ways. As stated by Robert Sylwester, "Educators might then view the [curriculum] as an ecological problem . . . which integrates complex environmental stimuli, and de-emphasizes basic skills and forms of evaluation that merely compress complexity" (1994, 48).

Authentic pedagogy should be an alternative perspective to the theories discussed in a majority of teacher education programs (most often students are taught to focus on Piaget's cognitive developmental model, which is limiting when working with children). As a theory and set of classroom methods, authentic pedagogy has been making waves in the field of education. If authentic pedagogy could be summed up in one sentence, it would be, "Knowledge should be socially created."

Like social constructivists, authentic educators believe that knowledge is constructed based on social experience and community interaction. Some useful suggestions offered by authentic educators include the following (see Burke, 1997; Caprio, 1994; Wolfe and Brandt, 1998; Woolfolk, 1998):

- *Useful knowledge may not be accurate knowledge*. Teachers need to be involved in ensuring that children review material accurately and in a useful manner. For example, children at a local graduation examination center were working on a problem-based project, the goal of which was to identify creative ways that the crew of the R.M.S. *Titanic* might have saved more passengers. Their instructor assisted them in identifying resources that would help them formulate hypotheses, rather than resources that would give away the answer. Once students learned how to research the topic, they were able to find creative solutions to the problem at hand.
- *Skills are closely tied to the learning situation and are difficult to apply to new settings*. To get children to generalize to other settings often takes practicing in those settings. As such, teachers need to provide opportunities for children to apply learned information and practice complex behaviors in the naturally occurring settings. Such activities take the shape of practicums, providing performance-based practice in career-related settings.
- *Authentic pedagogy should be built upon complex, authentic tasks, similar to miniature apprenticeships*. Students at Parkway West Senior High School in St. Louis, Missouri, who were completing their graduation equivalency degree (GED) requirements created internships in potential postgraduation jobs, where they were allowed to apply the information from the curriculum toward their daily activities. Assessment of achievement occurred with a portfolio that organized, represented, and applied the information to the site.
- *Children and teachers should share responsibility for learning*. Rather than organizing the learning of his children, Jeff Ford of Wayne Township Schools in Indianapolis, Indiana, had them create individual units related to their personal and professional interests. By empowering the students to guide their learning actively, Mr. Ford helped them to see the interrelatedness of the core subjects and how each might impact

their career performance (as well as get them interested in learning for the sake of learning).

- *There are multiple ways of looking at material.* No one way of examining information is necessarily correct, although accuracy does need to be considered. Sometimes authentic instruction errs on the side of being too flexible and too independent (Bruer, 1997). Primary and intermediate teachers who use authentic curriculums would be wise to concentrate on a standard curriculum that provides the flexibility and opportunity to be individually organized and situated in a number of activities and assignments.
- *Instruction is based on that which is good for the students in that situation.* Authentic instruction, like all good teaching, gives students and teachers the chance to work together to find effective ways of organizing learning. As such, both must be involved in ensuring that learning occurs and that information is applied practically.

An authentic approach to learning would be one where, through a process of social negotiation (group meeting), the teacher and student review individual and group responsibilities, discuss the value of multiple representations for a single concept, and emphasize the importance of process over getting the correct answer (Dozier, 1992; Sylwester, 1994; Wolfe and Brandt, 1998).

Although authentic practice is believed to make the information more meaningful in the long run, some problems exist. For example, multiple representations do not mean that all representations are equal. Some ideas can be better than others. Also, the simple fact of a teacher putting children within groups designed to "socially construct" some piece of information does not mean that the processing of information will follow. Some amount of trust and interaction needs to exist. Groups must be held accountable for their own practices and mature enough to consider the responsibility of being in charge of their own learning. Finally, some children often value quick process over long-term learning. Children must be shown the dynamic nature of information and how interesting the classroom can become if children take an active role in shaping the environment and the nature of the curriculum (Edelman, 1989; Nummela and Caine, 1998).

Beyond needing to understand the nature of cognition or brain development, teachers look for suggestions in helping children to become involved in the classroom. Over the course of my experiences in teaching preservice and inservice teachers, teachers have indicated that the following suggestions have been of assistance in creating a functional classroom that is interesting to both children and teachers:

- *Be open to perceiving new information about children and looking at them as individuals and in unique ways.* If the curriculum is to be individually based, take the time to recognize your students as individuals and incorporate their strengths into activities.
- *Provide a multidimensional classroom/work environment.* Provide children with opportunities to work on a variety of different tasks using different materials at the same time.
- *Evaluate students privately.* Provide students with critical reviews of assignments that can guide future practice and hone learning skills, but ensure that assessment strategies emphasize growth and steady change over time, rather than the constant need for high achievement.
- *Effective evaluation of individual learners requires both norm-referenced and criterion-referenced assessment.* However, be sure that students are aware of the differences between the two forms of measurement and why it is important to use both.
- *Ask open-ended questions about students' abilities from the beginning of a unit.* When assessing them, ask questions like, What can you tell me about yourself? Why is this important?"
- *Listen attentively to what children say.* Too often we fail to accept that students might be expert in some areas that are weak for us. Providing them the chance to organize and educate others may be a motivating factor in their own growth.
- *Help children identify their own abilities, strengths, and potentials.* Be sure that children participate in assessment strategies, so that metacognitive skills are improved, and they have the opportunity to see growth over the course of a class.
- *Help children feel competent in multiple areas.* Motivating students to be their best in several subjects helps children to feel responsible for learning and become adept at seeing the interrelatedness of curricular subjects. Providing opportunities for choice, initiative, and autonomy will help to ensure that students maximize their potential.

- *Provide new challenges and provide comments on positive attempts.* Children are more likely to learn when they are challenged and are provided with novel situations. By giving students a variety of different experiences, we grant them the chance to think about all of the many ways that learning can be unique. Further, when they identify a novel situation when information or skills might be used, such "teachable moments" should be supported and encouraged.
- *Teach strategies to accomplish tasks, not just factual information.* As with the example of the group who worked on the R.M.S. *Titanic* activity, students need to be instructed in procedural and declarative knowledge (D'Arcangelo, 1998; also see Woolfolk, 1998; Wolfe and Brandt, 1998).

IMPORTANCE FOR FUTURE PRACTICE AND CRITICAL DISCUSSION

Teachers need to realize that their implicit ideas about the construction of the mind and the construction of the classroom affect their perceptions and those of children. D. Cunningham states,

> If learning is best conceived, not as learning and remembering information, but as connections with and within communities of practice, then we will come to give full value to the collaborative nature of cognition, investigate the role of culture and community more thoroughly, and provide better opportunities for nurturing these connections. (1999)

It has become clear that our perceptions of the roles of teachers and learners have implications for our practice within the contexts of the classroom. Teachers need to be aware that there is an ongoing evolution of meaning that is made regarding the relationships between learners, teachers, and the curriculum. This awareness can become an intentional element of the curricular process.

The impact of the classroom meaning-making process and the role that implicit theories of cognition play in changing the nature of the classroom have implications for the metacognition and actualization of children. Teachers are to help learners to become competent and critical thinkers by being aware of how theories of cognition and effective pedagogies can assist them in maximizing the potential of their pedagogy.

Teachers can help children learn more effectively if educators create opportunities for students to relate the curriculum to their personal lives, provide an environment that reveals the multiple meanings of material, and allow children to see the dynamic nature of information.

REVIEW OF CHAPTERS

The remainder of this book highlights how an understanding of authentic learning can improve children's performance in the classroom and children' interest in learning and ability to learn. Research has shown that if students relate the curriculum to their personal lives, they are more likely to see the dynamic nature of information. Children also may be more likely to identify the multiple meanings of material.

Chapter 2: Development and the Brain

Much of the review from this chapter will be based on the article I wrote for the National Association of Secondary School Principals, "Brain Science in the Classroom" (2003a). The chapter reviews the pioneers in the field: Marian Diamond's (1988; Diamond and Hopson, 1999) work on the physiology of the brain, Mark Rosensweig and Edward Bennett's (1977) research on learning and brain morphology, as well as some of the current thinkers in the field who have written previously on this subject: Robert Sylwester, John Bruer, and Maurice Donald. I will supply information that is current in its approach, but I would like to write this chapter as a parent and teacher, using language and wording that makes the subject recognizable (as if to say, See! Some of the things you were doing were authentic and very effective, and you weren't even aware of it!).

Chapter 3: Brain-Based Learning

Chapter 3 reviews facets of brain-based learning and theories of cognition that relate to the morphology of the human brain. Learning environments in homes and schools need to be organized to provide for very specific behaviors and actions. Again, a review of the old model of schools will occur, along with suggestions for home and school environments: how they should be constructed, what they should include, and what behaviors should be seen to confirm that learning is occurring.

Chapter 4: Developmentally Appropriate Practices

Chapter 4 introduces readers to the notion of DAP. It will continue to rely on information drawn from chapter 2, but apply it to learning by suggesting that learning requires connecting prior knowledge to present information. Moreover, in order for learning to be dynamic and appropriate for the demands of today's market and technology-driven economy, we must begin to differentiate between knowledge-based learning and skills-based learning. Teachers and parents today should be less concerned with what their children know and more interested in their ability to find information and organize it to create something new.

Chapter 5: Problem-Based Learning

This chapter will review the current ideas surrounding problem-based learning (PBL), a pedagogical strategy that has largely been found in the medical and business fields. The theory will be reviewed, as will three of the applications of this theory, with case examples of how PBL and experiential education have transformed our understanding of the role of schools and community involvement in our children's education.

Chapter 6: Learning through Themes

One of the strongest concepts involved in brain-based education is working with children to understand how concepts and skills are interconnected. By recognizing how ideas are related through themes, youth can better recognize the implications for learning and later development. This chapter will provide an opportunity for parents and teachers to consider the importance of prior knowledge and the notion that prior experience helps guide children in future learning. With future pursuits in mind, then, it is critical that teachers provide opportunities in the classroom that mirror what children do outside of school. This chapter also includes examples of teacher practices and parent practices that make learning interesting for children through themes.

Chapter 7: Learning through Service

Much of effective pedagogy requires that students be active and involved in making decisions in the classroom. Student-centered practices, student power, and democratic strategies will be blended with brain-based terminology to demonstrate the parallels between effective teacher practice, brain-based pedagogy, and service learning.

Chapter 8: Democratic Classrooms

Democratic classrooms create an environment where all individuals involved in the education process have a part in decisions made that involve the students and classroom. The decisions should be reached in a democratic fashion. Every student in every classroom should have the capability to achieve high standards and be successful without hurting anyone else's opportunity to achieve (McDermott, 1999). As such, democratic methods of instruction encourage student learning and development through active participation in thoughtfully organized service that is conducted in, and meets the needs of, a community. Such practices provide teachers and students the opportunity to learn about civic responsibilities while supporting the needs of the community through active dialogue with community partners. Demonstrating the real-world implications of information reviewed and the action involved in learning enhances the academic curriculum. This chapter reviews the implications of such practices on the future of education.

Chapter 9: Enhancing Creativity: Learning for the Twenty-First Century

Chapter 9 describes an approach to creativity enhancement that is being applied and evaluated with students at a number of nontraditional and innovative schools. The model is largely based on the belief that creativity suffers in light of the preponderance of myths and stereotypes about learning that limit the potential of classrooms and students. Creativity appears to be an important component of problem solving and other higher cognitive abilities. This chapter debunks some of the myths surrounding creativity; practicing problem-solving tasks and coordinating reflexive thinking around specific areas of expertise can improve students' abilities to utilize their creativity.

Chapter 10: Where Do We Go Now? (Not Conclusions, Further Opportunities)

The book's conclusion will rest on the notion that teachers and parents who have read its pages will begin to consider altering their practices. The final chapter serves as a call to arms, challenging them to begin the steps needed to remodel their communities, schools, and homes to create stronger learning opportunities for their children.

Chapter Two

Development and the Brain

Before we can consider discussing how the brain develops and how it is organized, we must first understand the importance of the brain as it relates to who we are. The brain is so unlike any other part of the human body that to divide it up into its separate parts neglects its purpose and functionality. The brain is not only the control center of the entire human body, organizing our behaviors and biological functions, but it also is the seat of our humanity. It defines who we are, how we act, and the very nature of our species. Without the brain's power and integrated functions, we could not begin to understand ourselves, to have metacognitive functions (to know what it is to know about our own thinking).

Human beings are in a very unique position as a species. We may be one of the few creatures ever to inhabit this planet with the ability to evaluate our own growth and learning. As such, human beings have recognized the importance of modifying our environments to help us adapt and develop. Further, human beings can improve their learning and their growth by modifying their environments; what an extreme evolutionary opportunity for a species to be in the position to enrich its environment in order to strengthen its potential in the future! Educators and developmentalists understand that in order to maximize the abilities and opportunities of individuals over time and over generations, all children must be granted certain types of environments and experiences if they are to be in a position to succeed.

The human brain is also unlike any other organ because, as we develop and interact with our surroundings, it radically changes. Not only does its physical form change, but its functions change—it adapts to its environments, modifying how it works and what it does in order to meet the needs defined by the environment. No other organ can so actively and purposefully redefine itself in order to meet both our genetic and environmental needs. And although we start this discussion with a dichotomy between the genetic and the environmental, when it comes to looking at how the brain develops and works, the dichotomy is a false one. Rather than considering what the environment's impact is or how genetics factor into the development of the brain, it is better to see nature and nurture as two sides of the same coin. As such, nature and nurture cannot be separated and must be considered simultaneously in order to recognize their influence on learning. A better analysis may involve a different question, a question that sees learning as a process rather than an end product: What is development? In order to know how we can improve the learning of students (as a process and not a product), we must first understand what development is. Only then can teachers, parents, and researchers begin to recognize the full impact of the human brain.

DEVELOPMENT: THEORIES AND CONTEXTS

What is development? This question has plagued, and continues to plague, developmentalists since the beginning of the discipline. A simplistic response is that development is the scientific study of changes in a human being's biological, social, cognitive, and emotional behavior from conception until death. Though this definition is given, it is by no means complete (see Neugarten, 1976—development means everything, and so it is nothing). Development is a lifelong process, and development typically relates to relatively permanent change overtime.

Positions over the past century have varied in the context of the questions asked by the field. Charles Darwin's evolutionary perspective and the biological bases of behavior were primary themes during the beginning of developmental theory. Darwin's model emphasized the idea that species grow over time through enriched experiences with their surroundings: those with good environment-species fits tended to do well; those without strong supporting environments died off (very similar notion to our earlier example of Daniel in chapter 1, no? Without the proper fit in his classroom environment, Daniel struggled rather than evolved).

As many in education and as my parents and their parents will tell you, much of the twentieth century was guided by a vastly different theory of how we learn, grow, and develop: that theory was called behaviorism. Behaviorism states that children were raised to be vessels to fill with information, completed by successive reinforcements with rewards, gifts, bribes, stickers, candies, and other external reinforcers.

Teachers and parents got really good at recognizing subversive ways at modifying children's behaviors and thoughts, though the learning and the functioning of these kids were often simplistic behaviors and simplistic notions. Learning was nothing more than input driven—provide successively harder and challenging information to children and reinforce it enough, and the children will learn. (This pattern of thinking about learning as an end product, rather than a process, continues in our government's most recent attempts to quantify education through standardized testing: input in, output out = learning.) As educators have better understood what it means to learn and develop, we also have recognized that these mechanistic approaches from behaviorism were weak and inefficient. Though reinforcers work well with simple behaviors and simple ideas, stickers and gold stars fail when it comes time for children to think in an advanced manner or behave in complex ways (perhaps this is why our simplistic norm-referenced, standardized tests with their emphasis on superficial learning often don't measure what we are attempting to do in schools?).

Perhaps we can't easily quantify what output learning should be, and doesn't this make sense? Why should all students be expected to learn in the same way and in the same patterns? If children arrive in schools having had vastly different home experiences with different expectations placed upon them by their communities, wouldn't an education that diversified instruction to meet the individual needs of these students make the most sense? As such, development and learning would be organized around different experiences for different students, and learning would be seen as a process driven by the needs of the child, not as an end step or end product.

This more mechanistic, behavioral viewpoint (human as machine) followed the work of Watson (whose original piece on learning theory, his dissertation, was published ninety years ago in 1913). Learning theory in its various forms is predominant in this position. Developmental studies following World War II were guided by theories from experimental psychology, which believed that change (response) was a function of stimulus (input leads to output). The stimulus-response model guided experimental psychology and development, filtering to the general public that learning was nothing more than rote memorization and retention of basic facts through reinforcement schedules.

Over time, developmental theories came to hold that response is a function of the stimulus. However, there were limitations to this argument: developmental change is not likely to result from a one-to-one, linear relationship. In a sense, this superficial notion that behavior and learning are responses to environmental factors weakened the sciences. What behaviorists forgot, and what most people who have children of their own will tell you, is that bribes and redirections sometimes don't work. Darn the luck, but children do have free will and are sometimes guided by forces more powerful than extrinsic rewards and bribery! As such, a more powerful theory is required to explain how they grow and how they learn. Reinforcers and modeling ("do as I do" as a strategy of learning) work with simple ideas and concepts, but fail in connection with complex processes or when adults want children to learn divergent ideas (e.g., moral questions, philosophical beliefs, or values education).

HUMAN DEVELOPMENT: MORE THAN A MACHINE

William Kessen in the 1960s attempted to move developmental research beyond an experimental model (the model that saw human beings as machines: input in, output out). By focusing on how (operational) definitions of developmental terms were organized, Kessen created a novel approach to looking at human behavior and human learning. No longer could we just examine changes in children as simple relationships between what we thought was occurring outside the child and the outcome behaviors evidenced. No longer would learning be considered the physical state that results following the environmental antecedents to a behavior. Rather than focusing on the environmental factors that lead to a behavior, developmentalists, teachers, and parents should spend time observing the behavior they want to know more about (or sometimes, the learning they want to know more about). By learning more about the functions of learning itself, rather than the environments that shaped them, perhaps parents and teachers will be more likely to assist children in developing adaptively. In other words, if we understand the processes that lead to learning, then educators are more likely to assist children in succeeding at learning.

Throughout the 1960s and 1970s individual variability became more important to developmental research (rather than seeing all children as being the same, educators became interested in looking at how children differed and how their learning needs might differ). Three lines of inquiry grew out of this movement: (1) the role of biology in shaping the growth of human thought and behavior (for a review, see Gilbert Gottleib, 1976, and Gerald Edelman, 1989), (2) the role of learning and experience in perceptual development (for a review see Donald O. Hebb, 1949), and (3) the importance of cognitive development during infancy (for a review see Jerome Bruner, 1976).

THE ROLE OF BIOLOGY IN SHAPING
HUMAN THOUGHT AND BEHAVIOR

Biological bases for learning and development have seen a resurgence of interest during the last several decades. Not since Darwin in the late 1800s has there been so much discussion of natural selection and organismic variables in the areas of development. The content of today's developmental studies tends to be guided by biological bases of behavior, interest in the emergence of social relationships, and the desire to study children's cognitive capacities. Scientists also have examined child development as it relates to the evolution of our species. Just prior to the birth of human fetuses, why does the brain naturally destroy approximately 50 percent of the neurons that it created during fetal development? Why does this apoptosis occur (more about this later)? While it is just conjecture, apoptosis may be the result of the human brain's need to regulate itself in preparation for what it expects to occur immediately following birth (the pruning of certain cells may result from what it anticipates it will experience due to environmental circumstances). So, if a child were to be born in a world with limited energy sources and no natural light, it is likely that over time, the human brain would adapt to such a world, reducing the connections in areas of the brain that prepare the body for a sunlit environment.

Such biological themes also have been applied to understanding the development of human behaviors. Gottleib refers to the psychobiological approach as one that studies the development of behavior from physiological, biochemical, and anatomical interests. Development from a psychobiological viewpoint looks at species-typical behavior in an organism's usual environment. Thus, in order to understand how the brain typically develops and how this shapes the learning of children, we also need to look at the contexts that surround the child.

This concept is key to understanding why we need to recognize the role of development in how the brain affects the learning of children. If biology is critical to the development of the child, then a formative piece in this puzzle must be not only the development and functioning of the brain, but also the environment in which it is shaped. For example, it is now generally believed that the processes of the brain are shaped by not only an individual's context (as late behaviorists and early cognitivists like Piaget would have us believe), but also by the child's understanding of that context, prior knowledge of situations, and the biological constraints that limit these processes in the first place. The question of past decades that guided such studies may have emphasized the response of individuals (such as Piaget's cognitive developmental theory, with its emphasis on stages and cognitive limitations solely based on the child's age).

Developmentalists would ask, Can this individual do or learn *x*? Presently, we seem to be asking a different question: Can this individual do or learn *x*, under what task conditions, and to what extent can that capacity be demonstrated?

Four general biological principals also have been discovered in the area of development. First, organisms tend to progress from a homogenous state to a relatively heterogeneous state (see Sandra Scarr's work on the impact of genetics on development; Scarr and McCartney, 1983; Scarr and Weinberg, 1977). In other words, we tend to all start out with relatively similar genetic and biological makeups, but our experiences and the modifications to our neuronal connections that result affect who we are and what we are as we age. The range of responses (the differences in abilities) that define who we are and what we can do at birth are relatively small. By the time we graduate from high school, our experiences and the organization of our brains are significantly different, and the range continues to spread as we grow older.

Second, Gottleib also discusses that the behavior of organisms has a preadapted, forward-referencing quality. In other words, early neural development and early behavioral development impact later behavior.

Third, there are periods of development where the organism requires certain forms of stimulation in order to develop typically; such optimum stages of development negate the notion of the equipotentiality of stages in the life span (not all stages of development are of the same importance — what we experience early on has a huge impact on who we become, when compared to the relative importance of later life experiences). Despite our recognition that early experience with concepts and behaviors is critical in the organism's growth, theories of development (and many schools) continue to adhere to a theory of stages. Could this be why we continue to offer foreign-language instruction in middle school and high school despite our recognition that human beings learn languages better before they are eight years old?

Fourth, as an organism develops, its behaviors become more differentiated and versatile.

Homogeneity to Heterogeneity

First, organisms tend to progress from a homogenous state to a relatively heterogeneous state (states that similar functions are typically found in associated areas). The "old theory" of brain functioning was more static in its approach: information in — routed to specific area — routed to associated area — processed out as new information. Just as behaviorism was a simplistic model to describe development, this outdated theory of brain functioning is too simplistic. Sure, we can dissect human brains and chart how various areas are responsible for specific functions. Does this help cognitive neuroscientists to understand behaviors and learning further? Possibly. Does that help laypeople or teachers to better educate? Not really. Rather than subdividing each area, it is better for educators and parents to understand that most learning requires a variety of brain areas to be stimulated. Rather than learning information or skills in one way, it is better to learn them in a variety of ways to illicit activity in these various areas, stimulating growth in several interconnected areas rather than in just one area.

The new networking model discusses how information brought into the brain can simultaneously stimulate several areas with extremely different functions. Moreover, the brain may route this information through several systems before it is rerouted out as new information. Marcel Kinsbourne (1982) also makes it clear that localization works as a function of suppressory/inhibitory stimulation from associated areas. When damage occurs to one of these centers of function, alternate areas are free to provide similar function, since inhibitory stimulation no longer exists.

Preadaptation

Gottleib also discusses that the behavior of organisms has a preadapted, forward-referencing quality. In other words, early neural development and early behavioral development impact later behavior. Psychobiologists have identified that genes set limits on behavioral development, and aspects of the genetic code of humankind make it more likely that certain behaviors appear throughout the life span. The prior notion of maturation versus experience is better explained from an interactionist framework. That is to say, behavior development is inherently tied to the environment of the organism (see Ogbu and Simmons, 1998), which impacts the development of the brain (see Diamond, 1988; Diamond and Hopson, 1999), which impacts the phenotypic expression of the genetic code (see Plomin and McClearn, 1993), which ultimately impacts the organism's choosing of environmental niches (see Scarr and Weinberg, 1977). Whew! In other words, the nature-nurture or genetic-environment debate is a waste of time. Each interacts with and impacts the other; thus, they can't be pulled apart or separated out.

Windows of Opportunity

Third, there are periods of development where the organism requires certain forms of stimulation in order to develop typically; such optimum stages of development negate the notion of the equipotentiality of stages in the life span; however, biological theories of development continue to adhere to a theory of stages.

Versatility and Adaptability

Fourth, as an organism develops, its behaviors become more differentiated and versatile. Brain development is currently the hot topic in the cognitive sciences and is another important part of development that is being examined from a biological perspective. A theme that has advanced beyond cognitive neuroscience and is being applied to other areas of development is plasticity. Robert Plomin (1990) has advanced the notion that brain development is a direct result of a reduction in plasticity in the organism as a result of experience over time. Though an organism has the potential for a broad variety of behaviors, as a result of experience, these potentials are reduced and only a certain few are ever realized. Experience modifies the physical structure of the brain, and not all experiences are equal in providing the opportunities for future learning to be successful. Therefore, whatever experiences young children have should be strong enough to help assist learning throughout their lives.

Plasticity can be defined as malleability or formability. With respect to brain development, plasticity is an important concept. Santiago Cajal discussed the brain in terms similar to the networking model almost a hundred years ago. However, the brain has previously been seen as rigid and difficult to alter following the first few years of childhood. Over the last thirty years, thanks in large part to the work of Marian Diamond and her colleagues (see Rosenzweig and Bennett, 1996), scientists now think of the brain as being malleable, continuously changing in form and function. This malleability can be as simple as changes in chemicals across a cell wall (such as with Hebb's [1949] neuropsychological theory of learning), or as advanced as lateralization of language functioning in humans. Plasticity can refer to two concepts: (1) the brain's ability to adapt, following insult or damage, and (2) the desire of humankind to have the human brain work at its maximum potential.

Plasticity can be thought of as the brain's ability to reroute functions to alternative brain networks following some type of damage to a primary area. Such situations could exist following a stroke or trauma to the head. With some functions, such as with language, the brain seems hardwired to provide several networked areas. For example, while Broca's area (critical to the formation of speech and syntax) and Wernicke's area (critical to the physical movements required for speech) provide different specialized abilities that make speech possible, when one area is damaged, the other area can take over that function. This alternative system is typically thought to have limited functioning when compared with prior abilities.

THE ROLE OF LEARNING AND
EXPERIENCE IN PERCEPTUAL DEVELOPMENT

The view that has tended to guide development most recently has been that developmental change is a function of the interplay of the organism, the context of the environment, and the stimuli that exist in the environment. The current themes that surround development include a greater variety of contexts under study than originally conceived early in this science.

Recent developments in brain research and improvements in imaging technology have increased our understanding of the nature of the human brain. Largely thought of for nearly a century as separate areas and separate networks connected by "highways of knowledge," the brain is now thought of as a complex, interdependent ecosystem, that allows for singular functions to be organized and performed by multiple areas (Kosslyn and Koenig, 1992; Sylwester, 1994). The ancient notion that knowledge is constructed along singular pathways that connect one area to another has been reorganized to reflect a dynamic, interregional system incorporating multiple levels. These neural systems parallel knowledge schemas, which is why learning and brain systems tend to develop along similar time-frames (Case, 1991).

Gerald Edelman, a Nobel Prize–winning immunologist who studies the brain, has suggested that the nature of the brain is much like a jungle; pathways of information are naturally selected for continued use if the organizer uses them, and this information serves a purpose (1988). Neural networks are consistently reorganized as a result of experience and have the capacity to develop throughout the life cycle. As students learn information and skills that prepare them for jobs and careers, they improve in their awareness about their careers and themselves (Tomlinson and Kalbfleisch, 1998). Many teachers agree that the most effective way to teach children is to provide them opportunities to make knowledge meaningful and relevant (Burke, 1997; Dozier, 1992; Sylwester, 1994). Such experiences also improve motivation, increase retention of knowledge, improve the authentic nature of the material, and reduce the likelihood of boredom and failed retention in child populations.

When the information reviewed in class is seen by children as authentic and within their control, they become empowered learners, responsible for their own goals and motivated to identify connections between concepts. Children who are in charge of their learning are more likely to make deeper connections with material. Even though this is sound pedagogical practice, it is critical for another reason: in changing their relationship to material, children also may be changing the way they think. Learner empowerment and personalization of information is thought to make neural connections stronger than they would be without student empowerment (Brandt, 1997).

However, reorganization is based in large part on whether or not the student takes ownership of their learning. By becoming involved in decision making and applying information to their lives, students can increase the likelihood that information is meaningful and is retained. Neural pathways and the hardwiring of information depend on (1) the richness of the learning environment and (2) the interest and prior knowledge of the student.

Marian Diamond has studied the physiology of the brain and its relevance to education for over forty years. By studying the cerebral cortex of rats, Diamond identified that improving the learning environments of students fosters growth in areas of the brain responsible for higher-order thinking. Diamond separated two groups of rats into impoverished environments (where the rats had limited socialization or limited play) and enriched environments (where the rats were free to socialize, explore, and play with objects). Diamond found when comparing the cerebral cortex of the two groups of rats that the cortex of rats from enriched environments were thicker and more complex. Such thickness and increased nerve endings (dendrites) provides the opportunity for increased learning in the future, as new pieces of information are connected with similar information stored on dendrites (D'Arcangelo, 1998; Diamond and Hopson, 1999).

By enriching the environments of students, Diamond and others believe that we provide them with opportunities to think in more complex ways, to improve their metacognitive skills, and to increase their ability to think for themselves. If teachers actively seek out novel situations that connect students' prior and new knowledge, then it increases the likelihood that students will find lessons meaningful. The more meaningful the lesson, the greater the chance that new dendrites will sprout and increase the growth of neural networks.

Also, the natural flexibility or plasticity of the brain is thought to provide human beings the opportunity to learn even after they have experienced limiting or dysfunctional environments. Even if students did not have the opportunity to learn as juveniles or didn't work to their capacity as children, they can continue to learn. When a strong interaction between the learner and the curriculum exists, the potential for neural networks to organize and thrive is limitless.

Although interest in subject matter is important, even the most motivated children must work for significant periods of time to master new concepts or unfamiliar information (Fisher and Rose, 1998; Languis, 1998). Because most human beings lose significant parts of their neural flexibility (or brain plasticity) after about nine or ten years of age, some teachers have shared that their students have lost the ability to learn. This couldn't be farther from the truth, as these "windows of opportunity," though important, don't close altogether. Sylwester suggests that children retain enough flexibility to continue to learn novel tasks and new information late in life. Children may have to work harder than juveniles with higher levels of plasticity do, but learning can occur.

However, it is perhaps just as critical to potential learning that teachers be aware of children's prior knowledge. Children vary in the skills developed during their primary and secondary school years; as such, the curriculum should focus on individual skill building. The greater the access to their prior knowledge, the more easily students are able to learn new information. If neural connections are to be made, students must be able to connect new information with information already stored in memory. By helping students to be aware of how new information is related to their prior knowledge, we provide children a greater chance to retain new concepts and skills. When teachers and students recognize that information is interconnected and that what one learns in history can be applied to other subjects, then we become better adept at recognizing, organizing, and applying information.

The field tends to have a greater emphasis on the interaction between systems. Rather than just examining aspects of development in one context, developmentalists have begun to examine variables from the perspective that each variable under study tends to impact a variety of others. As a result, it is impossible to study one aspect of development (for example, the development of the brain!) without an examination of the ways in which it impacts the individual as well as his or her surroundings.

THE IMPORTANCE OF COGNITIVE DEVELOPMENT DURING INFANCY

We discussed earlier that plasticity was the ability of the brain to be more malleable, continuously changing in form and function. However, plasticity also can refer to the human mind functioning at the highest level possible. It is estimated that the human brain has approximately ten billion neurons and glial cells. It is hard to imagine the vast network of interconnections and spines that exists between these cells. Gilbert Gottleib (1974), Sandra Scarr (1993), and Robert Plomin (1990) are just some of those interested in the biological effects on psychological processes. Their belief in plasticity refers to the effects of environmental systems on the level of functioning of systems within the brain.

In 1979, W. Maxwell Cowan discussed the development of the brain and localization of neurons. Cowan asserts that, following the spreading of neurons to specific areas of the developing brain, the brain develops more neurons and connections than (theoretically) it will need. The next stage of brain development typically reveals the degeneration of some of these connections and the destruction of approximately one-fifth of all the neurons previously formed. Why is this plasticity? I think it is the perfect example of how the human brain anticipates the needs of the developing organism, based on initial contacts with its environment.

Based on the interplay (or dynamic dance, as one of my best developmental professors put it) between the genetic aspects of an individual and the surrounding environment (perhaps the developing systemic environments within the individual), the brain sheds connections it does not believe will be important in that setting.

This concept is similar to the assertion that not all genes are turned on at all times and that the systems within the individual and their exchanges with the environment will dictate which genes are acting at any time (approximately 70 percent of all our genes are turned on at one time). An example of this can be found with PKU—the gene for phenylketonuria is only activated with the presence of phenylalanine in the system (also see Scarr and McCartney, 1983).

Plasticity, in my mind, speaks more to a way of thinking than it does to one concept in the field of development. I think that biology and psychology, in an attempt to understand better the dynamic and systemic processes involved in development, are moving away from a static, stage-like process guided by reductionist methodologies. Instead, I believe that the field is moving toward a view of development that is holistic, probabilistic, and epigenetically oriented and that seeks to identify the unfolding of the developmental path in all areas of growth, change, reduction, and alteration.

The neural network model discusses how information brought into the brain can simultaneously stimulate several areas with extremely different functions. Moreover, the brain may route this information through several systems before it is rerouted out as new information. While scientists previously thought that the brain was fairly mechanistic in is functioning (input–output), it has now been rediscovered in its dynamic and inter-linked form using the networking model.

Marcel Kinsbourne asserts that functions can typically be found to exist over interconnected and associated areas. Kinsbourne also makes it clear that localization works as a function of suppressory/inhibitory stimulation from associated areas. When damage occurs to one of these centers of function, alternate areas are free to provide similar function, since inhibitory stimulation no longer exists. The previous theory of brain function would not have asserted the presence of inhibitory functions. Networking sees it as essential, for it accounts for the difficulty some people have in doing similar tasks at the same time and retaining information.

The connections that exist between systems can be thought of as similar to Donald O. Hebb's (1949) neuropsychological theory of learning. Hebb asserted that learning occurred as a direct result of changes in chemical structures at the cellular wall. He believed that learning was simply the altering of these materials at the cellular level. He went further by stating that the associations made between pieces of information occur because there is a likelihood that as cells A and B fire together, the interconnection between these two areas grow as a result of the simultaneous firing.

Connections between environments have been shown to have altered brain functioning. Environments can be defined as anything that exists outside the cellular wall. True networking can account for the effects of environmental systems on the level of functioning of systems within the brain. Specifically, with the decline in the belief in epistasis, scientists began to search for a perspective that could account for differences that existed following experience. Marian Diamond and J. Hopson (1999) provide research that discusses how environmental factors can lead to changes in the wiring of the brain. Diamond has consistently shown that enriched environments can provide for thicker cellular walls, greater amounts of genetic material in the neurons, thicker glial cells, and more connections between cells. Once more, rats that have been provided with such environments have been known to run mazes faster than rats in traditional or impoverished environments (perhaps this means they have "learned more" or are "smarter"?).

However, not all areas of the brain function as associated areas. The olfactory system is a functionally specific area that functions within is own system with no associated areas. Despite this system being hard-wired to function on its own, associations and connections do exist with other areas of the brain. Though the sense of smell as a function results from one area of the brain, connections with other areas do exist—continuing to provide support for the networking model of brain function.

WHY THE GENETICS/ENVIRONMENT DEBATE IS OVER

During the past decades, our knowledge of brain functioning and genetic influences has expanded greatly. The nature-versus-nurture debate has ended and has been replaced with a dynamic model that emphasizes the equipotential that exists based on both genes and experience. If one or the other were missing, it would result in serious deficits in functioning from the cellular level to the behavioral level. I believe that intelligence is one area of human development that is impacted by genetics and environmental circumstances.

Zamenhof and VanMarthens provide evidence for genetic impacts on intelligence. Intelligence, in their study, was identified as maze-running abilities. Zamenhof and VanMarthens provided a group of normal-functioning rats with an impoverished environment. When examining the brains of these rats, they found fewer connections between neurons, fewer glial cells, less acetylcholine (a neurotransmitter that has been connected to learning), and less genetic material in the cells (Diamond and Hopson, 1999). Zamenhof and VanMarthens hypothesized that because of malnourishment and the impoverished environments the rats had existed in, their genetic structures had been altered. Their findings with the offspring of these malnourished rats tended to show that they were correct. They found genetic differences and brain-functioning deficits in each of the first two generations of rats. Each of these generations had deficits in maze-running ability, showing some insult on "intelligence." Normal functioning only returned with the nourishment of three generations of rats, with the third generation providing average maze-running abilities (the authors still found some sex differences on maze-running abilities, however, with male rats outperforming female rats).

Even the presence or absence of certain neurotransmitters has been shown to alter the abilities of individuals to learn. The presence of the neurotransmitter acetylcholine has been shown to improve retention of learned information in individuals. It is hard to discuss just the effects of genes on intelligence because so much of what we know about genetic material is impacted by the individual's environment. To discuss one without the other seems inconsistent with what we know about intelligence and genes.

The biological bases of social behavior have become a topic of revived interest during the last two decades. Genetics has been called upon to explain the development of specific behaviors, but also the unfolding of behavioral patterns across development. Aspects of temperament (see Kagan, 1985) and other social behaviors are being examined through the use of twin studies, as Robert Plomin and others attempt to examine the effects of shared and nonshared environments.

Plomin believes that this resurgence in interest in genetics will provide developmental studies with better measures of the environment and a better understanding of the nature-versus-nurture interaction. During the past decades, our knowledge of brain functioning and genetic influences has expanded greatly. The nature-versus-nurture debate has ended and has been replaced with a dynamic model that emphasizes the equipotential that exists based on both genes and experience. That one or the other would be missing would result in serious deficits in functioning from the cellular level to the behavioral level.

WHAT THIS MEANS FOR TEACHERS AND PARENTS

As was discussed earlier, human beings are in an extremely advantageous position to maximize their genetic potential by modifying their surroundings to improve learning and growth. Scientists have understood for some time now that if there is a fit between the genetic predispositions of an organism and the environment in which that organism exists, the greater the organism's evolutionary opportunities over time. It also is likely that these opportunities can afford individuals greater potential within one lifetime (that is, people don't have to wait for generations to see some improvement in their evolution—we can improve now and in the future).

Parents and teachers who advocate for children must understand the implications development and brain science have for education: there is much that we know, but there also is so much to learn! Although we are relatively sure about a number of concepts (plasticity of the brain and preadaptation, for example), we are not as certain about the environments and surroundings that can assist with such growth. What follows throughout the remainder of this text is our best guess at this time about what environments and strategies can assist children in developing to their fullest potential.

Some of those same biological principles that helped in understanding development also can be of assistance in recognizing the challenges facing child advocates as we move into addressing today's educational dilemmas.

Homogeneity to Heterogeneity

As stated earlier, organisms tend to progress from a homogenous state to a relatively heterogeneous state. This can be considered true from an evolutionary perspective, but also for an examination of an individual child in his or her environment. As we grow older, we tend to become more different. Though there are a significant number of similarities between children when they are born, within months they differ exceptionally based on the environment into which they are born. Such a notion has significant implications for educators who work with disadvantaged youth. If children are reared in environments that don't have the best fit for learning (limited experiences, limited opportunities for play, weak ties with significant peers and adults to love), it is likely that these early limitations will hold them back over time. If we as a society are to provide the maximum opportunities for all children to learn (a tenet of America's educational system), then it is critical that we provide opportunities for all children as early as possible. It isn't enough to provide them once children arrive in kindergarten (many areas are reducing funding for early childhood programs just as we learn about the critical nature of this period!). We must provide opportunities for all children as early as possible and to as many children as possible.

Preadaptation

Gottleib suggests that early neural development and early behavioral development impact later behavior. If educators are to make a difference in the learning of children when they arrive at school around the age of five, a number of things must occur prior to their formal schooling. Being prepared for school means being prepared for what learning requires. It isn't enough to know about the ABCs and to be able to share your address and phone number.

Can your child play alone and with other children? Can your child talk about what he or she did over the weekend? Does your child have the ability to organize objects by a common characteristic? Can he or she take out a book and review it with you (even if the child has to make up the story because he cannot yet read the words)? Does your child have the desire to learn? When children arrive at school interested in playing, growing, and interacting, they are ready for school. However, as a proponent of formal education and the public schools, it is critical that the responsibility for educating not be placed solely on the backs of teachers.

As with everything, learning doesn't end at 3:00 P.M. when kids go home or in May when the school doors close—it happens all the time, everyday, from the time a child wakes until the child falls asleep. As such, all interested adults are challenged to take part in creating that fit between what children need to develop and what windows of opportunity their surroundings offer.

Third, there are periods of development where the organism requires certain forms of stimulation in order to develop typically. The sooner we can begin to assist children by supporting them, the better their development over time will be. Much has been made of the idea that if learning doesn't occur by a certain age, kids won't be able to learn. While it is likely that learning will be tougher, it can always occur. Parents of a developmentally disabled child may feel the need to give up if the child has difficulty during the first years of school; yet, is that an option? Shouldn't we continue to work on identifying ways of modifying the child's school and home experiences until we find something that works for that child? If you are reading this book five years after you started teaching, using methods in your classroom that aren't working, it makes sense that you would adapt to find something that works. Same with parenting—we work until we find a match.

Versatility and Adaptability

Finally, as an organism develops, its behaviors become more differentiated and versatile. Experience modifies the physical structure of the brain, and not all experiences are equal in providing the opportunities for successful future learning Therefore, whatever experiences young children have should be strong enough to help assist learning throughout their lives. Adults should create environments where children are allowed to think, to question, and most of all to play. Learning isn't about flash cards or memorization of random pieces of information. Learning is about making sense of your surroundings and developing strategies for shaping new skills and abilities into already existing notions of how the world works. If we can get children from a very early age to manipulate their environments, play with a variety of ideas, and think about their communities and world in different ways, then they will be better prepared as they move through school and into adulthood.

The chapters that follow are divided into concepts that are meaningful in this process of adapting to environments. Each chapter reviews a different concept that may help parents do their best parenting and teachers do their best teaching. Each section will be written with information that can inform the environments with which children interact, so teachers and parents will find anecdotes, concepts, and skills that can assist in maximizing the fit between children and their surroundings.

Chapter Three

Brain-Based Learning

OVERVIEW

The purpose of the current review is to discuss the implications of brain-based learning for the instruction of young children. It is believed that by learning about the development of the brain, teachers and parents can better prepare students not only to learn, but also to understand how they learn. Brain-based learning is an educational learning system that is rapidly gaining popularity across the country. Educators must recognize that the human brain is the most complicated organ in the human body. Brain-based methods of learning emphasize how the human brain receives, processes, interprets, connects, stores, and retrieves messages (Greenleaf, 2003).

All stakeholders who are involved in education profit from brain-based instruction. Students, teachers, parents, and administrators all reap the benefits of a curriculum that is designed to support student learning based on the morphology of the human brain (Prigge, 2002). Further, by better understanding what students need in order to learn, parents and teachers can begin to work together to ensure that children are afforded rich learning environments. Children depend on both parents and teachers to provide opportunities to learn and become successful. In order to maximize their learning potential, parents and educators must know how the brain works and how to make brain-based learning a great experience for their children. Any teacher can transform a classroom into a brain-based environment; it needs only preparation and a commitment to provide the best possible instruction for the students. Through the use of real-life experiences, students have meaningful instruction that empowers them as learners. These experiences motivate the students to develop and achieve their own goals, resulting in conceptual connections that promote significant learning (Slavkin, 2002).

BRAIN-BASED LEARNING

Brain-based learning is defined as any teaching technique that utilizes information about the human brain to organize how lessons are constructed and facilitated. The practice emphasizes how the brain learns naturally. Brain-based instruction is based on current brain research and focuses on the physiology and anatomy of the brain and the components that make it run smoothly. Physiologically, the brain searches for meaning, pattern, interconnectedness, relevance, and useful applications (Greenleaf, 2003). The genetic structure of the brain searches for meaning and relevance in its surroundings; as information and skills are taken in, they are organized based on the meaning attributed to the information. Thus, not all students will learn in the same way, in large part due to the way they perceive information, their prior experiences, and their prior knowledge about a particular subject (Slavkin, 2002). Teachers who are willing to study the brain understand how it learns, and they tailor their instruction to enhance the students' learning. Brain-based learning provides teachers and educators with a framework that they can use to enhance learning. Brain-based educators constantly attempt to match their instruction methods with the brain's ability to receive, fully process, and successfully store information (Greenleaf, 2003).

An investigation into the origins of using the brain's physical structure to understand how people learn is couched in a long history. Brain-based learning began with the improvement of technology. Previously, brain researchers could only study the brain while conducting an autopsy. However, because researchers were investigating dead tissue, they could not study areas such as how humans speak and develop language skills. Now, technology (such as positron emission topography [PET] scans, which provides 360-degree images of functioning brains) allows researchers to study the brain of live patients (Wolfe, 2001). Since then, the capacity for development seems limitless. Knowing how the neurological pathways interconnect to obtain and retain information has resulted in leaps and bounds in the knowledge of how humans learn. Educators need to utilize these developments in a positive way and cannot mistake brain development with the number of years of school a child has completed. Rather, the development of the brain occurs simultaneously with the incorporation of new experiences as they occur. The thinking of children differs from experience to experience, based on what occurs in their environments—the thinking of a child around a particular concept is completely different following the child's interaction with that concept (especially if the child is given the chance to explore it, touch it, play with the concept, or have meaningful interactions with the concept in a real-world setting).

Previous models of the brain have focused on the similarities between the human brain and computers, likening thinking to the storage, retrieval, and organization of files of information. Such an image is a limited perspective, according to Robert Sylwester, author of *A Celebration of Neurons: An Educator's Guide to the Human Brain* (1995). Rather than thinking of the human brain as a computer, Sylwester suggests that the human brain is much more complicated. The brain has the ability to store billions of segments of information, more than any computer ever could. So why do we even try to compare the human brain to a computer? Previously, teachers and cognitive psychologists had only enough information about the structure and function of the brain to suggest that cognition was akin to the computations performed by a computer (Weiss, 2000). Educators now know that the brain is less like a computer, since computers store information in files that go unchanged, whereas the human brain constantly updates how it stores and networks information, based on that which the individual experiences.

Educators need to remember some important concepts when working with brain-based learning. The functions of the brain occur in parallel fashion, which means that the brain is able to process many different pieces of information at once. Teachers and parents need to utilize this fact and use colorful posters, interesting stimulations, and complexity when designing information to be learned. Each brain is complex and differs as children develop and interact with their environments. Because of this, educators need to use a wide variety of input. This gives them a greater chance of reaching more students (Reardon, 1998; 1999).

When children are only taught to memorize, they are only using one part of their brain. Moreover, some traditional strategies of teaching, such as rote recognition of material, the use of lecture-based instruction, and other passive forms of learning often lead to limited understanding and re-tention of material. Brain-based learning provides students with hands-on activities and problem-solving situations. Students also are provided with firsthand experiences and extensive coverage of prior knowledge. These activities help the students make connections and fully understand better than reading a textbook.

RELEVANCE TO STUDENT LEARNING

Brain-based education focuses on the students' differences in thinking. Somewhere between the ages of six and nine, children begin to think ab-stractly instead of concretely (Kantrowitz and Wingert, 1992). Therefore, the hands-on, real-life experience method of brain-based instruction is a logical choice for elementary school students. The associated physical ac-tivity, socialization, and feeling of competence and self-worth encourage learning by choice, not by fear. The students also are opened to a com-munity of learners through brain-based education. Instead of the students seeing themselves as individual learners, trapped at their own desks with no relations to their peers, they are a community of readers, writers, and mathematicians (Peterson, 1989). The children do not feel they are better learners because they are "smarter" or "memorized more," but they actu-ally make sense of what is being taught to them. They are able to explain concepts in their own words, including through written activities. The light bulb has been turned on, and the students are excited about learning at school.

Students need educational experiences that relate to their brains' strengths. Observing students' learning styles is one way to help students explore their interests and enhance their abilities. For example, children with spatial intelligence need activities that enrich their cortex and feed their abilities (Diamond and Hopson, 1999). Teachers can offer fun spa-tial activities for students, such as designing birdhouses, climbing on jun-gle gyms, making puppets, building models, or making potato prints.

Many educators are teaching children to memorize facts and spit them back out on a test without truly understanding the material. The associa-tion between school experiences and other life experiences also is very important. These two connect in countless ways. Everything a student has experienced outside of the classroom affects how and in what ways he or she learns (Parnell, 1996). Children need these links in order to understand fully the material they are being taught.

Teachers wonder why students do not read their assigned textbook selections and why pictures and graphs are often ignored. Textbooks are visually appealing, but they do not provide any rich sensory information that allows students to relate the new knowledge with their existing schemas (Wolfe, 2001). Through brain-based learning several senses are stimulated simultaneously. For example, if a student's mind, body, and hands are all involved in a learning activity, the information learned is much more likely to make it to the student's memory. The involvement of the senses enables students to store the memory with relevance to what they are supposed to learn from the activity. This type of learning is not possible through the reading of a textbook, though that is often what is expected of the students.

Educators also need to allow their students to express what they have learned in different ways. Teachers need to teach to their students' different learning styles. Howard Gardner, a pioneer in the field of multiple intelligences, proposes that there are at least nine different types of learning styles. They include the following:

1. *Linguistic:* Having a talent for using appropriate language; these students enjoy activities that involve writing or speaking in front of people
2. *Logical-mathematical:* Having a talent for understanding cause and effect and the ability to manipulate numbers, quantities, and operations; these students like to engage in activities that enable them to work their minds when working out problems
3. *Spatial:* Having a talent for being able to internalize the spatial world in one's mind
4. *Kinesthetic:* Having a talent for using one's body or parts of the body; these students like to participate in sports, dancing, or any other activity where they are given the chance to move around
5. *Musical:* Having a talent for hearing, recognizing, and remembering musical patterns and being able to think in musical terms; students in this category like to participate actively in bands, singing, or in a chorus

6. *Interpersonal:* Having the ability and talent to work with others; these students are comfortable working actively in groups
7. *Intrapersonal:* Having an understanding of one's self rather than other people; these students work better by themselves than in a group
8. *Existential:* Having a talent for being able to think philosophically and theoretically; these students have the ability to think about things on a much higher level than others
9. *Naturalistic:* Having a talent for understanding plants, animals, and rocks in the world around us; these students like to be outside whenever they are given the chance—a good activity would be letting them lead a hike

Learning styles are defined as the way in which each person begins to concentrate on, process, internalize, and remember new and difficult academic material. Teachers need to recognize their students' individual learning styles. When students are taught new and challenging material through instructional approaches that fit their learning style, the chances of their understanding and retaining the information greatly increases. The emotional state of the learner is crucial to the learning experience as a whole. To help the emotional well-being of children, teachers can implement activities that relieve stress, use activities that increase rapport, and allow children to release positive emotions. Information is best remembered when children are able to see the relationships between different ideas. Teachers can instruct their students in different memorizing techniques, use role-play and body movements, incorporate some humor into instruction, or use metaphors. The more complex the challenge, the better the learning (Reardon, 1998/1999). Teachers can use chunking as an effective means of presenting information to students. In doing this, teachers are able to arrange information in a more meaningful way so that children are more apt to understand (Roberts, 2002).

Teachers also must keep in mind the prior knowledge and previous experiences that children bring to school with them. For example, a teacher in a suburban Indianapolis school instructing students on state parks could jump right in with activities. Nearly all of the students in the classroom have seen a state park and possibly even a national park. On the other hand, a teacher attempting the same unit on state parks in an inner-city Gary school would need more background information on the subject.

Most likely, those children do not leave their neighborhoods often, much less go to great wooded areas like state parks. They do not have much of a concept of huge trees, trails, and nature in general.

School-age children often complain that they will never use the things they learn in school. As adults we know how much the skills they learn now can affect their future. Educators and parents need to help students connect their learning to prior knowledge and realize the uses such skills and information will have in the future. The differentiation of instruction based on students' learning styles is imperative for meaningful education.

Interactive experiences can be created to motivate students to achieve their maximum learning potential. Integrating strong emotional connections creates passion within the students, which drives inspiring learning attitudes. Music, games, debates, and role modeling are all ways to give these kinds of opportunities to the kids. If nothing else, allowing students to move increases oxygen flow to the brain, which results in increased student attention. Manipulatives, clapping, and dancing are easily incorporated into classrooms. Laugher also has a beneficial effect on student attention. A joke of the day can have a great impact on student learning. Teachers must be aware of internal and external attention, ensuring that students use external attention for the learning and internal attention for processing the information (Prigge, 2002).

IMPLICATIONS OF BRAIN-BASED LEARNING

Teachers have ties with brain-based learning because of its relevance to their classrooms. Through incorporation of these methods, every area of the curriculum is integrated. For example, using writing to learn mathematics enhances students' higher-order thinking skills. By applying mathematics to real-life experiences, students gain conceptual knowledge while applying the steps that are listed in the textbook. This teaching method also can assist in practices geared for test preparation. Using brain-based strategies while constructing mnemonic devices, instead of drilling facts into the students' heads, is one way that memorization can work with the brain (Wolfe, 2001). Tying brain-based instructional methods to everyday teaching practices benefits teachers by improving their students' learning abilities.

Teachers initially may view brain-based instruction as time-consuming and difficult to manage. With careful planning and good classroom management skills, incorporating brain-based teaching methods only requires teacher energy. Brain-based instruction leaves room for individualization. A teacher can still teach following the state standard guidelines, while providing students with meaningful instruction. Taking ordinary lesson plans and asking, How can the students be more involved with this activity? is a great way to begin the brain-based teaching method. With experience, teachers will find that the students are more willing to learn, and that is all the better for the teacher's disposition and attitude.

Further, many techniques that teachers already use in their practices that are identified as "effective pedagogies" or "best practices" also are brain-based pedagogies. A curriculum based on brain functioning could look much like the curriculum that already exists in many classrooms and schools, but with subtle variations. However, such pedagogy would provide the opportunity for elementary students to show what they know, collaborate with each other on projects, incorporate thematic curriculums, provide opportunities for reflection, and create goal-based learning opportunities that build upon each other over the school year. Schools could begin to take on the nature of an apprenticeship, providing experiences that will help to nurture well-rounded, functional professionals, who can reflect on tasks and the reality of the professional environment—one that is ever changing and ever diversifying. Wouldn't elementary students be better prepared for a technologically advanced society if they were given skills rather than information, goals rather than instructions, practical knowledge rather than organized information (also see Languis, 1998; Resnick, 1987)?

Brain-based pedagogy should be an alternative perspective to the theories discussed in a majority of teacher education programs (most often students are taught to focus on Piaget's cognitive developmental model, which is limiting when working with elementary students). As a theory and set of classroom methods, brain-based pedagogy has been making waves in the field of education. If brain-based pedagogy could be summed up in one sentence, it would be, Knowledge should be socially created.

Like social constructivists, brain-based educators believe that knowledge is constructed based on social experience and community interaction. The following are some useful suggestions offered by brain-based educators (see Burke, 1997; Caprio, 1994; Wolfe and Brandt, 1998):

- *Useful knowledge may not be accurate knowledge.* Teachers need to be involved in ensuring that elementary students review material accurately and in a useful manner. Dr. Sue Norman, a former elementary teacher from the panhandle of Florida, uses the "muddy/clear" method to ensure that her students understand necessary material. After a presentation, she asks, "Muddy or clear?" Students then write a reflection about what parts were understood and which parts were unclear. She reviews the reflections later and holds a review session, or completely reteaches the lesson, depending upon the muddy/clear feelings of the students.
- *Skills are closely tied to the situation in which they are learned and are difficult to apply to new settings.* To get elementary students to generalize to other settings often takes practicing in those settings. As such, teachers need to provide opportunities for elementary students to apply learned information and practice complex behaviors in their naturally occurring settings. Such activities take the shape of practicums, providing performance-based practice in career-related settings. For example, after a unit on making change, students could go to a grocery store. After observing the cashiers counting back change to customers, the students could talk with the cashiers about money, counting change, and how important correct change is.
- *Brain-based pedagogy should be built upon complex, authentic tasks, similar to miniature apprenticeships.* Michael Whicker, an English teacher at F. J. Reitz High School in Evansville, Indiana, published a book last year with his senior creative writing students. They researched the topic, wrote drafts, revised, wrote grants, and worked collaboratively with Mr. Whicker to produce a final product, which has now been published. The authentic task had a great reward, and the experience was something they will never forget.
- *Elementary students and teachers should share responsibility for learning.* Peer teaching and jigsaws are both great methods for sharing the responsibility of learning. Both activities require student preparation, organization, involvement, and responsibility. In order to teach the material, the student must have a thorough understanding of the information. Each

student takes a part in the sharing of information, and other students and
the teacher learn along with him or her.

- *There are multiple ways of looking at material.* No one way of examining information is necessarily correct, although accuracy does need to be
  considered. Sometimes brain-based instruction errs on the side of being
  too flexible and too independent (Bruer, 1997). Elementary learning
  teachers who use brain-based curriculums would be wise to concentrate
  on a standard curriculum that provides the flexibility and opportunity to
  be individually organized and situated in a number of activities and assignments.
- *Instruction is based on that which is good for the students in that situation.* Brain-based instruction, like all good teaching, gives students and
  teachers the chance to work together to find effective ways of organizing learning. As such, both must be involved in ensuring that learning
  occurs and that information is applied practically.

A brain-based approach to elementary learning would be one where,
through a process of social negotiation (group meeting), the teacher and
student review individual and group responsibilities, discuss the value of
multiple representations for a single concept, and emphasize the importance of process over getting the correct answer (Sylwester, 1994; Wolfe
and Brandt, 1998).

Although brain-based practice is believed to make the information
more meaningful in the long run, some problems exist. For example, multiple representations do not mean that all representations are equal. Some
ideas can be better than others. Also, the fact that a teacher puts elementary students within groups designed to "socially construct" some piece of
information does not necessarily mean that the processing of information
will follow. Some amount of trust and interaction is needed. Groups must
be held accountable for their own practices and must be mature enough to
consider the responsibility of being in charge of their own learning. Finally, some elementary students often value quick process over long-term
learning. Elementary students must be shown the dynamic nature of information and how interesting the classroom can become if they take an
active role in shaping the environment and nature of the curriculum
(Nummela and Caine, 1998).

STRENGTHS AND WEAKNESSES

One benefit of brain-based education is that preparing the learner is relatively easy. First, educators must teach the students about the ways their brains function. Students also are more inclined to help themselves learn when they are taught about how they think (thinking about thinking is often referred to as metacognition, a time-tested approach to empowering students to reflect on their learning and the most effective ways they learn). Brain-based instruction is not a secret; students should be aware of the teaching method being used and realize how much it benefits them as learners. Second, the teacher must set goals for the classroom and the learners. Goals help everyone stay focused and motivated to achieve the final product.

Teachers should give a small health lesson to their students about proper sleep habits and nutrition. In order for the human brain to concentrate and retain information, it needs a minimum of eight hours of sleep per night—no exceptions! Also, the brain needs nourishment for optimal performance. Brainpower is increased through increases in antioxidant fruits and vegetables and the vitamin B12. Water is important for brain function, too. Dehydration affects the brain's ability to learn. Lastly, the teacher must explain learning preferences to the students. Awareness of their own and their peers' learning styles promotes respect for and acceptance of learning differences.

Other physiologists find the brain-based theory to be incomplete. Physiologist John Bruer (1997) feels as though society does not know enough about neuroscience to claim that brain-based learning is the most effective approach in a classroom. In his opinion, neuroscience and education are two very different subjects. In his article "Education and the Brain: A Bridge Too Far," he points out that if teachers feel the need to focus on science and education, they need to focus primarily on behavioral and cognitive psychology, rather than neuroscience. He does not stray away from the fact that it is important for teachers to understand the basic conceptions about the brain, but he feels that teachers who concentrate too heavily on brain-based education are running the risk of entering a subject that they do not fully understand (Bruer, 1997).

Other physiologists based their negative opinions of brain-based learning on the fact that no two human brains are exactly alike. They primarily concentrate on the theory that because human brains are not alike, teachers do not have the ability to reach their students on the same level. Some scientists argue that there are vast fundamental differences between learning and education. They insist that brain-based research on learning is different from brain-based research on education. Many of these same scientists argue that much of the brain-based research has been done on animals. They maintain that the animal brain is much different from the human brain, so there is no possible way that the research could be completely accurate (Weiss, 2000). Like many other research topics, this issue will probably never be solved.

There is some speculation as to whether brain-based learning is the best route for teachers. Because many school reforms target low-performing schools, teachers have opted to take the road less traveled and chosen to work with a high-performance school, Valley Park Elementary School in Kansas City, Kansas. They went in with one main goal: to make the school even better. They concentrated on the following research findings:

- The brain changes physiologically as a result of experience.
- Emotion influences learning.
- Intelligence is multiple.

Valley Park Elementary School created a different culture using a safe, nonthreatening learning environment, active and meaningful learning, rich and stimulating input, and accurate feedback. Not only did the Valley Park staff bring the virtues of trust and respect into the school, but they were also models for the students, making them aware of their thoughts and emotions. Because of this, a well-built sense of emotional and physical safety was instilled into the minds of the students. The staff based yearlong themes around district objectives. The content areas would overlap across the different grade levels, differing only in the difficulty level. During the project, certain tests were implemented into the school to measure the students' performance. The tests showed significant increases in students' reading ability, math computations, and basic skills. In examining the results at Valley Park, researchers found that schools could become more enriched when using brain-based learning techniques (Caulfield and Kidd, 2000).

Setting up a brain gym is another method used in elementary classrooms (Saunders, 2003). This idea incorporates body movement with thinking activities. The teacher sets up stations around the classroom that students visit either with a group or individually. The stations have various activities that entice the children: jumping jacks, passing a ball, reading a story, performing a puppet show, making a small craft, and so forth. The brain is involved at a high level throughout the gym. The movement stations get oxygen flowing to the brain, which in turn allows the students to think more clearly. One drawback to this idea is that the excess movement can cause the children to get rowdy. Some teachers are uncomfortable with noise and chaos. This is where excellent classroom-management skills come into practice!

One example of intermediate brain-based learning occurs at Westmark School in Encino, California. Their fifth graders incorporate math, science, and visual arts concepts to write and produce a television station. Each day, the students broadcast news on a closed-circuit television setup called Westmark News Network (Wagmeister and Shifrin, 2000). The students write the stories, add sound, graphics, and announcements to make the show interesting for their peers. The awesome responsibility and the satisfaction of the final product spark great enthusiasm in the students. The collaborative effort makes the integrated, hands-on project both meaningful and educational for the students.

IMPLICATIONS FOR TEACHERS

Many teachers are extremely excited about the future of brain-based learning. Educators should look with favor upon any method or technique that can enhance or improve student learning; however, like any other new technique, teachers must do careful research and become comfortable with the format to become effective. Brain-based instructional strategies are gaining popularity and will continue to do so. This method has numerous strengths to consider for use in the classroom. The hands-on approach has been in use for many years and will continue to grow and become stronger.

Information also is better held over time if it is personalized in some way, or if the information is closely connected with prior knowledge held by the learner. Information and the cognition that supports it are now being reinterpreted as reflexive, plastic, and dynamic, an interconnected and interdependent network, with a whole that is seen as being greater than the organized singularities (Donald, 1991; Wolfe and Brandt, 1998).

IMPLICATIONS FOR PARENTS

Parents are interested in brain-based learning because they discover what home practices benefit their child's brain development and what practices hinder development. They also learn about how to be involved in their child's education and don't so feel disjointed from the academic process (Diamond and Hopson, 1999). If the parents feel like they are a part of the academic process, they are more likely to get involved in the school. This in turn encourages student-parent relationships, which strengthen as the years progress. Through brain-based instruction, children will enter school better prepared for the classroom environment, and parents will feel more ready to act as their child's second teachers (Zigler, Finn-Stevenson, and Hall, 2002).

In order for parents to help their children attain a higher learning level, they need to be educated about brain-based learning. Parents need to understand that learning starts at home and increases when children start school. Parents should strive to begin working with brain-based learning at an early age with their children. Hands-on activities are a great way to promote early brain-based learning. Some examples of simple activities for parents are having children compare prices at the grocery store, letting them press buttons at the gas station, reading them stories every day, having them point out certain details on walks or hikes, or just simply letting them help with simple recipes in the kitchen.

Since learning is highly affected by emotions, parents need to make their children aware of how to handle the different emotions they encounter (Meoli, 2001). Parents also need to understand that their children should not be placed in environments or situations where they will feel threatened. Just as in a classroom setting, feeling threatened or stressed can reduce the likelihood that learning will occur deeply (for long-term storage and use).

As educators, it is important that we challenge our students, not threaten them. The fact is, if a human brain feels a real threat, its capabilities are automatically minimized. The brain will try to find balance, which causes it to work at lower levels of functioning. This occurs until the brain finally reaches homeostasis. When teachers place their students in a rich environment, the brain maximizes its learning capabilities, and the students are able to increase their thinking skills (Reardon, 1998; 1999).

AUTHENTIC ASSESSMENT

It is hard to define what good assessment is. There are numerous ways to assess students, and not every way will work all the time. E. Weber (1998) states that some of the best ways to use brain-based assessment are collaboration of students, teachers, and parents; authentic assessment, even in traditional settings; conflict resolution for small group assessment; and rubrics that define expectations and provide guidelines. By allowing interaction of students, teachers, and parents, the teacher can have valuable input from the students and parents that can help make the assessment more useful in the classroom. This allows the students and parents to feel like they are making a difference in the student's education. Other teachers may also be included in brain-based assessment. When teachers review and modify a peer's assessments, it makes a more cohesive assessment tool.

Brain-based learning requires interaction of the students, including group work. While it is preferred to have utopian groups, it is more common that there are going to be some disagreements among the students. A way of assessing the students in a brain-based classroom is to use conflict-resolution tactics for their group work. Conflict resolution is a more effective approach to conflicts in a group than removing the unhappy or troublesome group member (Weber, 1998). Students are encouraged to listen carefully to every member, define each person's responsibilities, value each member's contribution to the group, and to promote fun and humor in the group's activities. Teachers need to provide rubrics that give guidelines and define the students' expectations.

Assessment for brain-based learning can be completed in several forms. Brain-based education seems to lean toward the individual side. Students are seen as very different and unique in brain-based education. One of the most popular methods is the performance assessment (Lankard, 2003). In a performance assessment, the student completes a problem or an experiment that involves the application of the previously learned material.

These tasks are generally criterion referenced, based on a rubric or check-list. Portfolio assessment also is commonly found in brain-based class-rooms. The purpose of a portfolio is to allow the learners to create a por-trait of themselves that reflects their best evidence that learning has taken place. Their best talents and accomplishments shine through, and students generally take great pride in their portfolios. The teacher should include both formal and informal feedback to the students' portfolios.

During brain-based assessment, teachers are asked to use authentic as-sessment in traditional settings. An example of authentic assessment is to have students complete projects instead of taking short-answer paper-and-pencil tests (Weber, 1998).

Normative testing is still used even in brain-based classrooms (Weber, 1998). The difference is that students are not put under great pressure to succeed. The authentic assessment has equal bearing with the normative tests, so the students do not feel stressed to cram for a test. In the end this proves to be helpful, because students do not memorize for the sake of the test and forget everything by the end of the term. Brain-based learning as-sessment keeps the learner in mind and evaluates in a variety of ways to ensure a valid, accurate evaluation.

IMPLICATIONS FOR THE FUTURE OF EDUCATION

Child advocates should glean from the above information that brain-based education has its place in today's education system. Brain-based teaching can be incorporated into any classroom relatively easily, as long as the teacher's background knowledge of the brain and brain-based learning is sufficient. A measure of a good brain-based teacher might be how well he or she teaches for the students, not to them. The teachers should be guides for learning, rather than just lecturers trying to cover academic standards. By using group work, peer teaching, and field trips, a teacher can make learning fun as well as worthwhile.

Any classroom in the United States should be full of information with colorful displays and workstations scattered throughout. These hands-on and visual materials can help any learner to be a better student. The visu-als can help the students to retain the information better, but more impor-tantly, the students will have personal experiences that will stay with them about the information. By showing through experiment, acting out a play, or listening to old radio programs, a teacher can get a child to grasp learning opportunities for life. By using meaningful lessons and teaching techniques, teachers can effectively cover pertinent material in an interactive way for the students to retain the information better.

It is very likely that brain-based learning will continue to grow in popularity as our knowledge of the brain increases. While the topic of brain-based education and learning is very important, it is unlikely that this will be the only method that teachers dwell on in organizing their classrooms. Neuroscience is a very complicated form of biology, one that should not be taken lightly. As such, it is imperative that teachers and parents who consider using information about the brain do so based on solid information grounded in research (you will notice I have not mentioned improving the learning abilities of students through the use of classical music or VCR tapes . . . not very active experiences, listening to music or watching television, are they?).

Teachers already might be using brain-based teaching methods in their classrooms just by assessing students' learning styles and varying their instructional methods to accommodate the needs of students. Instead of teaching the lessons directly out of the teaching manual, children can be called upon to participate actively in learning by having a stake and a say in what occurs within their learning environments. When brain-based learning is successfully implemented in a classroom, no child is left behind.

Chapter Four

Developmentally Appropriate Practices

OVERVIEW

Developmentally appropriate practice (DAP) is defined as including an integrated curriculum based on children's natural interests, allowing for construction of concepts through exploration of concrete materials and adjusting to the diversity in our society relative to culture, gender, learning styles, and exceptionalities (Charlesworth, 1998). These guidelines are relevant for children from birth through age eight, but also have implications for teaching at all levels. DAP is a method that focuses on student-centered curriculum involving materials and activities that relate to the emerging physical, social, emotional, and cognitive development of young children. This program can assist teachers in developing a curriculum that successfully teaches all children at their own individual levels (Jambunathan, Burts, and Pierce, 1999).

DAP is a set of guidelines created in 1987 by the National Association for the Education of Young Children (NAEYC), based upon the views of constructivist theorists and cognitive developmentalist Jean Piaget. However, in 1997 NAEYC was required to restate the DAP guidelines in order to allow children with disabilities to receive an education that is developmentally, culturally, and individually appropriate (Quick, 1998). DAP encourages teachers to use appropriate educational practices related directly to children's development as they progress. A developmentally appropriate program educates a child using activities that the child enjoys (Kostelnik, Soderman, and Whiren, 1993). Teachers using DAP must not only focus on the basic facts of a child, but look deeper into the child's individual life. A teacher should create a curriculum that is appropriate to the child's age, family, culture, and community (Charlesworth, 2000). Educators must remember that children aren't little adults, but learn in a completely different way.

The purpose of DAP is to give hands-on experiences to students to engage them in active learning so that they will be more interested in the learning process. If students are more interested in learning, they will, in turn, be more likely to enjoy school and the experiences that it has to offer. DAP is commonly known as hands-on learning; however, the program has more in-depth aspects than just learning tactilely. Through partaking in activities that require student involvement, it is hoped that students will submit what they learn to their long-term memories and will be able to recall in the future what they learned from the task at hand.

This chapter reviews how DAP is essential to teachers meeting the learning needs of students. DAP, much like hands-on learning, plays a critical role in education. Teachers interacting with students need to be aware of children's abilities and various developmental stages. Teachers' lesson plans and activities should reflect the learning styles and developmental abilities of students. To inform others on this subject successfully, the chapter discusses specific aspects of DAP and differentiated experiences.

It is important for both parents and teachers to gain knowledge of DAP and to understand how this pedagogical practice is critical to the development of their children. It is believed that DAP can support teachers and parents in meeting the diverse needs of children as they grow and learn. The challenge for each is to create curriculums that match each child's developing abilities while also providing the right level of challenge and interest. Child advocates follow a process of raising and teaching young children based on an understanding of children's stages of development. The more knowledgeable child advocates, such as parents, teachers, and school administrators, become on this subject, the easier it will be for each person involved to formulate his or her own educated decisions regarding DAP. Teachers and parents are both responsible for providing children with the best possible education. By discovering relevant information on how to successfully educate children, parents and teachers ensure bright futures for our youth.

DEVELOPMENTALLY APPROPRIATE PRACTICES

As previously stated, DAP is a set of guidelines created by NAEYC in 1987. The primary reason for publishing these guidelines was to clarify the requirements set by the NAEYC accreditation process. Accredited programs were required to show evidence of developmentally appropriate instruction, including activities, materials, and expectations. Also, the guidelines refuted the increasing tendency of teachers to use a more formal approach to instruction and assessment. The guidelines linked DAP to specific ages and individual appropriateness. This publication identified the essential components of excellence in instructional practices with young children better than any preceding publication (Charlesworth, 1998).

Students learn as a result of interactions with the environment. Information that is to be functional to the learner must be explored and interpreted a number of times before neural pathways can be hardwired for long-term use. As is similarly found in Howard Gardner's theory of multiple intelligences (see chapter 3), information that is to be remembered by a variety of different learners should be represented in multiple ways, so as to stimulate simultaneously multiple neural networks, multiple areas of the brain, and in multiple formats so that diverse groups of students can learn the material. Information also is better held over time if it is personalized in some way, or if the information is closely connected with prior knowledge held by the learner. Information and the cognition that supports it are now being reinterpreted as reflexive, plastic, and dynamic, an interconnected and interdependent network, with a whole that is seen as being greater than the organized singularities (Donald, 1991; Wolfe and Brandt, 1998). Because of this recognition of the need for different students to have access to different formats of learning, DAP is both timely and essential as teachers attempt to teach ever-diversifying populations of students.

DAP requires teachers to involve students in the learning process while taking into consideration their individual skills, interests, and backgrounds. It is geared toward students' comprehensive abilities and the rate at which a student's brain will take in and absorb information. DAP allows children to make choices based on their individual differences, which promotes every student's success. Through this program, teachers provide instruction to students according to the diverse development of each individual child physically, socially, emotionally, and cognitively. Teachers who implement a DAP curriculum establish the best environment for students to participate actively in learning experiences, facilitate and guide student learning, make provisions that ensure the success of each child, and promote self-esteem and a desire to learn (Jambunathan, Burts, and Pierce, 1999). DAP will cover objectives based on state standards while also meeting each student's individual needs. DAP today focuses on developing language abilities and letting students be more creative in the classroom (Dunn and Kontos, 1997). DAP helps with students' confidence and facilitates a better learning environment. If good DAP is created for students, social development is accomplished, emotions are controlled, and learning becomes more comfortable for students.

Students' levels of experience are an important consideration to take into account when developing lessons to be taught in the curriculum. All students will not have the same experience levels (Meisels, Stetson, and Marsden, 2000). Teachers should get to know the students' differences in experience and adjust the instruction to fit their needs. Teachers need to be careful that they are not facilitating a one-size-fits-all classroom. They need to be aware of the individual differences within the classroom and be prepared to repeat important ideas and provide individual guidance as needed (Tomlinson and Kalbfleisch, 1998).

Another important concept to take into account in a child's educational development is preparing for a technology-driven economy. DAP also may infuse real-world skills into lessons, such as those relating to the area of technology. Children today are motivated by electronic devices, and teachers are discovering more interesting ways to involve technology in lessons, such as by using videos, television, computers, and other devices (Shearin Karres, 2003). For example, students in middle school (technology class/old industrial arts class) can use wireless laptop computers to follow the lesson the teacher presents to them. While the students get familiar with a program called PowerPoint, they also are analyzing data about the students' likes of ten music groups, ten movies, and ten foods, and then finally the students present the results of their findings on a screen. Another activity that students might perform includes using preapproved websites that have steps for building catapults and air dragsters (introducing and defining terms such as lift, drag, friction, gravity, and weight-to-mass ratio). In this wireless age, these gadgets are highly engaging and interesting to children (they know more about technology than most adults).

The cognitive psychologist Jean Piaget stated that children progress at different cognitive levels according to the child's age level. The first stage of Piaget's cognitive developmental model, the sensorimotor stage (from birth to the age of two), suggests that children learn through sensory and motor (sensorimotor) modalities, starting to grasp, crawl, and utter sounds. A good example of this stage is when a child grasps a toy that makes a sound when moved by the child—as soon as the toy is taken out of the child's sight, the toy is no longer present to the child's senses.

In Piaget's preoperational second stage (age two to seven), a child starts to recognize and pronounce letters and some words by identifying the symbols that represent the letters. Children start to learn at this level by observing others and repeating the actions that they see. The children start to group like things together by color and shape.

In the third stage, the concrete-operational stage (age seven to eleven), a child is able to recognize the weight and mass of objects and starts to learn logical sequence with objects and events. A child is able to read a book and figure out the next event to happen in the story's sequence.

The formal-operational stage is the last stage (age eleven to adult) of Piaget's cognitive developmental theory. In this stage students learn to test theories and think about the future (Charlesworth, 2000). These stages are very important for teachers to keep in mind as they develop appropriate activities to enhance learning.

A teacher needs to understand that there are exceptions (some children at the same age understand and progress developmentally faster or slower then average) to this rule of child development. These exceptions could be due to the child's maturity level or physical or mental disabilities.

IMPLICATIONS FOR STUDENTS

DAP appears to have significant relevance for students, because it encourages teachers to use the best educational practices to promote student learning. These practices should consist of instruction that is individually, culturally, and age appropriate. The DAP approach allows children to play a part in their own learning experiences. Through DAP children can construct their own ideas, knowledge, and understanding by engaging in relevant activities and explorations that require them to discover information on their own, rather than having it given to them (Quick, 1998). This also is known as a learner-centered approach. Research shows that classroom environments that are learner centered significantly enhance learning, social, and emotional outcomes for young children. It is easier for children to understand concepts if they can actually perform activities relevant to their developmental process.

Teachers who use DAP are "attentive to issues surrounding children's cognitive and metacognitive development, the affective and motivational dimensions of instruction, the developmental and social aspects of learning, and individual differences in learning strategies that are, in part, associated with children's cultural and social backgrounds" (Daniels and Perry, 2003, 203). In a learner-centered classroom that uses DAP, teachers often provide a variety of educational activities that are applicable to children's lives and customized for different stages of development, but teachers also need to be prepared to speed up or slow down the pace of the lesson. They should not get so caught up in the lesson that they lose certain students without realizing it. Teachers also frequently interact with students, which allows the teacher to thoroughly monitor students' progress, while providing each student with individual help (Daniels and Perry, 2003).

In *What's Best For Kids* (1991), Anthony Coletta summarizes a list of six DAP principles to help parents and educators make better decisions about raising and teaching children:

- *Principle #1: Give equal attention to all areas of development: physical, emotional, social, and intellectual.* Many people believe the theory that if a child's intellectual ability is developed, everything else will fall into place on its own. This theory could not be farther from the truth. Physical, social, and emotional maturation are closely related to self-esteem. Children start to define themselves at a very young age. If all of the emphasis is put on intellectual growth, children could suffer in other areas. Every child must develop in each level to be well rounded. If a child is not allowed to develop socially, he or she will not have the ability to make friends and, therefore, will not be able to fit into school or society as easily. This could definitely have a direct effect on his or her intellectual abilities.

- *Principle #2: Reduce stress in children's lives.* When it is time, children move smoothly from one stage to another of their emotional, social, physical, and intellectual development; stress can seriously impair the ideal progression through each of these stages. This can be especially true if a child experiences a major setback, such as loss of a parent, divorce, hospitalization, parental drug abuse, or child abuse. It can also be true if a child is pressured to achieve too early. Every child develops at a different rate. Children will develop on their own through these stages if they are given adequate time and support.

- *Principle #3: Create respect for adult leadership.* Some parents are too indulgent with their children. This weakens what child development experts regard as a crucial prerequisite for learning: a child's respect for the parents' ability to define and enforce household rules with consistency and fairness. If children cannot or do not accept limits set by their parents, they will not be able to accept them from other adults in leadership roles. At a young age children need a relatively consistent routine. If children are allowed to govern their own actions at a young age, they will never be able to accept authority as they get older.

- *Principle #4: Protect children from school failure at the beginning.* Children pass through the same stages of development in a sequential and universal manner but at different rates. Not every child is going to be ready to enter kindergarten at the age of five. Children under the age of eight sometimes need to be protected from the damage to self-esteem that can occur if they are repeatedly confronted with tasks that are beyond their maturational levels. Some children will not be able to function at the same level as other children. A constant fear of failure will only lead to low self-esteem.

- *Principle #5: Support a developmentally appropriate curriculum.* Many child development experts and early childhood educators believe that young children need interactive, meaningful, and concrete learning experiences. We cannot expect an eight-year-old child to sit in a classroom hour after hour and listen to a teacher talk. Children need to be able to get up and move and be active in the classroom. This is how they get excited about learning. Not only children, but people in general, learn better through interaction and manipulation.

- *Principle #6: Support alternatives to standardized achievement tests.* In most states, standardized achievement tests are used instead of assessments that better judge a child's capabilities. Standardized testing shifts the curriculum toward goals that are easily measured. Measurable goals should not be the fundamental objective for young children. This is a very heated debate. Standardized testing is not the most accurate way of testing young children, but in our society, there must be a measurable goal. Most children need to have another form of testing to rate their capabilities accurately.

THE IMPLICATIONS FOR DEVELOPMENTALLY APPROPRIATE PRACTICES ON ACHIEVEMENT

Many research articles supporting DAP have been published. In most cases, the DAP program has had positive effects on children's social, emotional, and cognitive development. Researchers have found that students are more likely to remember things that they have learned with a hands-on approach, which is the founding belief of DAP. In classrooms today, the diverse population of students all have very different backgrounds and experiences. Students who have had more experiences in life are apt to learn more easily, based on the fact that they have more prior knowledge to tie the new information to.

Research on preschool children enrolled in child-initiated programs has discovered that the children show less test anxiety and stress behaviors than children in academic programs (Dunn and Kontos, 1997). One study of 293 first-grade students in inner-city public schools found that students with teachers who used DAP scored significantly higher in social skills than students with teachers who used developmentally inappropriate practices (DIP) (Jones and Gullo, 1999). Also, results from another study indicate that the DAP approach promotes students' self-competence, because it gave them independence to direct their own activities and behaviors (Jambunathan, Burts, and Pierce, 1999). Preschool and kindergarten students in DIP classrooms exhibit double the stress levels of students in DAP classrooms, have lower academic achievement, poorer study habits, and are less social (Charlesworth, 1998). More research into the cognitive effects of DAP shows students in these programs have higher creativity levels and stronger verbal skills than those in DIP classrooms (Dunn, Beach, and Kontos, 1994; Dunn and Kontos, 1997; Hirsh-

Pasek, Hyson, and Rescorla, 1990; Jones and Gullo, 1999; Marcon, 1992). The DAP approach also is beneficial for special-needs students, because the guidelines allow for provisions that meet each child's specific needs (Duncan, Kemple, and Smith, 2000).

There are many strengths to the DAP approach. Multiple studies say that the less developmentally appropriate preschool and kindergarten classroom experiences are linked to poorer academic achievement, lower work-habit grades, greater distractibility, and less prosocial/conforming behavior during the early grade school years (Charlesworth, 2000). Sometimes DIP looks more appealing because these practices can demonstrate quick short-term gains, typically in achievement scores, which may initially be attractive and persuasive to administrators and parents. A closer look at the long-term effects of DAP, however, shows a definite benefit over DIP for children (Haupt and Ostlund, 2002).

Hands-on learning is definitely considered a strength for DAP. According to C. H. Wolfgang and M. E. Wolfgang (1992), play activities are the central method of learning for young children. At a very young age, children do not know how to add and subtract or spell out words; they only know how to play. This play helps to show them the act of manipulation

A second DAP strength is that students can learn a lot by participating in activities that involve them in exploration and the learning process. This helps get them excited about learning. For students to enjoy school and learn more, educators must keep them enthralled with learning and show them how exciting and interesting it can be, as well as foster an I-can-do-it! attitude. When students are more self-assured, they can learn so much more than if they have feelings of self-doubt.

When standardized test scores and report card grades are compared, students who have been in a DAP classroom score higher in reading and mathematics in kindergarten through second grade than those students who have not been in a DAP classroom (Dunn, Beach, and Kontos, 1994). DAP has been found to have greater benefits then a traditional classroom on both immediate and a more long-term basis (Burts et al., 1993; Frede and Barnett, 1992; Marcon, 1994). Children in first grade who were in a DAP room in preschool progressed better academically than those who weren't (Frede and Barnett, 1992).

DAP classrooms also help students of low socioeconomic status (SES) (Burts et al., 1993). It levels the playing field, allowing them learn with their higher-SES counterparts. Students of lower SES in DAP classrooms did equally well as students of higher SES on the California Achievement Test, but students of higher SES who were in DIP (Developmentally Inappropriate Practices) classrooms did better than their lower-SES counterparts on the same test. This demonstrates the long-held belief that standardized tests favor students of higher SES (Charlesworth, 1998). This also indicates that lower-SES students generally do not perform as well as their higher-SES peers on standardized tests, but shows as well that it is possible for all students in DAP classrooms to achieve similar test results, as DAP gives students more experiential knowledge, rather than just pencil-and-paper knowledge.

CHALLENGES FACING DAP AS A SOUND METHOD OF INSTRUCTION

Those who disapprove of the DAP guidelines argue that the program is not for every child, because everyone is different. DAP is said to provide guidelines for teaching all children, but these opponents state that all children cannot be taught the same way. The guidelines are said to be a "common core of beliefs, values, and goals"; however, people who oppose DAP say that not everyone shares this common core of beliefs, values, and goals, because of the diversity between individuals (Lubeck, 1998). One person stated that the concern is that DAP's underlying guidelines are based on a "white middle-class perspective" and have the most success with "typically developing children from relatively 'advantaged,' Anglo home environments," as opposed to children who come from "disadvantaged" backgrounds, who may not benefit from DAP because they lack the knowledge, skills, and perspectives that the DAP program supports (O'Brien, 2000).

Further, not all research reflects positively on DAP; there are some inconclusive and contradictory results relating to this pedagogical practice. The study on the 293 first-grade inner-city students discussed earlier (Jones and Gullo, 1999) indicated that the DIP students scored better in language arts than the DAP students. The mathematics results for the same students showed no significant difference between the two groups. One study shows that students in child-initiated classrooms have higher reading and mathematical achievement; however, results from another study indicate that academic-focused classrooms have higher literacy achievement scores than those in child-initiated programs. Some studies have shown no differences in achievement between child-initiated and academic-focused programs. These types of results make it difficult to determine whether DAP is beneficial.

The opponents of the DAP method have highlighted some of its weaknesses. For instance, Sally Lubeck (1998) stated that although special-needs students may benefit from the DAP method at times, "many young children with disabilities are less likely to engage spontaneously with materials in their environments." In order for the method to work for these types of children, the teacher must constantly encourage them to engage actively with learning opportunities (Duncan, Kemple, and Smith, 2000).

IMPLICATIONS FOR TEACHERS

All children learn and respond to settings differently; for this reason, many teachers consider the DAP approach beneficial for most children. DAP is gaining supporters in education due to its emphasis on meeting the needs of individual students. At a time when educators are working with more and more divergent populations of students, differentiating practices based on each individual student's needs is critical. This approach has a huge impact on all teachers, but especially on special education teachers. The Council for Exceptional Children's Division for Early Childhood has recognized DAP as an essential ingredient in programs for young children with disabilities. In order to better serve parents and students, special education teachers must keep up not only on DAP, but also on developmentally appropriate curriculums for different age groups (Sadler, 2003). Most teachers really enjoy using this method because students have fun learning. That, after all, is our ultimate goal as teachers—to show our students that learning can be fun.

Further, teachers are expected to develop lessons for the curriculum and base them on state standards. They should state objectives and set goals that the students should strive to obtain. There is much to consider as a teacher assembles a lesson that teaches students, namely, the skills students need to learn and what is interesting to them. The trick is for the teacher to put it all together and make it work consistently (Cambron-McCabe et al., 2000).

Teachers have differing views on using DAP in their classrooms, and their opinions affect their performance in educating their students using this method. There are certain personality traits that come into play when making the most of DAP. Odds are that students are not taught as effectively and are simply being prepared on a daily basis through DIP for the standardized tests that they are required to take.

Teachers do suffer from some stress due to what the school system demands of them. They are expected to not only cover the requirements in a small amount of time; they also are responsible for instigating community responsibility and both personal and community values. While doing all of this, many teachers find it difficult to equalize teacher-initiated activities and child-initiated activities (Lubeck, 1998). Expected to find a happy medium in all of these areas, the teacher is overwhelmed just by having to find information to teach on these issues and enough time for instruction.

Burnout is common among teachers, as they feel that they work so hard and are expected to do too much in a cramped time period. Another common feeling among teachers is that no matter what they struggle to teach in class, there always is the matter of parent support. Most teachers feel that not having the support of parents, colleagues, and administrators makes it hard to teach using DAP, and they find themselves focusing on skill development and direct teaching geared toward standardized tests (McMullen, 1999). If teachers feel unsupported and burned out, they are more likely to abandon conscious efforts to make their classroom practices the most effective for their students and, instead, will do what is easier for them. By taking the easy route, chances are that they are probably not meeting the academic needs of their students, thereby cheating their students out of the quality education that was initially a priority.

Studies have been conducted on teachers' beliefs and practices. Some confusion and inconsistencies have arisen from these studies, but for the most part, teachers' beliefs appear to reflect effective teaching in their classrooms. Most teachers tend to have developmental beliefs, but do not always use DAP techniques (Smith and Croom, 2000). Although their practices aren't always consistent with their beliefs, a majority of teachers and administrators are in support of DAP (Hoot et al., 1996). It seems logical that teachers would want to teach in a fashion that supports the level of cognitive and emotive understanding of students.

Teachers also should be prepared to assist parents with understanding the concept of DAP. Parents would benefit from understanding the instructional techniques that work best for their child so they can effectively help them with homework. During parent-teacher conferences, teachers should be prepared to share tips with the parents. Also, parents are a good resource when teachers are trying to get to know their students.

The difference between the knowledge to be learned and the students' present skills base should be considered as part of a child's learning development. Though the findings of studies of the effects of DAP on children are inconsistent, the strengths of the program are still numerous. Nearly all of the studies conducted have shown that using the DAP approach helps students gain self-confidence in their attitudes and abilities and provides a less stressful environment for their learning. Having self-confidence and less stress gives children a desire to learn more, allows them to enjoy learning, and gives them the opportunity to work cooperatively with and learn from their peers without the stressfulness and competitiveness of formal assessment and working individually (Jambunathan, Burts, and Pierce, 1999).

Students might enjoy learning more if they learn in a hands-on environment that combines hands-on education and traditional academics into one interesting form of learning. That which keeps students' attention gives them a better learning experience. While conducting some research, one writer discovered that there might be no need to separate developmental and academic learning, as the two might be very effective when combined (O'Brien, 1997).

Students involved with DAP are positively affected socially, emotionally, and cognitively. They enjoy learning more, because they can grasp the concepts through experimentation and learning activities. Also, the activities they learn directly correspond with their developmental levels; therefore, they are not expected to learn information they are not developmentally ready for. Their social skills improve through working cooperatively with their peers and the positive support they receive from their teachers. They become more confident in learning because they do not feel intimidated by this type of instruction, as opposed to more formalized academic instruction. Overall, students greatly benefit from being taught through DAP.

In a primary classroom, DAP might appear as a first-grade math activity that has students work in groups and make estimations on how many pumpkin seeds are in their group's pumpkin. After the groups come to a consensus, each group has the teacher put their estimation on the number chart. All groups then count their seeds by using grouping methods (fives, tens, twenties, etc.). When all the seeds have been counted, each group has the teacher put its actual number of seeds on the chart. All the groups share how they found their answers, and the class decides which group had the closest estimate. This activity is DAP-based, because students are actively involved in their learning process; rather than abstractly estimating numbers on a worksheet, they actually see how math applies to real life. Also, they are interacting with each other to gain social skills and learn how to cooperate. This activity is fun and not stressful, and students may not even realize they are learning!

In a secondary classroom, students could cover a unit on the Civil War by conducting interviews and researching fascinating facts about the period, such as discovering interesting little tidbits of information that we do not hear as much about. Students could then relay the information they have discovered through any representation of their choice. For instance, they could create, write, construct, or invent. These types of activities are developmentally appropriate because they focus on students choosing their own method of demonstrating what they have learned.

WHAT DO PARENTS THINK ABOUT DAP?

A major emphasis of the DAP method is parent involvement. It would be helpful to have parents' input as to how their children's classroom should be run. According to D. R. Powell (1994), there are many ways to reach parents with the DAP information. These suggestions include talking to parents about how programs provide developmentally appropriate care and education and also how DAP supports a child-centered approach to early education.

Parents can be invited to share ideas and materials for a classroom project, helping to extend the learning to the home. Parents also can volunteer their time to help with in-class projects. Parents do not have to wait for teachers to contact them, but can take the initiative to facilitate the communication. Parent-teacher conferences also can be another place to make a conscious effort to form alliances with parents that encourage DAP activities at home. The most important thing is that parents feel involved and understand what their child is being taught in the classroom. If parents do not understand the instruction that is taking place in the classroom, they will be less likely to want to help.

Teachers have the opportunity to exert an important influence in both the home and school settings as they assist parents to become involved in their children's appropriate educational experiences. For example, teachers can make parents aware of DAP activities connected to current topics being studied in the classroom that they can participate in at home. Teachers also can send books home with students that are related to the topic they are studying in the classroom and provide suggestions for parents on follow-up activities.

For the most part, parents want to see physical evidence of what their children are learning, such as test scores, report cards, or written activities. Some ways to show parents this tangible evidence of learning is to include various types of assessment with the activities, such as checklists with learner-centered and developmentally appropriate performance indicators. Also, teachers can put student work in portfolios to show their progress and accomplishments. Another good idea is to send letters or reports home so that parents can see what their child has learned (Daniels and Perry, 2003).

A study was conducted on parents in the United States, Finland, China, and Ecuador to determine their perspectives on DAP. Nearly all preferred clear-cut instruction, such as the use of workbooks and textbooks and frequent formal assessment, rather than using learning games or other DAP activities. Parents from the United States were less supportive of DAP than parents from some of the other countries, and they supported greater use of practice and repetition activities for the development of reading skills (Hoot et al., 1996).

It might be difficult for parents to understand the concepts of DAP at first, as the odds are that they were not educated in this manner. Parents are generally skeptical of new ideas in education because they feel that their children should be learning in the same way they did. They think that what worked for them will work for their children and do not accept changes in education well. Parents probably think that their children will not learn as much in a DAP format, so teachers will have to arm themselves with critical evidence of what the children have learned through DAP activities.

With the above in mind, parents need to be familiar with DAP in order to help the students properly with any schoolwork they bring home. A parent should take an active interest in their children's homework. A parent should not do homework for the student, but should know the right way to help a student with homework. Give the students every opportunity to solve any homework problems on their own. A parent can answer a student's question with a question (where do you think you can find that answer?) to encourage a capable student to achieve an independent response (Glenn and Brock, 1998).

There are both strengths and weaknesses in this method of instruction, but the strengths outweigh the weaknesses. One strength is that teachers are being prepared in different ways than ever before so that they will be able to meet the needs of all of their students, with the emphasis being on students from culturally and linguistically different backgrounds (Moores, 1999). Using this method will increase the self-esteem of these diverse students, because it attends to everyone's specific needs and developmental levels. All of this will lead to the students receiving the best education possible. A weakness, however, is that teachers' beliefs differ from their teaching practices. Findings showed that in many cases, teachers said that they believed in DAP, but did not actually practice it in a manner that reflects their beliefs (Jones and Gullo, 1999).

AUTHENTIC ASSESSMENT

DAP is not a system that requires comparison of and competition between students, but rather assesses them through alternative assessments and mastery of abilities and information. Since DAP instruction involves age- and individually appropriate teaching practices according to each child's developmental stage, alternative assessment is suitable; it provides students, teachers, and stakeholders in education the opportunity to confirm that students can master particular academic expectations. Through assessment, a teacher can monitor a student's progress, let the student see his or her own growth and development, and pick out students that may need an additional challenge or some specific type of instruction to help in his or her growth (Neuman, Copple, and Bredekamp, 2001).

Most of the assessment that takes place in a DAP classroom is conducted through observation and interviews; by observing the student you can tell if the child is improving and also how he or she is working with other students. Other appropriate methods of assessment for DAP classrooms include checklists, rating scales, photographs, audiotapes, videotapes, work samples, and narrative recording systems, such as anecdotal records, running records, time sampling, and event sampling. Checklists are a list of behaviors or traits that the teacher is observing in a particular area. They are easy to use and require little training, and the teacher can develop them in a relatively short time. Also, rating scales can tell the reader more about the degree of a student's mastery of or the frequency of a behavior; they also take a minimum amount of time to complete, are easy to develop, and require little training to use. Photographs can be used to record development in all areas by showing the increased complexity of structures as children get older or show a student's ability to work with others. Anecdotal records are used to record specific events that demonstrate a particular behavior in nonjudgmental language; they tell what happened, where, and when. The running record is a detailed description of the events that take place over a specific period of time. Through this method, objective language is used and the child's language is recorded verbatim. Time sampling is used to record what happens within a specified period of time, which is usually short in duration. Any assessment used with this method should have a purpose and should incorporate curriculum content to achieve the goals of the lesson. Used correctly, developmental assessments enable a teacher to identify the needs of all students and especially of students that need extra help. Once a student is identified, the teacher can develop an appropriate curriculum for him or her to accommodate individual needs (Moore, 2000).

DAP considers what is appropriate for the age level and cognitive abilities of students and encompasses many hands-on activities to engage children in more beneficial learning. When students are actively involved in learning, they are apt to take more knowledge away from planned and self-directed exploration, which makes the use of Criterion Referenced Assessments (CRTs) relevant. Assessing through CRTs encourages students to think for themselves and use their own creative abilities to solve problems, instead of giving them only one possible way of figuring something out. When given options, students learn such life skills as logical reasoning and discovering things in their own ways. There are many ways to arrive at the same conclusion, and that is what makes learning so exciting—that we can unveil fresh, new ways of gathering the same results that someone else gathered. Sometimes, differing routes of thinking can catapult us into previously undiscovered, uncharted territory! This can sometimes be the most exciting part of exploration. If students arrive at different results when conducting the same experiment, even more questions are raised as to why the same two experiments yielded contrasting outcomes.

IMPLICATIONS FOR
THE FUTURE OF EDUCATION

DAP is likely a surefire way to help all students learn successfully. Although all approaches have their faults, this program seems to have mostly positive effects on student achievement. Since all students clearly learn differently, it is critical that parents and teachers provide them with age-related activities that meet individual student's needs and relate to individual goals.

Students can gain other benefits from this program, as well. DAP encourages interaction and cooperation, and it indirectly promotes acceptance of diversity. Using group activities in the classroom helps students develop social skills and learn how to cooperate, skills that they will use all of their lives, in and out of the classroom. Teaching according to each student's individual needs helps others understand that everyone is different in some way and may learn slightly differently, which is okay. They will learn to be accepting of special needs, cultural diversity, social diversity, and even the diverse personalities among themselves.

Through the DAP approach, the teacher is a facilitator, rather than a lecturer. This allows students to construct their own ways of learning and to take responsibility for their educations. By doing this, students will gain a sense of achievement and pride. Lesson plans should center on the developmental levels of the students, which requires teachers to take the time to assess their students and identify individual needs. Information that teachers should gather includes culture, interests, learning styles, backgrounds, skills, and academic abilities, and this information can be gathered in various ways. For instance, a teacher should interview parents at the beginning of the year to gather information on students and test students to gain an understanding where they are academically. Observation and student interviews are also effective tools. Students' active involvement in their education improves their ability to understand because they teach themselves and their peers.

Culturally enriched lesson plans—developmentally and culturally appropriate practices (DCAP)—are becoming more common in the classroom (Moores, 1999). Lessons that include antibias educational practices will be of interest to students who may have felt left out before. For instance, a DCAP lesson might involve inviting a parent from another culture to share with the class or visiting cultural museums or culture-related events.

In this day and age, when children are barraged with standardized tests, it would be wise for teachers and parents to consider using forms of teaching prescribed by each child's interests, needs, and abilities. Teachers using the DAP method put more emphasis on progress than on perfection. Students who are brought up in a DAP environment feel more confident in their cognitive abilities and are therefore less intimidated by tests and grades.

Chapter Five

Problem-Based Learning

This chapter reviews the current ideas surrounding problem-based learning (PBL), a developmentally appropriate pedagogical strategy that has largely been found in the medical and business fields. The theory will be reviewed, as will three of the applications of this theory, with case examples of how PBL and experiential education have transformed our understanding of the roles of schools and community involvement in our children's education.

OVERVIEW

On Monday morning a class of fourth graders walk into their room and find that a small area of the room has been taped off with police tape. Confused, the students all gather around the area to find their class pet missing. The teacher walks over to them and begins, "The class pet has been stolen. The police have taped this area off because it is now a crime scene, and we have to solve the crime." She continues by telling the class that in the next few weeks they are going to conduct an investigation and try to figure out where the pet is. Throughout the unit they will conduct fingerprint analysis, perform handwriting analysis from the ransom note, generate diagrams and spreadsheets of the crime, make predictions, and see if the predictions can be proven. This is an example of PBL. "Problem-based learning is an instructional method that encourages learners to apply critical thinking, problem-solving skills, and content knowledge to real-world problems and issues" (Levin, 2001, p. 1). Learning through the solving of a problem usually involves group work, but is not limited to a team approach.

75

This chapter identifies the characteristics of a problem-based curriculum, its advantages and disadvantages, and its strengths and weaknesses. It also shows PBL's effectiveness in working with diverse groups of students and its implications for twenty-first–century education. In order to recognize whether PBL is an advantageous learning strategy for students, teachers and parents should further understand it as a pedagogical strategy.

HISTORY OF PROBLEM-BASED LEARNING

PBL originated in the medical field as a method of instruction to prepare future physicians. Howard Barrows (1986) created the problem-based instructional method as a substitute for the typical approach to teaching medical students. He felt that medical students would benefit from a problem-solving method that focused on real-life problems rather than the use of a lecture format that did not test critical-thinking skills. Because students would be learning information in an environment constructed to simulate professional expectations as realistically as possible, students were given the chance to see the implications of learning the information immediately, improving the likelihood that they might use it in the future.

PROBLEM-BASED LEARNING

As it relates to P–12 education, PBL is a relatively new teaching strategy that is making its way into many of today's classrooms. However, early in the twentieth century, John Dewey said, "organizing education so that active tendencies shall be fully enlisted in doing something, while seeing to it that the doing requires observation, the acquisition of information, and the use of a constructive imagination, is what needs to be done to improve social conditions" (quoted in Delisle, 1997, 137).

Teachers today are finding the need to reach a broad base of students who require more than just the traditional methods of instruction. Students today, reared on a healthy diet of television, the Internet, and advanced technology, enter the classroom interested in learning, only to find that the methods used are static and fairly benign. Students today expect that classrooms will afford them the opportunities they already have at home: an active environment that may be educational and hands-on.

Diana Wood described PBL "as a small group teaching method that combines the acquisition of knowledge with the development of generic skills and attitudes" (2003, 329). Students explore the problem and also investigate the strategies necessary to resolve the issue, strengthening their problem-solving skills, inductive reasoning skills, and creativity. Teachers take on a much different role from that typically expected in a problem-based classroom. The instructor first selects a topic, or problem, for the students to explore. She then allows her students to examine the problem and form their own solutions, whether as a group or individually.

Student-centered learning and problem-stimulated learning are two major versions of PBL (Waterman, Akmajian, and Kearny, 1991). In student-centered PBL, the students create their own learning objectives after evaluating the problem. Students engage in self-directed learning outside the classroom. The students are required to cover and evaluate resources. Also, students can identify their own learning goals with maximum flexibility. Problem-stimulated learning gives students resources and learning objectives. Students are encouraged to choose an objective that they have little prior knowledge about. Problem-stimulated learning is more efficient and allows students to cover more crucial information than traditional teaching strategies (Bridges and Hallinger, 1991).

Although this approach may seem completely uncharacteristic of a typical classroom, the method has a great foundation. It is a commonsense approach to classroom learning. Students are not tested on their memorization skills or their ability to read a textbook. Instead, they are asked to put their knowledge into practice by solving a problem that they could potentially encounter in the world around them. Further, students are called upon to perform research on their own before returning to their group for a discussion, increasing individualized problem-solving skills.

PBL is an instructional practice that arranges the curriculum or topic around a major problem that will be beneficial for students in the future. The students are engaged and involved in problem solving, from figuring out the root of the problem, understanding what the problem is, and then finding a solution to it on their own. The teacher is to be a problem-solving facilitator by modeling problem-based strategies and encouraging inquiry from the students. The environment should be set up to encourage the use of problem-solving skills and make needed materials available to the students.

Problem-based means that the curriculum is carried out as a series of model problems that could happen in real life. These problems are designed to challenge the learner to determine and achieve the curriculum's objectives. The students approach the problem without prior preparation. They apply their previous knowledge as well as the curriculum that needs to be reviewed in order to examine the problem and retrieve relevant information. By providing students with the flexibility to apply their individualized skills and prior knowledge to novel issues, students gain practice in relating previously learned skills and information in alternative contexts. Such experiences provide a stronger understanding of the richness of learning and hopefully demonstrate the need for students to apply information in a variety of formats. It is critical for students to realize that there may not be a single solution to a particular problem. It is their duty to research and identify possible solutions (Levin, 2001).

THE CONTEXT OF THE PROBLEM: AUTHENTICATING THE LEARNING ENVIRONMENT

Using ill-structured problems is the key element of PBL. The problem sets the context for the entire unit experience. Problems should not be the traditional issues that were written on the board or that are easy enough for everyone in the class to understand. Rather, these are real-world problems that students will be faced with outside of the classroom; they are likely to be issues or events facing their local communities and are unlikely to be solved through only one process or solution. As such, each student will often interpret these problems differently, having differing prior knowledge about the subject.

Further, PBL also offers students an opportunity to see the diversity of knowledge, as there is often more than one right way to reach a solution. The teacher directs students to challenge one another and come up with different ways of finding a solution; the teacher serves not as an "expert," as in traditional classrooms, but as a mentor or facilitator, guiding students toward information, experiences, and systems that can provide them with what they need to resolve the problem.

GOALS OF PROBLEM-BASED LEARNING

PBL has four basic goals. First, teachers begin the process of PBL by examining their role and redefining themselves as facilitators, tutors, or guides, rather than as disseminators of information. Teachers then work to choose a worthy topic that can withstand a predetermined period of focus and encompass many standards of learning. The topic also should be an interesting real-world situation.

Second, the PBL process further requires students to examine their own roles within the classroom and the way PBL changes their involvement in the learning process. It gives the students a chance to use the skills they have been taught, as well as to come up with their own strategies to use them. Students lay claim to their work and will hopefully show their excitement by their willingness to complete the assigned tasks. PBL also offers students an opportunity to see the diversity of knowledge, as there is often more than one right way to reach a solution. Group work is encouraged, but not necessarily required.

Third, PBL creates a novel approach to assessing student learning, moving away from a summative form of evaluation (chapter tests following a review of information or midterm and final examinations) to a more formative process (exploring information consistently over time and evaluating the changing project rather than just reviewing it at the end).

Finally, and perhaps most importantly, PBL alters the role of parents and communities in the learning process of children. In the course of a unit the students should use the community as a reference, as well as have community leaders come into the classroom as experts. The parents' involvement will occur outside the classroom, while they assist the student in the research of the community and its properties, as well as helping to foster the excitement and enthusiasm of the student.

A standard problem-based approach is a complex blending of prior knowledge, basic lecture, and problem solving. Students may require brief informational lectures to familiarize themselves with a topic, especially if the subject is complex. There are a few guidelines instructors should follow when creating an effective PBL scenario:

- The learning objectives set for the students should be consistent with the facilitator's (teacher's).
- Problems should be age- and grade-level appropriate so that the children can comprehend the problem.
- The assignment should be interesting for the learners and relevant to their education or their future.
- Cues should be given to encourage and direct the discussion of the issue presented.
- The problem situation should encourage, rather than restrict, discussion early in the process.
- The problem should promote participation from all group members.
- When researching information, students should be able to locate data from various learning resources.

CHALLENGES FACING PBL CLASSROOMS

Though this is an advantageous system for students to recognize the connections between curriculum and community issues, some problems do exist in certain contexts. In order to recognize whether PBL is an advantageous learning strategy for students, teachers and parents should further understand it as a pedagogical strategy.

While PBL provides students with the opportunity to review information in practical and purposeful ways, it is unclear whether it is a more effective approach to learning. Kochhar (2003) examined students from eight medical schools in the Netherlands. The result showed that students from a problem-based curriculum knew no more than students from a lecture-based classroom. Kochhar (2003) also reported that previous studies actually showed that students gained less medical knowledge from a problem-based curriculum. However, while she does acknowledge that traditional assessments conclude that there is little to no differences between a problem-based and a traditional curriculum, Wood (2003) reports that students in problem-based curriculums seem to have better knowledge retention and a greater ability to apply this information contextually.

IMPLICATIONS FOR TEACHERS

Teachers are faced with working with a diversified population of students. Oftentimes, the biggest challenges come not from the racial, but the economic, challenges evident in most school corporations. Poverty can lead a child down a path to low self-confidence and a feeling of worthlessness. Today's society often views money as a sign of power, prestige, and poise. A person of low income may feel disadvantaged in situations such as finding a career or pursuing an education.

Further, all students learn differently. Some students learn very well through direct instruction, while others learn well through group work. PBL has been shown to work well with all types of learners, making its strategies ideal for heterogeneous classrooms where students with mixed abilities can pool their talents collaboratively to invent a solution (Delisle, 1997). PBL is a strong pedagogy to get a wide variety of students to work together toward a common goal. A group that contained gifted and talented students as well as special-needs students would be able to work together and combine ideas to find a solution to the problem.

A problem-based curriculum, among other methods, can aid a teacher in building the confidence of a student. Bettina Lankard Brown (1999) reviewed the effects of PBL on self-efficacy in "Self-Efficacy Beliefs and Career Development." Teachers in the study used a poorly structured scenario to offer students the opportunity "to test their skills and confront the internal and external barriers they may perceive as limiting their successful achievement of a goal or objective" (Brown, 1999). Brown found that PBL offered many chances to build a child's confidence. As a result, she asserts, teachers should provide these opportunities and make a difference in a child's life.

With PBL, the teacher provides students with opportunities to learn independently as well as from one another and coaches them in the skills they need to do so effectively (Solomon and Geddes, 2001). Teachers are pressured to prepare students for the challenge of work and life beyond school. Torp and Sage (1998) encourage teachers to begin using PBL by making a list of learners' characteristics. Teachers also can add to these lists as the lesson progresses. The teacher should then decide on a topic that will cover a lot of ground and be interdisciplinary, meaning it should cover all the subjects, while intermingling them. The teacher should present the problem, but not the content of the problem, which is up to the students to uncover throughout the unit (Bridges and Hallinger, 1991). The units should involve the students in active learning and relating to the world around them (Torp and Sage, 1998). The units need to be challenging and thoughtful, while teaching skills in a more authentic way (Torp and Sage, 1997).

The teacher should begin to assess what students are learning and what they don't understand and make accommodations for such occasions. She should be carefully overseeing the groups and evaluating their input to the unit, as well as helping the groups get the information they need to complete their tasks (Savery and Duffy, 1995).

By using a problem-based approach to teaching, instructors can avoid students learning material for a test and then forgetting what they studied. Brown found that PBL offered many chances to build a child's confidence. Teachers who use active learning in their classroom say that they have seen their students learn more material, understand more ideas, and find school more enjoyable (Delisle, 1997).

A teacher might feel a bit tested when developing and transitioning to a problem-based classroom. An educator must plan thoroughly in advance to ensure the problem is valid, understandable, and challenging. This might require hours of outside research and careful alignment with the curriculum standards. The PBL problem should incorporate local and state educational goals, build on prior knowledge, and require active student participation.

In order to alter traditional methods, development programs will need to be offered so teachers can make the transition to PBL (Brandon and Majumdar, 1997). This transition will not be an easy one. The teachers take on a completely new role; they go from being experts and facilitators to being coaches. Teachers are referred to as coaches because of the position that they take in PBL. Athletic coaches usually watch from the sideline and support players' decisions and strategy selection. The hardest part about this pedagogical practice tends to be that teachers have to become questioners instead of tellers (Torp and Sage, 1998).

Teachers who use PBL in their classrooms will enrich the learning experience for their students in many different ways. Research has shown that problem-solving, decision-making, modeling, and reasoning-process skills increase in students who learn from teachers who use

PBL. PBL students also gain group and communication skills. PBL uses a jigsaw-puzzle approach for some of the instruction. What takes place in a jigsaw is that the students become experts on a particular topic. After all research is done, students serve as experts in their localized domains. Students are able to split into groups and discuss and explain their topics to their classmates. This is a great way to get students to work well not only on their own, but also in groups. These are skills that students need to acquire.

WHAT DO PARENTS THINK ABOUT PBL?

Parents involvement in the PBL units can consist of, but is not limited to, classroom involvement as an expert in a topic being covered, at home as an access to the outside community, or at home as the excitement builder for a topic. Basically, all of these ideas can be used in any form of teaching, but are exceptionally important in the long units of the PBL process. Parents should be encouraged to participate in the learning process of their children, and they should be given explanations for all that goes on in the classroom. The open-door policy should apply in every classroom, not just a PBL classroom.

Teachers encounter mixed emotions from parents about implementing PBL into a traditional classroom. Some parents trust the teacher and stand behind whatever educational decisions they make. On the other hand, there are a few parents who do not accept PBL at all. Those parents were probably taught in a traditional classroom, and they believe that their child should be taught the same way. One question that parents often ask is, Will it work for my child?

When using PBL in the classroom, parents will see their child's self-esteem increase because everyone participates in activities. Parents will also see an increase in their child's enthusiasm, which will result in a higher attendance rate (Bartels, 1998). Parents might hold different views about a problem-based curriculum; however, most should see the intrinsic value this teaching method holds. When the students are involved in the learning process and doing things outside of the classroom to find a solution to the problem, this demonstrates that they are enjoying learning. Parents report hearing about what is happening at school without having to ask

(Torp and Sage, 2002). If the students are active learners, everyone involved should be pleased. Parents are a little hesitant about PBL in the beginning, but once some information is given to them regarding this new approach, they are usually very accepting of it.

Parents support PBL because of the excitement that is shown by their children. When students became excited about PBL, they transmit the excitement to their parents. Children are led down a path of problem solving that most classrooms do not offer. Critical-thinking skills are formed, and teamwork is developed. Children most often develop a desire for learning when they feel they hold a connection between what they learn and the world around them.

PROBLEM-BASED LEARNING: AUTHENTIC ASSESSMENT

While students are persistently encouraged to be engaged in the learning process, assessing the students' learning can be rather difficult because assessment is often focused on the final product (Ngeow and Kong, 2001). A valid assessment system assesses students' competencies based on real-life problems (Baxter and Shavelson, 1994). When solving problems, the assessment of knowledge is the most important. Test items require students to apply their knowledge to important problem-solving situations (Segers and Dochy, 2001). PBL assessment methods should follow the basic principles of testing the student in relation to the curriculum. Assessment of PBL groups is advisable. It also is important to judge the group as a whole. The goal within the learning environment is to work effectively in a team (Wood, 2003).

In assessing students throughout the PBL unit, the goal is to see how students got the conclusions they did and the steps they went through in getting there, rather than just assessing based on the final answer. By examining the process the students take to solve a problem and determining why they took that path, the teacher can focus more on the cognitive learning of the student (Zvacek, 1999). The assessment should encourage the students to be creative, work collaboratively with others in the groups, and think about their own learning process (Herman, Aschbacher, and Winters, 1992).

The assessment method should be a more formative process of looking at the students' work from an improvement, rather than a comparative, point of view. That is, are the students improving throughout the unit, changing their methods to fit the lessons, and using past knowledge in co-operation with the newly learned information to complete the lessons? This can be evaluated by observing the students throughout the process and comparing observations with the end product. The assessment should consist of comparing one individual student's final product with his achievement over the course of the unit.

PBL can be assessed in a number of ways. For instance, the six most common forms of assessment in a problem-based curriculum are (1) grades, (2) written comments from the facilitator, (3) a group evaluation from the facilitator, (4) an individual evaluation from the facilitator, (5) a peer evaluation, and (6) self-assessment. Unfortunately, not all institutions take advantage of the numerous ways to assess students in this environment. Conclusions from a survey taken in five Ontario medical schools indicated that feedback was infrequent. Students were not satisfied with the amount and type of assessment used in their curricula. It was concluded that learners prefer peer and group feedback, although these two types of assessment were not widely used by educators (Parikh, McReelis, and Hodges, 2001).

According to B. R. Levin (2001), all forms of assessment used should focus on the cognitive objectives, the content to be learned, and the skills used in a specific process. Specific forms of criterion-referenced assessment include rubrics, checklists, individual learning logs, and evaluations by outside observers. Teachers also may make informal assessments by asking questions, making observations, and guiding discussions. Final projects, such as portfolios and group presentations, may serve as a type of formal assessment. To evaluate individuals, teachers may request self- and group-assessments, as well as giving the students feedback.

PBL assessment is virtually all criterion-referenced assessment. The students should be encouraged to keep some type of journal along the way. The teacher could look at these periodically to assess the students' work. The Need to Know chart also is something that the educator can use to assess the students' work and progress. Ralph Tyler said that learning takes place through the students' active learning (Torp and Sage, 2002). The educator needs to be clear about what they want the students to accomplish.

B. Bloom's taxonomy is often mentioned in the assessment of PBL (Bloom, 1956). In PBL teaching and assessing are merged through the guidance of the coach through the problem-solving process. Many times this assessment is done through nongraded assignments. This could be in the form of feedback, adjustment, refocusing, and coaching (Torp and Sage, 2002). Along with the process of PBL, assessment is also a whole new endeavor for the teacher. It is something that will require patience and perseverance.

IMPLICATIONS FOR THE FUTURE OF EDUCATION

PBL has become a very popular term in education. The information acquired from this research identifies teaching strategies and techniques for educators to pursue in the classroom. Teachers are pressured to prepare students for the challenge of work and life beyond school. They also are confronted with the challenge to provide more authentic instructional contexts and activities than traditional knowledge-based curricula. Students of all ages retain information best and demonstrate increased depths of understanding when they are more actively involved at higher levels of thinking (Dods, 1997). If PBL is used correctly, our students will develop learning strategies that will help them to become lifelong, self-directed learners. Instead of leading a discussion or lecturing, teachers are able to create a problem that students will take ownership of. Students can become observers, coaches, and advisors in order to work out a solution to the problem. PBL lets students take a more active role in the classroom. Further, students will learn how to formulate complicated learning issues in order to prepare them for future learning. PBL can be used with students of all abilities and ages in almost every subject area.

Once child advocates know the benefits of PBL, teachers and parents recognize that children will be able to develop skills needed in a complex world. PBL gives students the opportunity to demonstrate what they have learned in the past, as well as in the current year, and to use that knowledge in a constructive, real-life situation. There is more emphasis on improvement and collective learning and less on individual memorization. The students get the chance to utilize more resources in the classroom and community from these the units than is typical of standard teaching methods. The topics chosen for problem-based lessons can range from their current neighborhood problems to the world problems that will affect them later in life. Further, their community involvement ideas expand and their role in the community and world becomes much clearer at an earlier age. With proper training, PBL is an instructional tool that can be used to integrate the disciplines and create positive changes in our students' achievement, social skills, and motivation.

Chapter Six

Learning through Themes

Michael Slavkin
and Melba Wilderman

It is taken for granted, apparently, that in time students will see for
themselves how things fit together. Unfortunately, the reality of the situation is that they tend to learn what we teach. If we teach connected-
ness and integration, they learn that. If we teach separation and discon-
tinuity, that is what they learn. To suppose otherwise would be
incongruous. (Humphreys, Post, and Ellis, 1981, xi)

Interdisciplinary learning reflects the current trend in education to provide
meaningful and authentic activities in the classroom. Schools are moving
away from teaching isolated concepts toward a more constructivist view
of learning, emphasizing a more in-depth acquisition of knowledge. This
trend is also reflected in the nation's cry for accountability (Manning,
Manning, and Long, 1994). Studies have found that programs using integration or an interdisciplinary curriculum "almost always produced equivalent or even better scores on standardized achievement tests than those
where students were taught through the traditional discipline-oriented format" (Lubeck, 1998, 165).

WHAT IS INTERDISCIPLINARY LEARNING?

The term *interdisciplinary curriculum* refers to a "knowledge view and
curriculum approach that consciously applies methodology and language
from more than one discipline to examine a central theme, topic, issue,
problem, or work" (Jacobs, 2002). In other words, overlapping concepts
in subject areas such as science, social studies, math, health, and physical

education are integrated into our language arts program. This method capitalizes on natural and logical connections between the disciplines. The students are able to see connections to learning and the real world. The aim is to develop a unit that incorporates at least two disciplines that have a common theme and central questions.

The primary goal of interdisciplinary teaching is to incorporate subject matter and standards more strongly into a set day. Integrating the curriculum allows teachers to teach the standards and the other disciplines required of them (Lawton, 1994). For example, a first-grade teacher has 149 state indicators in math, science, language arts, and social studies that he or she is required to meet each year. Teachers are always looking for ways they can focus on language arts while continuing to meet the objectives and standards of science, math, and social studies. Because of the significant number of standards required for review in a year, teachers may find it difficult to find time to cover all areas. By teaching thematically and via an integrated curriculum, teachers may find it easier to review all the information required and in a deeper and richer manner (Engelmann and Carnine, 1982).

BENEFITS OF AN INTERDISCIPLINARY CURRICULUM

The benefits of an interdisciplinary curriculum are numerous, but the following key factors should show teachers the strength of this method:

- *Providing valuable focus:* An interdisciplinary curriculum focuses the student on the mastery of objectives. It also increases student motivation and interest in learning because there is a high level of engagement throughout the integrated thematic unit (ITU).
- *Helping students understand why they are doing what they are doing:* The interdisciplinary curriculum focuses on the processes of learning. Higher levels of thinking skills, such as problem-solving and decision-making skills, are emphasized in the ITU.
- *Demonstrating coherent connections among disciplines that allow a transfer of learning from one discipline to another:* The concepts, strategies, and skills taught in an ITU are portable. The students are able to transfer those concepts easily to other subject areas.

- *Helping students to grasp the relation of content to process:* The emphasis of an interdisciplinary curriculum is on improved learning. Effective student learning occurs through the use of cooperative learning strategies and hands-on activities.
- *Facilitating the acquisition of an integrated knowledge base (Ritter, 1999):* The students are actively involved throughout the learning process. They are able to develop knowledge, skills, and values through the activities of the ITU. An ITU helps students to develop new ideas and concepts from the existing skills.

First, a teacher must look at the big picture. What standards and skills need to be taught at that specific grade level? Heidi Hayes Jacobs (2002) stresses three important areas that need to be considered:

1. *Content:* Identify a direction and intent for the unit. An appropriate theme would reflect the current curriculum and student interests, experiences, issues, or problems.
2. *Skills and thinking processes:* Consider three or four specific objectives you wish students to master by the completion of the unit. These objectives must tie into the state or national standards. You should think about activities with which to accomplish the objectives, activities that extend beyond pencil-and-paper worksheets.
3. *Assessment:* Interdisciplinary teaching allows teachers to expand their assessment strategies. The focus of assessment is on demonstration of those skills and thinking processes that are gained and practiced throughout the ITU. Effective assessment incorporated into an ITU has several characteristics. The assessment tends to be open ended, meaning that it does not have one definite answer, but multiple possible answers. It also is not solvable by a single method. The emphasis is on process, not product. Therefore, the means of getting an answer is more important than the answer itself. Effective assessment requires a depth of understanding. Mere memorization of facts and concepts is not enough. Higher levels of knowledge are evaluated with greater importance. Students are required to pull together of a number of ideas from varying contexts. The students, at the end of an ITU, should be able to link the learned thinking processes to other subjects. The students are also required to demonstrate through performance the skills

learned. Finally, the connection between learning and the real world is realized through assessments involving realistic situations. Learning becomes real to the students through these realistic situations. They see the real-world implications of what they have learned.

In organizing a classroom around an integrated curriculum, teachers should develop a blueprint for revising their existing curriculums.

DESIGNING AN INTERDISCIPLINARY CURRICULUM

When you are implementing an interdisciplinary curriculum, it is best to work with one or more of your colleagues. This is especially true at the intermediate and middle school levels, where teachers are more apt to teach specific content areas. Faculty who use teaming might find this process simpler than those who do not have as many opportunities to work with colleagues will. Teaming on ITUs can be done not only at one grade level, but also across grades. Further, it is important to include your students in the planning process, since students can suggest many creative ways to address the standards within units focused on their personal and social concerns (Akerson, 2001).

The title of the theme should attract the interest of the students. Teachers must remember that the theme is designed to bring students into a position of curricular power—the theme must therefore support students' interests. Further, the theme should be broad enough to incorporate at least two of the disciplines. More than just supporting their interest, it also should support their intellectual growth by supporting concepts in their formative stages. While we want students to be excited about learning, we also want the learning to be meaningful and valuable. The theme should broaden students' understandings of the world and how they fit into it.

While some thematic units instantly sound fun to students, not all themes are created equally. Teachers should avoid creating themes solely based on the "cute factor." Cutsey curriculums may limit how deeply students can learn certain material. So, while themes like bears, penguins, and bugs may be of interest, it takes an expert teacher to create meaningful activities that will support learning across all areas of the curriculum. Some stronger examples of themes might relate to meaningful areas of the community or society. Examples could include global concepts, such as family, love, friendship, anger, hate, service, or exploration, or specific concepts, such as space, weather, nocturnal animals, storytelling, the environment, the human body, the pioneers, or the Underground Railroad. A critical facet of introducing a theme to a classroom community is to be sure to invite support and feedback from key stakeholders, such as principals, parents, and other cooperating teachers (Schubert, 1993). Some teachers find it helpful to create a thematic letter to send out to stakeholders, explaining (1) what the unit theme is, (2) what will be covered during the theme, (3) and possible ways for stakeholders to interact with the curriculum to support student growth.

BENEFITS OF INVITING STUDENTS TO HELP

There are many benefits to inviting students to help plan a thematic unit. First, they are given the opportunity to develop critical-thinking skills. The students envision what it is they want to learn and then utilize their creative abilities when they brainstorm the ideas and activities to be incorporated into the unit (Flores, 2000). Secondly, when students are asked to plan a thematic unit, the message is relayed to the students that their ideas are valued. The students take ownership of their own learning when they have input into the direction of their studies, increasing the likelihood that learning will take place. Finally, students see that education is a matter of serious concern for our entire society. They will see the community's willingness to encourage their endeavors through the community's support of the students' studies (Vars and Beane, 2000).

Once a theme is decided on, then a concept wheel can be constructed (figure 6.1). This serves as a visual tool during the planning process. The theme should be in the middle with an arm for each discipline teachers intend to consider (Akerson, 2001; Jacobs, 2002).

Teachers should make sure that the curriculum is coherent, cohesive, and well integrated among the various classes (Alder, 2002). One strategy for developing units for the school year is to send home a survey for the students to fill out. Invite the students to list some goals they have for themselves and also to list three topics they would be interested in learning about. Then, look at the surveys and pick several topics that you think

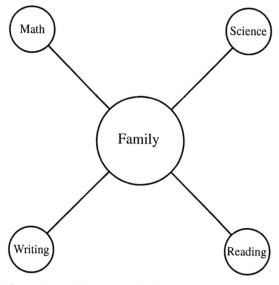

Figure 6.1.   A Concept wheel

would be interesting for the students to explore and to learn about. Try to base your decision on their interests, as well as the standards and material you are expected to cover.

ENSURING A COHERENT, COHESIVE, AND INTEGRATED CURRICULUM

The key to ensuring a coherent, cohesive, and integrated curriculum is in the planning. An integrated thematic unit is not something you can throw together overnight. You must spend some time planning your unit. Before you can begin to coordinate your thematic unit, you must reflect upon several initial considerations (Seely, 1995).

1. *Assess your student population.* You need to familiarize yourself with the students so you can tailor the unit to serve their needs. You need to know which students struggle in certain areas, which students may be pulled out for various reasons, and which students are potentially on the higher end of the spectrum. This will allow the teaching group to plan the unit around these learning concerns. Portfolios may be one way of looking at

the student's development. It is very important for teachers to build on prior knowledge, rather than teaching above a student's level. Look at the ability of your students so you can plan activities that will not be too difficult for them. Ask yourself how your students learn best.

2. *Familiarize yourself with your national and state standards.* Your unit should be centered on the standards you are planning to teach. The purpose of integrating two or more disciplines is to be able to meet a variety of standards in one unit. It is one way of saving time. The core concepts you are teaching should come directly from the standards. Ask yourself what standards and skills are worth knowing.

3. *Consider the environment in which you are teaching.* In an elementary school classroom you need to consider such things as how much time you have for the unit and whether your day is seamless. Time plays a big factor when planning any unit. Ask yourself how can students learn to look for and make connections within and between subjects (Jacobs, 2002).

STEP ONE: CREATING A THEMATIC STATEMENT

Thematic statements allow teachers to think about a theme that can organize the curriculum and explain its purposes to others. While the teacher may be comfortable with this form of pedagogy, most parents, administrators, and students are not. They haven't seen this type of teaching and learning, and for many it can be intimidating. As such, the thematic statement can be a brief introduction to the method of thematic teaching, the reasons for it, and its implications for student learning. The thematic statement need not be more than one or two pages in length, but it must reflect four primary parts: (1) a chosen theme, (2) the implications for the theme for student learning, (3) the goals of the unit, and (4) the objectives of the unit.

Choosing Your Theme

Perhaps one of the most critical steps in organizing your curriculum also happens to be the first step that a teacher must take; the first step in developing an integrated thematic unit is to create a thematic statement. This statement should include your rationale, or purpose, for choosing the theme you wish to teach. While teachers should be motivated to teach the theme that will organize their curriculum, it is critical that they remember that it is not their interest that must be piqued, but the students'. As such, the teacher should concentrate on thinking about the unit from the perspective of the students, organizing a theme that is inherently of interest to them.

Implications for the Theme on Student Learning

The theme that the teacher chooses should attract the interests of the students. More than anything, one of the key goals expressed for the unit will be to get them excited about learning. Further, the theme should broaden students' understandings of the world and how they fit into it. According to P. C. Schlechty (2000), material should also be connected to the students' backgrounds and experiences to increase the likelihood that learning will occur (see Gamberg, 2003). The key to thematic teaching is that by reorganizing the curriculum into a package that piques the students' interests, it is more likely to connect with their experiences and values, making the information and skills more approachable and learnable (see also Newmann and Wehlage, 1993).

Schlechty (2000) also states that the unit is to be meaningful to the students in that it is both purposeful and authentically engaging. Having meaning, as Schlechty sees it, is fundamentally different from being interesting. Interest speaks to the students' prior knowledge and belief systems; to be meaningful requires that the unit be a powerful transmission of information and skills. The teacher should construct lesson plans that amaze the students, challenging them to think that they are playing when in reality they are learning deeply and richly.

As an example, Jessica and Jenn, two first-grade teachers from Indiana, created a thematic unit on family to help their students better understand the various facets of our communities (including citizens, corporations, countries, communities). The teachers started their unit by sending home a letter (a form of thematic statement) to all their parents, reviewing the key points of the unit and why they were drawn to teach the curriculum from a thematic structure:

> The first-grade teachers decided to choose the theme of family and culture for our thematic unit. We believe it is appropriate to be taught at the first-grade level because first graders will be able to understand their cultural

background and what makes up a family. During kindergarten, students learn about themselves and their capabilities. First grade is when curriculum shifts from a focus on the individual to emphasize the world around the individual. At this age, it is important for students to examine the relationships between themselves and others, and understand the importance of ideas or concepts and how they relate to them.

First grade is a very critical time for students to examine the topics in this thematic unit. Their classroom will be made up of many different types of students from different family backgrounds and cultures. With the diversity of our student population increasing, it is important for students to see differences and learn to accept them as alternate lifestyles that differ from their own. We hope that teaching this thematic unit on family and culture will broaden the students' knowledge of differences within families and communities and decrease prejudices between students and other individuals they interact with throughout their lives. (Jessica and Jenn, Yankee Elementary, 2003)

STEP TWO: ORGANIZING
VIA ASSESSMENT—GOALS AND OBJECTIVES

After teachers identify a meaningful and engaging theme with which to organize their curriculums, they need to identify goals that can describe to stakeholders like parents and administrators what they expect the unit to do.

Goals for the Thematic Unit

Thematic goals are not measurable; nor do they typically give us specific outcomes that will guide our lesson plans. Instead, goals give teachers an opportunity to share expressive values and beliefs about what impact the theme will have on their students. The goals, much like the thematic statement, should incorporate how the theme of the unit relates to the curriculum. Jessica and Jenn's goals are specific to the unit, but do not mention any areas of the curriculum specifically. Further, they aren't measurable; nor would they clearly assist a teacher in organizing a lesson plan. They do, however, provide some sense of what the unit will cover and how it will impact their students:

Instructional Goals for Family and Culture: A Thematic Unit for First Grade
   After the unit students will be able to recognize the different types of family structures and different cultural makeup within families.

After the unit students will be able to recognize the different communities and learn the definition of family. (Jessica and Jenn, Yankee Elementary, 2003)

Objectives for the Thematic Unit

The final part in creating a thematic statement is to express clearly the goals and objectives of the unit. This will help people to understand what you expect from the students, much like the goals. However, the objectives for the unit are critical to assisting teachers in designing units that meet state standards and provide a foundation for the assessment of the students' development.

Goals are global statements that organize a teacher's thoughts for the unit. They aren't measurable and tend to be very lofty. On the other hand, objectives help to organize thoughts and zero in on what the students will be doing. They are measurable, observable, and achievable, and most importantly they provide a teacher with the tools to recognize whether the unit was successful and whether the students met the curricular standards. Objectives are comprised of three parts:

1. *An initial introduction:* AITSWBAT—"After instruction, the students will be able to . . ."
2. *An action verb:* Or, what we expect the students to be able to do. Action verbs should be specific and clear. Further, teachers should avoid such generic words as "know" or "understand," which tend to emphasize rote memorization of material and superficial learning. Teachers who teach thematically should want to encourage higher-level thinking, so choose verbs that denote the application, analysis, evaluation, or synthesis of information and skills (for further information, review the levels of Bloom's taxonomy of cognition; see table 6.1).
3. *An outcome:* "As evidenced by . . ."—List the outcomes you anticipate. Outcomes are the products that the teachers will expect to see as confirmations of learning. Outcomes can be used for comparative purposes, in the form, for instance, of a normative test or quiz, but they tend to be performance-based activities, such as essays, presentations, projects, and other hands-on representations of learning.

Table 6.1. Bloom's Taxonomy of Cognition

Knowledge *Typically, this level is not considered appropriate for thematic learning due to its weakness*	Memorize, recall, identify, label, define, list, match, name, spell, tell, underline, state, recall, locate, fill in the blank	• Label an insect • Memorize parts of a worm
Comprehension	Describe, discuss, paraphrase, convert, explain, restate, rewrite, trace, translate, summarize, retell in your own words, put in order, interpret	• Write a summary of a chapter of *James and the Giant Peach* • Retell the ending of a story on caterpillars • Explain how butterflies grow
Application	Construct, demonstrate, make, apply, conclude, demonstrate, draw, give an example, show, state a rule, use, operate, illustrate, determine	• Apply information to a math story problem involving more than one step • "Dragonfly" math story problems • Follow directions to make an insect out of food and craft supplies

continued

Table 6.1. Bloom's Taxonomy of Cognition (*continued*)

Analysis	Categorize, order, diagram, classify, analyze, compare, contrast, specify, infer, debate, deduct, differentiate, diagram, determine the factors, diagnose, distinguish	• Do bug graphing • Create a survey of the grossest bugs • Do bug reports • Categorize insects and noninsects
Synthesis	Hypothesize, combine, create, estimate, write, suppose, suggest, reorganize, rearrange, pretend, plan, invent, generate, design	• Perform science experiments • Invent your own bug • Create a story or poem
Evaluation	Interpret, judge, decide, discuss, assess, appraise, compare, conclude, defend, give your opinion, evaluate, justify, rate, rank, value, support, select	• Support a position • Render an opinion • Compare and contrast the movie and book versions of *James and the Giant Peach*

Source: Bloom, 1956.

Each objective should look as follows:

After instruction, the students will be able to (action verb), as evidenced by (performance or outcome).

In the case of Jessica and Jenn's unit at Yankee Elementary, they had a number of objectives, each of which would later be connected with the state standards to support the learning of their students:

Instructional Objectives and Alignment with Indiana State Standards

Objective 1 — After instruction, the students will be able to understand the different components that make up a family, as evidenced by a painting, family tree, webbing, writing, or by differentiated multiple performances.

Objective 2 — After instruction, the students will be able to explain the differences between communities and homes, as evidenced by a model of a home, collage, and sharing interviews with family members.

Objective 3 — After instruction, the students will be able to define what a family is, as evidenced by their completion of a portfolio of the unit and final presentation. (Jessica and Jenn, Yankee Elementary, 2003)

Thematic statements, as the first step in organizing a thematic unit, may be the most important. Without a solid theme, the students will not be engaged in learning. Without understandable goals, parents and administrators may not buy into the reasoning behind teaching from a thematic pedagogy. Without solid objectives teachers may not know whether their unit has been successful. Because of its critical nature, teachers should spend the necessary time to ensure that all facets of the thematic statement are present and that it is strong enough that all are interested.

STEP THREE: ALIGNMENT WITH STANDARDS

The prevailing attitude in education is accountability. Principals, school curriculum directors, school boards, and departments of education at the state and federal levels are challenging teachers to align what they do in their classrooms with curricular elements that detail requisite skills to be mastered by students. While standards were originally designed out of a desire for greater school and teacher accountability for meeting the standards, standards-based practice has been warped to suggest that accountability, or curricular alignment, is only to be performed as it relates to high-stakes assessments. This couldn't be farther from the truth. Academic standards should be key knowledge, skills, and dispositions that all students in a particular grade or subject should master.

Alignment with State or National Academic Standards

Every state's standards differ to a great extent. As the United States is not currently under one form of curriculum (although this may change by the No Child Left Behind legislation), teachers need to become familiar with their state academic requirements. Further, it is critical that they understand their school corporation and building principal's relationships with the standards. While many administrators previously have not emphasized the role of the standards in curriculum planning (focusing more on textbooks and other curriculums chosen by committees), in today's schools, failure to understand the impact of the standards can limit the success not only a of teacher, but also of students. Novice teachers should work with master teachers to discover what requirements exist in their schools to align daily lessons and units with the standards. However, even if principals are not driven to examine whether standards are being met by each unit, it would be highly suspect if teachers in twenty-first-century schools were not identifying how their lessons were meeting standards (and this would perhaps demonstrate that teacher's lack of professionalism!).

Teachers need to recognize the role of the standards in curriculum planning—standards do not drive instruction, instruction drives the standards. While academic standards detail necessary skills that students should perform and knowledge that they should gain, they were not designed to be taught as items on a checklist to be marked off as they are reviewed (Lipson et al., 1993). Academic standards are to be mastered; that is to say, students should be able to demonstrate effectively the standards for a curriculum in a variety of settings and in a variety of formats following instruction. As such, teachers should be looking for ways to review multiple academic subjects and identify the strands that connect concepts—writing skills are often reviewed not just in language arts, but also in social studies, mathematics, and science. Reviewing skills and knowledge bases that support one another can help teachers to streamline their curriculums, making for smarter pedagogy and richer experiences.

Alignment of the standards to a unit requires patience and skill. The process remains thematically based—teachers should work hard to keep the theme at the forefront throughout the process of curricular alignment, rather than looking through the standards randomly or haphazardly aligning standards that are the easiest to identify. Teachers should start the process by first remembering the theme—when a teacher thinks about the theme that her students selected, what subject area is the first to come to mind as being relevant? Mrs. Elpers, a middle school mathematics teacher, reviewed her beliefs about how curriculum and theme were connected in her thematic statement about her sixth-grade thematic unit on mysteries:

My integrated theme unit is a mystery theme for 6th grade. My goals for this unit are not only to teach specific concepts, but to also help the students learn to think critically. I think that beginning in the primary grades, students are "taught" just to regurgitate facts and figures they have learned. However, do they really understand the concepts and are they able to decide when and how to apply these concepts in their daily lives? I think as teachers we need to teach students to become independent and critical thinkers so that they can actually use what they have learned. Also I have tutored more and more students who struggle with using context clues and inferences to form a conclusion. I think mysteries would be a great way to help students develop these skills. Through mysteries, students would not only try to use the clues to figure it out, but they must also decide which clues are important.

I think this unit would be motivating to a variety of students because it can be used in any subject, and it lends itself to a variety of projects that the students could choose to do. Students could write their own mysteries, share them with the class or perhaps even perform them for their parents. They could use the Internet to research various mysteries throughout history or in different cultures. They could build models of Stonehenge or the pyramids and analyze the mystery behind how they were built. They can create artwork, videos, a radio mystery, and countless other projects. It's also fun because students could choose to work in a group and that also motivates students.

Students also can better see the interconnectedness of the curriculum while they work through these problem-solving situations. Social studies helps students to recognize the similarities and differences between groups and cultures, identifying salient points to assist in better knowing other

groups throughout history. Science relies on similar skills, using information presented to us in a systematic manner to strengthen the objectivity of
our understanding of our world. Finally, this theme can assist my students
in reviewing the importance of mathematics as a necessary skill for life—
without math, many of the problems reviewed for this mystery would be
subjective, without boundaries, and hard to quantify. As such, math provides the link to the other subjects as we work to resolve the mysteries set
up in this unit. (Mrs. Elpers, Fairlawn Academy, 2003)

After teachers have identified which area of the curriculum might provide a foundation for their unit, they should start aligning this subject to
their objectives. Teachers should only align standards that support mastery
of knowledge, skills, and dispositions. If after the completion of an objective, it cannot be said that a student has mastered a standard, then students shouldn't be expected to review it for the unit. Teachers should continue from subject to subject until such time as they can effectively see the
links between content areas that support the standard. Teacher education
candidates from the University of Southern Indiana represent effective
alignment of the State of Indiana Academic Standards for eighth grade in
their unit on journeys.

Goals and Objectives

Goal 1—After the unit, students will learn through various historical journeys how America became the country it is today.
Objective 1—After instruction, students will be able to display how physical journeys in American history can relate to personal journeys, as evidenced by a written journal. Standards:

English

8.3.5 Identify and analyze recurring themes (such as good versus evil)
that appear frequently across traditional and contemporary
works.
8.4.1 Discuss ideas for writing, keep a list or notebook of ideas, and
use graphic organizers to plan writing.
8.4.2 Create compositions that have a clear message, a coherent thesis
(a statement of position on the topic), and end with a clear and
well-supported conclusion.
8.4.4 Plan and conduct multiple-step information searches by using
computer networks.

8.4.5 Achieve an effective balance between researched information and original ideas.

8.4.6 Use a computer to create documents by using word-processing skills and publishing programs; develop simple databases and spreadsheets to manage information and prepare reports.

8.4.7 Review, evaluate, and revise writing for meaning and clarity.

8.4.8 Edit and proofread one's own writing, as well as that of others, using an editing checklist or set of rules, with specific examples of corrections of frequent errors.

8.6.4 Edit written manuscripts to ensure that correct grammar is used.

8.6.5 Use correct punctuation.

8.6.6 Use correct capitalization.

8.6.7 Use correct spelling conventions.

Social Studies

8.1.16 Describe the abolition of slavery in the northern states, conflict and compromises (1820), and the continued resistance to slavery by African Americans.

8.1.20 Explain the influence of individuals on key events and developments of the early United States.

8.1.27 Recognize historical perspective by identifying the historical context in which events unfolded and by avoiding evaluation of the past solely in terms of present-day norms.

Objective 2—After instruction, students will be able to evaluate how one aspect of American cultures led to a significant event in American history, as evidenced by a video project. Standards:

Social Studies

8.1.27 Recognize historical perspective by identifying the historical context in which events unfolded and by avoiding evaluation of the past solely in terms of present-day norms.

8.1.31 Examine the causes of problems in the past, and evaluate solutions chosen as well as possible alternative courses of action. Consider the information available at the time, the interests of those affected by the decision, and the consequences of each course of action.

8.3.9 Identify ways people modified the physical environment as the United States developed, and the types of problems that resulted.

8.5.9 Describe changes in entertainment and recreation, such as the growing interest in sports of various kinds in the mid-nineteenth century, and explain how these changes related to urbanization and technological developments.

English

8.3.6. Identify and analyze recurring themes (such as good versus evil) that appear frequently across traditional and contemporary works.

8.4.1 Discuss ideas for writing, keep a list or notebook of ideas, and use graphic organizers to plan writing.

8.4.2 Create compositions that have a clear message, a coherent thesis (a statement of position on the topic), and end with a clear and well-supported conclusion.

8.4.4 Plan and conduct multiple-step information searches by using computer networks.

8.4.5 Achieve an effective balance between researched information and original ideas.

8.4.6 Use a computer to create documents by using word-processing skills and publishing programs; develop simple databases and spreadsheets to manage information and prepare reports.

8.4.7 Review, evaluate, and revise writing for meaning and clarity.

8.4.8 Edit and proofread one's own writing, as well as that of others, using an editing checklist or set of rules, with specific examples of corrections of frequent errors.

8.6.4 Edit written manuscripts to ensure that correct grammar is used.

8.6.5 Use correct punctuation.

8.6.6 Use correct capitalization.

8.6.7 Use correct spelling conventions.

Art

8.7.1 Create works of art based on sensitive observation from real life and personal experience.

8.7.2 Demonstrate ability to utilize personal interests, current events, experiences, imagery, media, or methods as sources for expanding their artwork.

8.7.3 Utilize themes and symbols that demonstrate knowledge of contexts, values, and aesthetics to communicate intended meaning in their work.

8.9.1 Selectively utilize the visual characteristics and expressive features of a given medium to enhance meaning in their work.
8.9.2 Demonstrate appropriate use of different media, techniques, and processes to communicate themes and ideas in their work.

Multiple objectives can meet the same standards, reinforcing particular skills in different contexts. Similarly, different content areas can help to support learning in multiple ways, so that students can see the depth of the curriculum and the interconnectedness of concepts from subject to subject.

STEP FOUR: LESSON PLANNING

Perhaps the greatest struggle that teachers have in thematic teaching is the requirement to create lesson plans that support the unit. In order to ensure that the unit remains focused and organized, it is critical that teachers spend the time to create curricular plans that can drive the instruction, as well as document what has been covered. Again, as a facet of teacher accountability, it is critical that teachers be able to show key stakeholders (and in particular, students) what they are learning and why they are learning it. While it is unlikely that students will ever see a lesson plan, the supporting documentation to the unit, such as thematic statements, standards, rubrics, checklists, and procedures can be shared. Moreover, principals, parents, and curriculum directors will want to see plans, and lesson plans provide a clear picture of what is expected throughout the unit.

Organizing Lesson Plans

Different teachers and principals have different expectations for what is to be included in a lesson plan. For the purposes of a thematic unit, it is critical that there be at least four key areas: (1) a section for objectives and aligned standards, (2) a procedures section, (3) an assessment section, and finally (4) a supporting document section.

Objectives and Aligned Standards

Since the primary purpose of thematic units is to demonstrate the effective and systematic teaching of various areas of the curriculum, a lesson plan should be sure to include details as to what students should be able to do or know following a lesson. Further, this section is critical if the unit is to be based on an assessment-driven practice, as teachers need to know what is expected of students (objectives) in order to assess them effectively.

Procedures

Procedures for the lesson should be clearly delineated descriptions of what teachers and students are expected to do on a daily basis throughout the course of the lesson. Procedures should be written in such a way that another teacher, a substitute teacher, or a principal could enter your classroom, and quickly take over for you. As such, these sections should be rich with pertinent characteristics of who is doing what and when and in what context they are doing it. This section also assists others in understanding how your objectives will support meeting the standards (a teacher should be able to review the procedures section and see a link between the standards and the assessment sections).

Assessment

As stated previously, good assessment should drive instruction. For teachers, this should be the most important (and perhaps lengthy) section of the lesson plan. Whereas in the past this section might have included immeasurable statements such as "The students will be assessed through participation," or "I will be sure to evaluate how creatively they perform this task," professional teachers must share in this section how the standards have been met and how students will evidence the outcomes. For example, in the assessment section below, note how the teacher reviews what standards were met, how they were met, and how the objective was evidenced:

Evaluation/Assessment
    Students will be evaluated using the rubrics below. I have tried to cover all the standards listed, and hopefully the students will now have a better understanding of the meaning of patriotism and American symbols. Standards:

English/Language Arts:

   1.1.3 Recognize that sentences start with capital letters and end with punctuation, such as periods, question marks, and exclamation points.

Students demonstrated by the three sentences they wrote on their Liberty Bell fact sheet and also by the sentences they constructed on their U.S. symbol fact cards.

1.1.11 Read common sight words (words that are often seen and heard). Students demonstrated by comparing the words on their patriotic word wall with the words on their common sight words word wall. They used a combination of common sight words and the new patriotic words in their sentences and made note of them in the stories we read.

1.2.1 Identify the title, author, illustrator, and table of contents of a reading selection. Students demonstrated by learning about the different parts of a book when we read *America* by Louise Borden, and by having the children review the parts of book as we read the other stories.

1.7.7 Retell stories using basic story grammar and relating the sequence of story events by answering who, what, where, why, and how questions. Students demonstrated by giving their oral reports on American symbols.

Math:

1.1.1 Count, read, and write whole numbers up to 100. Students demonstrated by using the unifix cubes that were grouped in tens, to measure themselves and the eye on the Statue of Liberty, and then recording their measurements. Also counted the number of stars and stripes on the flag.

1.1.2 Count and group objects in ones and tens. Students demonstrated by using the unifix cubes to measure themselves and the Statue of Liberty's eye. They also learned that our flag has fifty stars that are five groups of ten.

1.5.1 Measure the length of objects by repeating a nonstandard unit or a standard unit. Students demonstrated by participating in the Just How Big is Lady Liberty math activity.

1.5.2 Use different units to measure the length of the same object and predict whether the measure will be greater or smaller when a different unit is used. Students demonstrated by participating in the Just How Big is Lady Liberty math activity.

Science:

1.2.2 Use sums and differences of single-digit numbers in investigations and judge the reasonableness of the answers. Students demonstrated by recording their estimates of how big the Lady Liberty's eye was, and then after actually measuring it, adding or subtracting from their earlier estimates to see how close they had been.

1.6.1 Observe and describe that models, such as toys, are like the real things in some ways but different in others. Students demonstrated by looking at the small scale models of the Liberty Bell and Statue of Liberty and discussing orally as a class how they look very much like the real thing but are much smaller.

Social Studies:

1.1.3 Identify American songs and symbols. Students demonstrated by doing various activities such as giving reports, making posters, recording facts, and singing patriotic songs in class.

Art:

1.1.1 Understand that art reflects the culture of its origin. Students demonstrated by making a replica of our American flag and by memorizing facts and giving reports about our country's unique American symbols.

1.1.2 Identify works of art and artifacts used in the customs, festivals, and celebrations of various cultures. Students demonstrated by examining the designs of various American symbols and by creating their own examples of these symbols in class (craft activities, posters, etc.).

1.7.3 Identify and use symbols to express ideas. Students demonstrated by creating their own personal symbols and also by creating their posters to tell about their group's assigned symbol.

Music:

1.2.3 Keep a steady beat on a percussion instrument. Students demonstrated by playing musical instruments in class during patriotic activities.

1.8.3 Discuss suitable music for various occasions and rituals. Students demonstrated by using the instruments to demonstrate that music, marching, and the playing of instruments is often associated with patriotic occasions to express pride in our country.

Each standard details what students will do in order to demonstrate mastery of the standard. One assignment can support multiple standards from a variety of areas, and stakeholders should be able to see clearly evidence of what students are doing to master a standard and cover the objective (Alder, 2002).

STEP FIVE: PUTTING IT ALL TOGETHER

Once thematic statements, goals and objectives, academic standard alignment, and lesson planning have occurred, all documentation needs to be organized into a cohesive unit. Teachers who spend time prior to teaching a unit by putting all the unit artifacts together find that teaching the unit is a much more fluid process—organization is key! Without having all of the necessary documents to teach the lesson effectively, teachers may find thematic teaching overwhelming, not as a result of the method, but because of their lack of organizational skills.

Supporting Documentation

The final component of a lesson plan should include all materials that will be required to teach the lesson. This can include, but isn't limited to, handouts, assignment descriptions, templates, advanced organizers, rubrics, and checklists. For further review, see the attached thematic lesson plan from a third-grade unit on animals at the end of this section.

Resources to Assist with Integrated Teaching

To ensure that students have the ability to make their learning meaningful and powerful, teachers should construct resource areas throughout their classrooms to support student access to materials. Some items that teachers should consider having on hand for use throughout their units include the following:

- Fiction and nonfiction books (twenty to thirty books on hand for the students to read during self-selected reading)
- Magazines (*Ranger Rick*, *Highlights*, and *My Big Backyard*)
- Internet (teacher resources)
- Specialized people (parents and people in your community)
- Videos (informative facts about bugs: *Bug City*, *James and the Giant Peach*)
- Field trips (places in your community)
- Manipulatives

It is essential for teachers to take advantage of these resources as they lead their students through their educational experience. One very beneficial resource for elementary teachers when designing an interdisciplinary curriculum is nonfiction books. These books can be shared with students during read-aloud time. After reading the teacher can guide discussions that lead into other disciplines. They can look for scientific accuracy in the book. Another important resource at any grade level is parents (it is hard to plan crafts and group activities without an extra set of hands!). Parents can send in many great fiction and nonfiction books and videos and also can assist in making snacks and crafts.

It is critical to remember that although the interdisciplinary approach is an effective one, these units should be spread out throughout the school year. Doing five to eight a year tends to be adequate for motivating students and ensuring that students stay involved.

CONCLUSION

Using this approach, teachers will discover many benefits of an interdisciplinary curriculum. In other words, overlapping concepts in subject areas such as science, social studies, math, health, and physical education are integrated into our language arts program. This method capitalizes on natural and logical connections between the disciplines. Not only are students able to see the connections between content areas, but they are able to learn in the real world.

Chapter Seven

Learning through Service

What similarities exist between effective practice, service-learning, and authentic pedagogies? Both service-learning and authentic pedagogies are tools that challenge administrators and faculty in the schools to reconsider what occurs in the classroom to provide a more real-world and student-centered approach to education. It has been shown throughout the professional literature on both topics that if students relate the curriculum to their personal lives, then they are more likely to see the dynamic nature of information. Yet, as schools face times of pressure for accountability via standards-based practices such as No Child Left Behind (Page, 2002), are such pedagogical practices relevant or appropriate? This review investigates the overlap between service-learning and authentic pedagogies. Further, I discuss some examples of the positive results of service-learning and provide a template for similar curricular realignment in other schools in light of the current accountability movement.

Students who engage in service-learning activities participate within the school curriculum while providing a service to their community. Such experiences are supported by authentic pedagogy, which suggests that classroom experiences be enhanced by individualized instruction, meaningful interactions with the community, and opportunities that support student interests (Wolfe, 2001). It is thought that these community and curricular integrations are likely to increase student participation within schools, creating a sense of ownership and active participation (Furco, 1996; Nix and Slavkin, 2002; Plucker and Slavkin, 2000; Schine, 1997). Further, such experiences may support the high-stakes unfunded mandates for school accountability that demand greater community involvement in what occurs in our schools.

AUTHENTIC PEDAGOGY

The nature of cognition, the functioning of the human brain, and the construction of knowledge are tied to one another. Largely thought of for nearly a century as separate areas and separate networks connected by "highways of knowledge," the brain is now thought of as a complex, interdependent ecosystem that allows for singular functions to be organized and performed by multiple areas (Kosslyn and Koenig, 1992; Sylwester, 1994; Wolfe, 2001). These neural systems parallel knowledge schemas, which is why learning and brain systems tend to develop along similar time frames (Case, 1991). Thus, the stronger the interactions between the information and skills that a student learns, the more likely those schemas are to be organized and assimilated for future use.

Neural networks are consistently reorganized as a result of experience and have the capacity to develop throughout the life cycle. As stated earlier in chapter 2, windows of opportunity may indicate that children are better able to learn skills at developmentally appropriate times. These windows may begin to shut as time progresses, but in almost all circumstances, learning can progress. Skills can be taught and encouraged by teachers and parents at all levels of education. Thus, even if students did not have the opportunity to learn as juveniles or did not work to their capacity, they can continue to learn (Fisher and Rose, 1998; Languis, 1998; Nix and Slavkin, 2002). Thus, the more individualized and meaningful experiences are, the more likely the students are to recognize, reuse, and engage in higher-order thinking skills with respect to those experiences (Slavkin, 2002; Tomlinson and Kalbfleisch, 1998).

Many teachers agree that the most effective way to teach students is to provide them with opportunities to make knowledge meaningful and relevant (Burke, 1997; Dozier, 1992; Slavkin, 2002; Sylwester, 1994). Students who are in charge of their learning are more likely to make deeper connections with material. Even though this is sound pedagogical practice, it is critical for another reason: in changing their relationship with material, students also may be changing the way they think. Learner empowerment and personalization of information is thought to make neural connections stronger than they would be without student empowerment (Brandt, 1997; Diamond and Hopson, 1999; Lowery, 1998).

However, reorganization is based in large part on whether or not the student takes ownership of learning. By becoming involved in decision making and applying information to their lives, students can increase the likelihood that information is meaningful and is retained. Neural pathways and the hardwiring of information depend on (1) the richness of the learning environment and (2) the interest and prior knowledge of the student.

Moreover, students vary in the knowledge and skills they developed during their primary and secondary school years; as such, the curriculum should focus on individual skill building. The greater the access to their prior knowledge, the more easily they are able to learn new information. When teachers and students recognize that information is interconnected and that what one learns in one subject area can be applied to other subjects, we become more adept at recognizing, organizing, and applying information (D'Arcangelo, 1998; Nummela and Caine, 1998; Renzulli and Reis, 1985). This concept is supported by initiatives such as Carol Tomlinson and M. L. Kalbfleisch's challenge for differentiated practices that support the individual interests of learners as they engage in interdisciplinary and integrated curricular experiences (1998).

Thus, it would largely make sense that learners would function better in an environment that is intriguing, provides multiple sensory experiences, and involves dynamic problems without singular answers. It seems relatively simple to suggest that teachers instruct in an environment that provides real-world problems that afford students the opportunity to collaborate and work with information in personal and individual ways. As Robert Sylwester states, "Educators might then view the [curriculum] as an ecological problem . . . which integrates complex environmental stimuli, and de-emphasizes basic skills and forms of evaluation that merely compress complexity" (1994, 48).

A curriculum based on authentic practices could look much like the curriculums that already exist in many classrooms and schools that use differentiated experiences to meet academic standards, but with subtle variations. However, such pedagogy must provide the opportunity for students to show what they know and to collaborate with each other on projects, incorporate thematic curriculums, provide opportunities for reflection, and create goal-based learning opportunities that build upon each other over the school year. Such a curriculum would expect that students and teachers engage in mini apprenticeships, creating experiences that will result in well-rounded, functional professionals who can reflect on tasks and the reality of the professional environment—one that is ever changing and ever diversifying.

SERVICE LEARNING

Similar to authentic pedagogies, service-learning experiences often require teachers and students to interact with members of the community to engage in higher-order thinking about some area of interest to all the involved parties. Service-learning has been utilized by schools as a curricular support that increases students' involvement with local communities and improves the philanthropic experience of youth (Billing, 2000b; Meyers, 1999; Nix, 2001; Schumer and Belbas, 1996). Service-learning also is believed to provide students opportunities for active involvement in the democratic processes of the school and community, though it is thought that the potential impact of such programs has not yet been realized (Rutter and Newmann, 1989; Schukar, 1997).

Many researchers have identified the importance of students moving from the theory of the classroom curriculum to reality via involvement with their communities (Lee, 1997; Meyers, 1999; Halsted and Schine, 1994; Neuman, Copple, and Bredekamp, 2001). Service-learning is intentionally designed "to equally benefit the provider and the recipient of the service as well as to ensure equal focus on both the service being provided and the learning that is occurring" (Furco, 1996, 396). While community service provides students the opportunity to give back to their communities, service-learning programs emphasize the connection between the service, the curriculum, and students' reflections on their experiences as they relate to the curriculum (O'Flanagan, 1997; Nix and Slavkin, 2002; Slavkin and Faust, 2003).

Certain effects have been observed in students who participate in service-learning activities. Students have found an increase in self-pride, an improved connection with their community, and a feeling of ownership of their community and their school curriculum (Sandler and Vandgrift, 1995; Schine, 1997). F. M. Newmann and R. A. Rutter (1983) showed that involvement in service-learning projects by secondary students modestly increased students' sense of social responsibility and personal competence. Green (1962) and Bucher and Hall (1998) have found that service-learning involvement with secondary students may provide them with the interventions necessary to succeed in school.

Students also have indicated that the opportunity to work with the community and relate it to the curriculum of the school have helped give them a sense of success not previously found at school (Billing, 2000a; Lantieri, 1999). S. Moores (1999) and M. Nix and M. L. Slavkin (2002) found that groups of high-risk students were more likely to show high self-esteem following involvement with service-learning projects that included an adult-mentoring component.

S. Meyers (1999) suggests that the curriculum of any school should include aspects of (a) experiential learning, (b) reflection about the learning as it occurs, and (c) an understanding of the workplace within the broader social context so as to improve students' sense of involvement with community. It would seem likely that these characteristics would be critical components of any service-learning program that a principal would want to initiate within his or her school. Thus, as authentic curriculums' challenge to develop individual ownership and identification with information and activities that resonate with prior experiences, so too does service-learning hold that in order for these projects to be successful, there must be some individual "buy-in" and ownership.

IMPLICATIONS FOR SCHOOL LEADERS IN THE FACE OF ACCOUNTABILITY

In the decades following 1983's U.S. Department of Education publication *A Nation at Risk* (in which the government largely vilified the public schools for their poor performance and the underachievement of students), schools have found themselves under increasing pressure to demonstrate student achievement. Whereas in the past American schools had been challenged to demonstrate student achievement through grades and performances on assignments, states are increasingly moving toward a system of accountability that mandates high test scores as indicators of achievement. Despite the protests of most experts in assessment and education, school systems throughout the country are being challenged to "teach to a test" in an effort to boost scores and regain public confidence.

Service-learning may be a tool that schools can use to meet the needs of students in a time of pressure from departments of education for accountability via standards-based practices. This chapter reviews the creative opportunities and challenges faced by an alternative school in Southern Indiana that has infused service-learning into the curriculum.

An alternative school, Stanley Hall Enrichment Center, Evansville-Vanderburgh School Corporation, in Evansville, Indiana, has moved away from an individualized alternative school program for truant students to one that infuses service-learning into its curriculum. The experience has provided curricular challenges and exceptional opportunities, many of which might be of benefit to other schools interested in infusing service-learning into their curriculums, while still meeting graduation standards or accountability mandates.

INDIANA PUBLIC LAW 221:
GIVING VOICE TO THE COMMUNITY?

School systems across the county are facing increasing pressure to align the performances in their classrooms with state standards, a challenge that on the surface is easily met and not of issue. However, most teachers are feeling the pressure to teach the standards that are evidenced on state high-stakes tests. Educators don't often support "teaching to the test" as a practice as it tends to reinforce rote memorization, superficial understanding of material, and limited higher-order thinking. Standards-based practices were initially designed to afford teachers the ability to understand what competencies students should master throughout their years in primary, intermediate, and secondary education. What has transpired, however, is that students are being taught to take a test, teachers are being forced to teach passively, and schools are reeling under the pressure to meet a system of accountability that may or may not have any validity in demonstrating student achievement (Sacks, 1999).

An example of such high-stakes, standards-based practices that are similar to accountability mandates evidenced throughout the country can be found in the state of Indiana. Indiana teachers and schools are well versed in a Department of Education initiative entitled Public Law 221, a legislative mandate that challenges school accountability by matching state standards with individual school needs. Indiana Public Law 221 is a recent initiative by the Department of Education to create a yearly accountability program that focuses on continuous school improvement by challenging standards-based practice, with achievement outcomes measured by a high-stakes gateway examination that must be passed if students are to graduate from high school. All public schools in the state of Indiana are under a mandate to create a professional development program for teachers, organize a community-based committee to investigate the performance of the school, and utilize a variety of source information to demonstrate how the school will improve the performance of students. However, the assessment of school improvement and the categorical organization of schools have largely been based on the yearly performance of students on a state-mandated standardized test, the Indiana Statewide Test of Educational Performance (ISTEP+). Because of this, more than ever schools are considering how they are meeting state standards and the curriculum.

Rather than supporting the pedagogical skills that we know are effective in supporting high achievement and cognitive growth in students, many teachers feel that this system of accountability only supports passive learning in a limited educational environment (Kohn, 2000). Informal evidence suggests that many of the schools have only become more ingrained in the practice of teaching to the test; as the pressure to demonstrate consistent performance on a measure of general factual knowledge increases, so has the effort to provide a curriculum in a traditional, factual manner. Some schools, especially those that work with marginalized populations or nontraditional student populations, cannot meet these performances (nor have they ever been able to), not as a result of inability, nor because of a lack of effort or dedication on the part of their educators. These schools tend to be limited by the lack of community investment and financial integrity to do what is required of them. Though Public Law 221 (like many other forms of standards-based, high-stakes testing accountability programs throughout the United States) hopes to assist these very same schools by getting the community involved with them, it is unlikely to have that desired outcome as most of these schools will be labeled as deficient because their labeling will be based on ISTEP+ (gateway exam) scores.

ACCOUNTABILITY FOR "OTHER" STUDENTS—
HOW SERVICE LEARNING CAN BENEFIT YOU

Schools who work with marginalized, multiethnic, or nontraditional student populations often are called upon to meet standards using an assessment package that was never designed with them in mind. Rather than utilizing standardized test scores to demonstrate proficiency and school improvement, schools are using their Public Law 221 committees and professional-development programs to create innovative and nontraditional curriculum shifts. Service-learning is an integral part of this process. Service-learning provides these schools with a loophole under Public Law 221: demonstrate performance via alternative means. Thus, what follows below is a brief account of how one school has created individual goals and performance indicators for itself that cannot be measured by standardized tests, but can only be demonstrated through civic literacy and community involvement.

STANLEY HALL ENRICHMENT CENTER: A MODEL
OF ALIGNMENT AND SCHOOL IMPROVEMENT

Stanley Hall Enrichment Center in Evansville, Indiana, has a history of dedication to the needs of students who have not fit into the classrooms of traditional high schools. Stanley Hall has met academic standards by providing an individualized curriculum that meets graduate standards. Within the last decade, however, the school has created a curriculum that is largely based on service-learning. As such, its goals are parallel with those largely found throughout the service-learning literature. Stanley Hall believes that all students can learn, deserve a safe environment conducive to learning, and should have equal access to curriculums that enhance opportunities to maximize personal growth, as well as to contribute to the society of which they are a part. The teachers of this school provide a safe environment conducive to learning with opportunities for success, growth, and wise use of time, talents, tools, and other resources; they also challenge all students to contribute to society, further their educations, and empower themselves (while still embracing the propositions set forth by the Indiana Department of Education and the National Board for Professional Teaching Standards).

The current status of educational programming is evidenced by measures taken on site that relate to the mission and three primary goals of Stanley Hall. Stanley Hall's measures its performance and accountability using indicators selected by its community committee that are inextricably tied to its mission as an alternative school. As a result of student transitions between home schools and Stanley Hall Enrichment Center, standardized test scores like those of the ISTEP+ do not demonstrate repeat performances on the test. As such, any normative or comparative purposes that a test might offer from semester to semester or year to year are of limited value. Also, the size of each semester's testing sample (average $n = 25$) may increase the likelihood that one student's scores skew the average for a semester significantly.

Community-connected assessments (service-learning and community service) are more appropriate and valid measures related to Stanley Hall's curricular goals and academic standards. As Stanley Hall has increased its use of service-learning components to provide coursework and meet Indiana state standards, it has taken steps to analyze the efficacy of this programming in meeting its three primary goals. Specifically, following service-learning performances, students have demonstrated improved sense of self-efficacy, increased connection with community, and increased involvement with the school curriculum.

Achievement expectations are geared toward fulfillment of the Stanley Hall mission to empower students to earn a high school diploma, advance to postsecondary education or gainful employment, remain lifelong learners, and serve as valuable community members. As such, these achievement goals, all of which are tied to service-learning, guide proficiency in and mastery of state standards.

Students who engage in service-learning activities participate within the school curriculum while providing a service to their community. It is thought that this community and curricular integration has increased student participation within schools, creating a sense of ownership and active participation. Moreover, it has helped the school maintain a level of success that was not achieved with these students in a traditional high school setting.

CONCLUSION

Whether such modifications to curriculums are referred to as authentic pedagogy or service-learning, these approaches should be utilized by schools as curricular supports that increase students' involvement with local communities, improve the philanthropic experience of youth, and invest in independent project-based models. Service-learning provides students opportunities for active involvement in the democratic processes of the school and community, at a time when state departments of education are mandating community involvement and dedication. Authentic pedagogies afford all students the opportunity to learn as educators are challenged to meet individual expectations in demonstrating mastery of state academic standards (doing justice to the philosophy behind President Bush's No Child Left Behind legislation, rather than just creating an unachievable unfounded mandate). It is believed that such transitions might afford a variety of schools the opportunity to meet the demands of accountability, by allowing alternative performances to serve as evidence of stability and consistent educational strength.

The impact of the classroom meaning-making process and the roles that student empowerment and student-centered pedagogical practices play in changing the nature of the classroom have implications for the metacognition and actualization of students. If teachers are to help learners to become competent and critical thinkers, they must be aware of how authentic practices can assist them in maximizing the potential of their pedagogy. Teachers can help students learn more effectively if educators create opportunities for students to relate the curriculum to their personal lives, provide an environment that reveals the multiple meanings of material, and allow students to see the dynamic nature of information.

Chapter Eight

Democratic Classrooms

OVERVIEW

What similarities exist between authentic learning and democratic pedagogies? Both authentic learning and democratic pedagogies are tools that challenge administrators and faculty in the schools to reconsider what occurs in the classroom to provide a more real-world and student-centered approach to education. Democratic pedagogical practice has been around for several years in school systems across the United States. But what is a democratic classroom, and why are so few teachers using the practice in their classrooms? It has been shown throughout the professional literature on both topics that if students relate the curriculum to their personal lives, then they are more likely to see the dynamic nature of information.

This chapter briefly reviews what a democratic classroom is and how it relates to the curriculum. The following pages will give parents and teachers an extensive look into how this teaching method can be successfully incorporated into the daily curriculum. This chapter also discusses the role of the parent in democratic classrooms and shows their importance in helping to create a successful program. Democratic teaching is an effective pedagogical practice for students and an opportunity for teachers, parents, and community members to demonstrate how learning within schools has real-world implications for community issues. Beyond this, democratic classrooms can help students to recognize the implications of learning and the real-world connections that knowledge and skills have.

After reading this chapter, the reader should have a clear image of how democratic classroom projects and democratic classrooms are structured, the strengths and weaknesses of the method, and the implications for students, teachers, and parents. All of this information is prevalent to both teachers and parents because it involves how students are taught and how they learn. The guidelines for running and developing these methods will be clearly laid out for teachers. Further, this information also should help parents understand why this tool will help their student learn more effectively and become a better part of the community. Parents, as active community members, need to recognize that democratic methods, when used correctly in the classroom, will help their student better retain knowledge, learn teamwork, take ownership in their community, gain self worth, develop values, understand characteristics of democracy, and take pride in the services they are providing.

Authentic learning and *democratic classrooms* are two separately defined terms that can be intertwined into one classroom. Both are rapidly becoming prevalent teaching methods in many classrooms. Democratic education processes have a part in the decisions that are made involving the students and classroom. The decisions should be reached in a democratic fashion. Every student in every classroom should have the ability to achieve high standards, and democratic classrooms create an environment where all individuals involved can be successful without jeopardizing anyone else's opportunity to achieve (McDermott, 1999).

Similarly, authentic instruction encourages student learning and development through active participation in thoughtfully organized service that is conducted in, and meets the needs of, a community. Both authentic instruction and democracy-based methods of instruction provide teachers and students the opportunity to learn about civic responsibilities, while supporting the needs of the community through active dialogue with community partners. The academic curriculum is enhanced by demonstrating the real-world implications of the information reviewed and the action involved in learning (Allen, 2003).

While democratic learning includes doing things to better the community of the school and its surroundings, there is a difference between community service and democratic learning. Whereas community service is an intended service volunteered by individuals or an organization to benefit a community, democratic learning is defined as community-based curricular programming that aligns with curricular needs and a sense of civic literacy.

DEFINITION OF DEMOCRATIC CLASSROOMS

Democratic classrooms create an environment where all individuals involved in the education process have a part in the decisions made involving the students and classroom. The decisions should be reached in a democratic fashion. Every student in every classroom should have the capability to achieve high standards and be successful without jeopardizing anyone else's opportunity to achieve (McDermott, 1999). Service-learning is just one of the many techniques that teachers have incorporated into their classrooms to help support civic literacy and engage students in their local communities. Such processes are considered under the umbrella of democratic pedagogical practices. A democratic classroom is an "environment where deliberate, conscious, caring, and ethical decisions are made for the well-being of everyone. A democratic classroom is alive with the singular possibility that everyone can learn and be successful but never at the expense of anyone else" (McDermott, 1999).

Setting up a democratic classroom sets the scene for an egalitarian style of learning within the classroom. In a democratic classroom, students should feel comfortable enough to express their viewpoints while learning to listen to opposing views. Every child is treated with respect. Students are actively involved in all aspects of the classroom. They can help develop classroom rules while making cooperative decisions about the curriculums they wish to study. The students also should be involved in meaningful lessons. A democratic classroom promotes values that are needed in a service-learning project such as freedom, decision-making skills, risk taking, dealing with consequences, and group participation (Allen, 2003). All of these values are important skills that are implemented in a service-learning project that works within the community.

Many teachers agree that the most effective way to teach students is to provide them opportunities to make knowledge meaningful and relevant. Students who are in charge of their learning are more likely to make deeper connections with material. Even though this is sound pedagogical practice, it is critical for another reason: in changing their relationship with material, students also may be changing the way they think. Learner empowerment and personalization of information is thought to make neural connections stronger than they would be without student empowerment.

Moreover, the knowledge and skills students developed during their primary and secondary school years vary; as such, the curriculum should focus on individual skill building. The greater the access to their prior knowledge, the more easily students are able to learn new information. When teachers and students recognize that information is interconnected and that what one has learned in one subject area and in prior years can be applied to other subjects, then they become more adept at recognizing, organizing, and applying information.

IMPLICATIONS OF DEMOCRACY FOR LEARNING

Parents, as active community members, need to recognize that these methods, when used correctly in the classroom, will help their students better retain knowledge, learn teamwork, take ownership in their community, gain self worth, develop values, understand the characteristics of democracy, and take pride in the service they are providing. Teachers will also need to understand why these practices should be an essential part of their classroom environment and how to implement these strategies effectively.

A substantial amount of research has investigated how this pedagogy affects student learning and academic achievement. Research has shown that there is a positive relationship between students' involvement in these methods and their ability to learn (Halpern, 1996). There have been four beneficial outcomes resulting from the use of democracy in the classroom: "increases in academic learning, civic responsibility, personal and social development and opportunities for career exploration" (Allen, 2003).

Generally, service-learning combined with a democratic classroom provides students with their choice of hands-on experience. The students are taken out of the classroom to work on projects that they have decided meet their needs best. When allowed to use a democratic approach in the classroom, students are more likely to take part in the activity fully. Service-learning is often referred to as "the students' project" because the projects have not been forced on the students by someone else, and they do not have to read about them in a book. Rather than teachers serving as "experts," they are there to facilitate and assess the task so that it will best benefit the students' attainment of pertinent knowledge.

When given the opportunity to do a hands-on project, students are more likely to have meaningful interactions with the knowledge and skills that they are to learn. Further, such involvement increases the likelihood that students will be able to utilize this information and the skills obtained during project completion in other experiences. The more students have real-world opportunities to use information within the contexts prescribed in their communities, the greater the chance that they will use that knowledge later.

Many researchers have identified the importance of students moving from the theory of the classroom curriculum to reality via involvement with their communities (Halsted and Schine, 1994; Lee, 1997; Meoli, 2001). Democratic learning is intentionally designed to benefit the teacher and the student equally; they move away from a provider-recipient relationship to one of egalitarianism. Such a change is designed to ensure equal focus on both the community being organized and the learning that is occurring.

Further studies have shown that students have scored significantly higher on "four out of ten evaluation measures including: school involvement, grades, core subject grade averages, increased overall G.P.A.s, and educational aspirations" (Education Commission of the States, 1999). Certain effects have been observed in students who participate in democratic activities. Students have found an increase in self-pride, an improved connection with their communities, and a feeling of ownership of their communities and their school curriculums (Sandler and Vandgrift, 1995; Schine, 1997). F. M. Newmann and R. A. Rutter (1983) have showed that involvement in service-learning projects and democratic experiences by secondary students modestly increased students' sense of social responsibility and personal competence. Bucher and Hall (1998) have found that democratic involvement in community events with students may provide them with the interventions necessary to succeed in school.

Students also have indicated that the opportunity to work with the community and relate it to the curriculum of the school helped give them a sense of success not previously found at school (Billing, 1999, 2000a, and 2000b; Lantieri, 1999). S. Moores (1999) and M. Nix and M. L. Slavkin (2002) found that groups of high-risk students were more likely to show high self-esteem following involvement with service-learning projects that included an adult-mentoring component.

Meyers (1999) suggests that the democratic curriculum of any school should include aspects of (a) experiential learning, (b) reflection about the learning as it occurs, and (c) an understanding of the community within the broader social context to improve students' sense of involvement with community. It would seem likely that these characteristics would be critical components of any service-learning program that a principal would want to initiate within his or her school. Thus, as authentic curriculums' challenge students to develop individual ownership and identification with information and activities that resonate with prior experiences, so too does service-learning hold that in order for these projects to be successful, there must be some individual "buy-in" and ownership.

Further, strong evidence exists that student learning is greatly enhanced because students are directly involved in controlling their learning experience and because the activity has meaning to them. The California Department of Education created a pyramid that displays the average percentage of a student's retention rate with each method of teaching. At the top of the pyramid, scoring only 5 percent is teaching by lecture. This means that only 5 percent of students remember what they learn when a teacher lectures to them. At the bottom of the pyramid, with 90 percent retention, is learning by teaching others. This means that students learn the most through teaching others the skills that they have learned (California Department of Education, 1999).

However, reorganization of the curriculum is based in large part on whether or not the student takes ownership of learning. By becoming involved in decision making and applying information to their lives, students can increase the likelihood that information is meaningful and is retained. The effectiveness of the service experience and the students' abilities to understand the connections between community and classroom depend on (1) the richness of the learning environment and (2) the interest and prior knowledge of the student. Service-learning in a democratic classroom allows students to learn by doing. Research has proven that these types of pedagogies are effective in increasing student learning, achievement, and retention of information.

When allowed to do a hands-on project, students are more likely to have meaningful interactions with the knowledge and skills that they are to learn. Further, such involvement increases the likelihood that students will be able to utilize this information and the skills obtained during project completion in other experiences. The more that students have real-world opportunities to use information within the contexts prescribed in their communities, the greater the chance that they will use that knowledge later. Service-learning provides students with the opportunity to experience life in their communities, but from an alternative perspective. When students are participating in a service-learning project they see many people with different lifestyles. This allows students to understand more and not to cast blame, perpetuate stereotypes, or view the receiver as inferior (Perreault, 1997). Seeing the challenges the students are facing today, educators are shortchanging them by not giving them the opportunities and programs, such as service-learning, that will be just as important to them as academics (Friedland, 2003).

Service to community and integration within the democratic framework of our communities has been shown to create higher moral concern, compassion, flexibility in thinking, a stronger drive for creativity in achievement, and higher self-esteem in the students who participated regularly (Waterman, Akmajian, and Kearny, 1991). Typically, people who feel better emotionally can perform better in an educational environment. Cynthia McDermott (1999), author of *The Search for Democracy*, claims that teachers should not be teaching students in a vacuum in twenty-first–century America, filling them with randomized information that they have a limited basis for understanding. Rather, teachers should be engaging students and involving them outside of classroom environments by exploring their local communities and addressing skills and information that can assist them in better understanding their place within society and the impact of learning on helping to strengthen our communities.

Although more research is needed, students have been shown to benefit tremendously from service-learning and democratic classrooms. Democratic classrooms encourage students to take an active part in the classroom. The classroom should be a community where everyone feels like an essential part of the environment. This is often a downfall of many students in a traditional school. They do not produce work to their ability level because they are concentrating on how to adapt socially in their classrooms. These feelings often result in misbehavior, lower grades, and the desire not even to be at school. Students should recognize the ideas of others as probable solutions and work together to create the best possible solution to a problem. When a student plays an active part in a community, whether it is school, home, city, or country, that student understands the workings of that community and takes more pride in maintaining or elevating it (Furco, 1996; Furco and Billig, 2002; Inskip, 1998; McDermott, 1999).

CREATING A DEMOCRATIC COMMUNITY THROUGH SERVICE: AN EXAMPLE OF CIVIC LITERACY

The first step in implementing a service project in a classroom is to decide what the project will be. It is important to listen to input from students about what they feel is important in the community. After deciding on a service, the teacher needs to find the agency that the classroom will build a partnership with. The California Department of Education recognizes these key components to ensure successful partnerships:

> Common goals need to be set among all who are involved. The service-learning activity needs to follow along and meet the teacher's standards while meeting the needs of the community organization involved. It may be a good idea to have the schools create a written policy that displays each group member's responsibility. The managers of agencies and school administrators need to give authority over a service project to the teacher who is working directly with the students. This will allow that person to make split second decisions without having to ask for permission first. The teacher needs to develop some form of evaluating the service-learning project. The evaluation will allow the teacher to identify any problems and make changes necessary to ensure that the program runs smoothly in the future. (California Department of Education, 1999)

Giving the students a voice in the planning and implementation of a service project will make it more meaningful to them. It is also important to incorporate reflection activities so the students can make personal connections between the activities and their own views. Teachers also must continue to receive preparation and professional development to assist them in continuing to learn as they develop deeper understandings of how to run a service-learning project (Nix and Slavkin, 2002). Other issues such as transportation and cost will have to be taken up with administrators within a specific school district.

RELEVANCE TO TEACHERS

An important group in service-learning is the teachers. While the numbers are slowly growing, many teachers still do not use service-learning in their classrooms. There are several schools that offer some service-learning, but only about 6.6 percent of American teachers use this practice in their classrooms (VanSickle, 1983). There is no true distinction in terms of age, number of years in teaching, or gender for teachers who use service-learning. However, the difference is that some of the teachers who use service-learning feel differently about the way young people learn, the proper instructional relationship between teachers and students, the importance of connecting their classroom to the outside world, and their students' ability to self-direct their own learning. These methods change the role of the teacher in a normal classroom. The teacher no longer controls the learning; he or she facilitates it. The student no longer acts as the passive receiver of information, but becomes an active participant in the learning process. The work style becomes collaborative instead of individual. The challenge that teachers find in their classrooms is getting students to understand the power that they have to influence others. Democracy through service-learning is a great way to help students see this influence.

Teachers tend to lean on this strategy for teaching because they are able to get involved in the learning of their students with a more hands-on approach. One important reason that teachers may find this practice useful in their classrooms is that studies have shown great gains in grades and test scores in language arts, mathematics, science, and other academic areas as a result of a well-designed service-learning project. In a society where education relies a lot on what test scores say about the students, teachers may lean toward this method of teaching to improve their classroom scores and possibly the schools in an effort to help their schools financially.

Teachers may also use this method in their classroom because service-learning has shown consistently that it can produce significant and positive change in students, schools, and communities (Fredericks, 2001). Teachers are constantly faced with negative words about and battles over their students and hearing that they are not doing enough to keep their students in line. This method would enhance the positive attitudes of their students by allowing them to give back to their community, but it can also help the community see the good things that the students are doing. Students become more engaged in studies and become more motivated to learn. Student attendance increases. Teachers and students report an increase in mutual respect, and the projects build stronger, more cohesive peer relationships.

Service-learning also helps prospective teachers develop skills and attitudes that can be beneficial to them as teachers, including sensitivity to diversity, increased self-esteem, strengthened communication skills, improved problem solving and critical thinking, stronger commitment to teaching as a profession, deeper engagement in critical reflection, and strengthened caring skills (Jones, Malone, and Stallings, 2002).

Like all facets of education, each strategy has its strengths and weaknesses. One key weakness to service-learning is the budget cuts that many public schools face each year. Because many schools are seeing their money going to other programs in their school systems, service-learning seems almost obsolete for their curriculum. One way to make this strategy work for schools is to work with community leaders to create relationships that are both beneficial to the companies and to the students (Horne, 2002). By building relationships with different departments in a community and state, a school can reach many goals through service-learning. Another weakness in service-learning is the number of teachers opposed to using it in their classrooms. While some teachers are diehard opponents of service-learning, many teachers are just conflicted about why or why not to use it. An important strength of service-learning to consider is that teachers are able to help participants discover the value of their academic knowledge in their service and vice versa. Because of this students are able to view their education with a more open mind and relate their service to their life experiences.

Another challenge is student interest versus curricular imposition. In simpler terms, what do the students want to learn versus what do teachers want them to learn? Sometimes, there is no agreement, causing a strain on a democratic atmosphere within the classroom. Classroom management is another challenge. It is normal for a democratic classroom to have some degree of chaos. It is sometimes difficult for teachers to decide what degree of chaos needs their intervention without being an abuse of control. The final problem is the lack of reflection time for both the teacher and the students. Teachers need time to focus on how democratic principles affect their classrooms. Often, the rigors of teaching overrun the teacher's free time (Beyer, 1996). Reflection is also vital for students involved in a service-learning activity. Reflection allows the students to direct their attention to the meaning and significance of the experiences. It is difficult to build in the time for such activities, but it is vital for the success of these pedagogies.

One example of a service-learning project comes from Indianapolis, Indiana, at Perry Meridian High School. Twelfth-grade students from Rosemarie Kuntz's government classes teamed up with local transportation officials at the Indianapolis Metropolitan Planning Organization to study ways to reduce traffic congestion in the city. The students did hours of research, attended neighborhood meetings, and conducted community surveys. One group proposed the construction of a monorail system to the officials (Allen, 2003). This is a great example of the students getting involved to help find solutions to a problem that not only affects those students, but their entire community. The students are able to work with local officials to come up with several plans to help their community. These students are able to get involved with local business officials and show them that they are interested in issues happening in their community and allow those officials to be a part of their educational experience.

A curriculum based on democratic principles and civic engagement could look much like the curriculums that already exists in many classrooms and schools that use differentiated experiences to meet the academic standards, but with subtle variations. However, such a pedagogy must provide the opportunity for students to show what they know and collaborate with each other on projects, incorporate thematic curriculums, provide opportunities for reflection, and create goal-based learning opportunities that build upon each other over the school year. Such a curriculum would expect students and teachers to engage in mini apprenticeships, creating experiences that will result in well-rounded, functional professionals who can reflect on tasks and the reality of the professional environment—one that is ever changing and ever diversifying. The teacher can incorporate all academic standards into a service-learning activity. The teachers often find a new sense of energy as they watch their students learn and realize what young people can accomplish when given the right tools (Jones, Malone, and Stallings, 2002).

There are many ways that a teacher can implement democratic procedures into his or her classroom. An example of a democratic classroom is having the students and teacher focus on getting to know one another during the first few weeks of school. It is important to develop the classroom expectations and rules as a collaborative group.

Another example of a democratic classroom is when a group of fifth-grade students created a community clean-up project. The students began by splitting into groups, deciding how to carry out the assignment, and voting on the best ideas. Then they listed things that need to be completed. Next, they assigned their classmates duties and broadened the list to include things the rest of the classes in the school could do to help the project succeed. One group found ways of connecting all subjects to the project and how to meet their state's standards, while other groups decided who, what, when, and how. Their school counselor stated, "You've got to engage all the senses. The more senses you engage, the more kids are going to learn" (see Dickerson, 1998).

Traditionally, teachers have the power in the classroom. Much of the power lies in praise or in the lack thereof. Praise in a democratic classroom defeats the democratic purpose. We want the inhabitants of our country to have a free voice and be able to express their own thoughts. Using praise in schools takes self-worth from the students and puts it in the teacher's hands. After several years of "conditioning," students in a traditional environment do not know if they have completed a worthwhile paper, reading assignment, math test, and so forth. They do not know if anything is good or bad until the teacher informs them. A democratic classroom should provide students the ability to understand and attain educational freedom, which is tied to responsibility (Larrivee, 2002). The teacher is the one who helps mold the responsibility needed to gain this freedom.

Grades are one example of praise used in the classroom. After a period of time students learn to do just enough work to get the grade they desire. They do not try to achieve a higher standard, and they are not concerned with actually learning the material. Many ideas are kept until a grade is received and then forgotten. If we as a community can pull students away from seeking the grade and guide them instead toward seeking knowledge, they will gain more from their educations.

In order for teachers to create the best service-learning environment, they need to have a network of willing individuals to support the students' education. Teachers must get the school, parents, and community involved to arrive at the best educational experience for the children. Teachers will do this by devising the best strategy for communication with all above-mentioned individuals and working together as a closely knit team.

IMPLICATIONS FOR PARENTS

Parents may be skeptical of new teaching strategies. It seems that students have been guinea pigs for the past few decades for variety of new teaching strategies. Parents may worry that the student will not acquire the knowledge needed to pass standardized testing and succeed in college. Educating parents about service-learning and democratic teaching should assuage these and other fears.

After immersion in an effective service-learning environment, parents should notice their child learning not only the theory being taught, but also experiencing it. They should gain more personal knowledge, have a blurred distinction between their teacher and themselves, be involved in corporate learning, and have knowledge of a wide variety of outcomes for given situations (*Academic Service-Learning*, 1997). Service-learning and democracy will typically increase a student's personal growth. This can include improving the student's self-esteem and personal responsibility (*Academic service-learning*, 1997; "Learning through service," 1998). Parents also should see improvement in their children's social development. They should have increased interpersonal skills, increased tolerance and understanding of diversity, and increased likelihood of future community participation.

Service-learning and democracy can be brought into the home. Students should be more excited about completing "work" outside of school. If the whole family can get involved in the child's project, this can help build the family unit. Frequently, parental involvement will increase the family's communication, self-esteem, and desire for involvement in education. Parents desiring the best educational setting for their student should get involved with their educational community and especially the teacher. A parent needs to connect with the teacher, understanding what is expected of their student, why, and how to help.

Parents and teachers can work together to form lines of communication that work best for their particular community. For some communities parents and teachers can communicate electronically via Web pages and e-mail. Other communities may prefer forming parent/teacher committees or receiving newsletters. After improved communication is established, it should be much easier for parents to help the student to have the best educational experience possible. They will be able to help their student more effectively with homework, and they should feel more comfortable volunteering their time in the classroom. Parents need to go beyond the forms of involvement mentioned above to achieve an ideal educational environment. They can network with the teacher, school, and community to provide education, resources, time, and new ideas to help students succeed in the new millennium.

Parents always want to know that their children are learning real-life skills within the classroom. Service-learning gets the children involved, which in turn gets the parents involved. All parents want their children to grow into responsible, good citizens. Service-learning in democratic classrooms gives students the tools and values they need to become responsible citizens. There are many positive outcomes possible for their children: for instance, perhaps the child will begin to foster preemployment or job skills, while he or she becomes aware of career options. Participating in a service-learning activity exposes children to the challenges of working with people of different cultures, backgrounds, and ages. These are skills and tolerances they will need to develop for survival in the real world. The child will become aware of life issues that exist outside of the classroom. Research has also shown that students who participate in a service-learning activity rate the value of having responsibility higher than other students their age. The child's self-esteem will improve, and there will be a decrease in problem behaviors. The students involved are less likely to participate in at-risk behaviors such as sexual activity or drug use. Parents will be happy to know that their child is developing many skills and competencies he or she will need in society (Brown, 1998; Education Commission of the States, 1999).

All of the implications on a student's home life will be positive. The student will learn values and gain an increased sense of responsibility. Students will develop stronger, more trusting relationships with adults, including parents. They will become motivated to learn and become active citizens in their homes, schools, and communities. Because of this standards-based service requirement, democratic learning requires a degree of parental involvement. Parental involvement can be as little or as much as a parent can put into a student's learning development. Parental involvement is important because it will keep students interested. It can include any number of activities, from helping with fund raising or supervising outdoor projects, to helping out within the classroom. Some parents may take this a step further in getting their employers or businesses involved with the democratic learning projects being planned at their child's school. By seeking out business or financial support, parents are engaging in a personal connection with their child's education. Just like teachers and students, parents can be active participants in making each new project a success.

An important strength for parental involvement in democratic learning is that parents involved in the democratic projects can connect to their children's educations on a more personal level. As students begin to see their parents get involved with their schoolwork and the projects they are doing in school, they may become more eager to participate and succeed in the classroom. This may also motivate the child, when he may be struggling with something outside of the democratic learning project at home, to ask for help from his parents because the child has seen that his parents have gotten involved in his education and are interested in his success.

ASSESSMENT IN DEMOCRATIC CLASSROOMS

Democratic learning and democratic classrooms would mainly use criterion-referenced assessment methods. CRTs "compare a student's performance to some pre-established criteria or objective" (Slavkin, 2003a and 2003b). In a democratic classroom, students should develop more critical-thinking skills, better communication skills, and a better ability to work cooperatively. A teacher can track a student's progress by using an alternative assessment method such as portfolios, checklists, or essays. These types of assessments do not have one right answer, but they test to see whether students have mastered a skill or objective. The students could write essays at the end of a democratic learning activity that describe the meaning the project had to them, what skills they learned, and ideas for more projects in the future. There is no right or wrong answer, but this form of assessment provides feedback to the teacher as to whether or not this was a worthwhile experience for the students.

Assessment in a democratic learning environment may seem a daunting task for teachers. Teachers should be able to create a sound evaluation effectively if they follow some basic steps. Small assessments are a major part of democratic learning. Assessment needs to be a consistent and ongoing process that teachers and students can work through to create the most accurate evaluation. Assessment needs to be continual so that both teacher and student will know if the project is understood and completed to the standards desired. Teachers need to evaluate their strategy for teaching the curriculum. They need to measure the degree of their students' understanding constantly. They also need to use accurate and consistent forms of evaluation (Melchior, 2001).

Students need to evaluate their own progress. They can decide if they need more help or clarification. They also can help their teacher create more effective teaching strategies. To create an effective evaluation for democratic learning, the teacher and student have to decide who is involved in the project, what that particular project needs to succeed, how they can help it succeed, what the outcomes may be, and what impact they will have. At each step in the process the team of students, teacher, and other project members will decide if the agreed-on criteria are being met. If there are problems, the team will work together to correct them so the students can achieve their goals.

The use of portfolios is becoming more popular in classrooms. The use of reflective portfolios involves the student in the process of evaluation. The students control the learning because they are involved in creating the expectations, so they know what needs to be done to achieve a desired grade. Assessment no longer becomes something done to them, but a tool for growth. A portfolio displays the student's skills and knowledge. The student picks out what pieces of work he or she wants to display. The student, teacher, and parents can see how the child is progressing.

One strength of democratic learning is that it can be tied to the curriculum through academic standards. Democratic learning brings to education a whole new idea of teaching the standards by allowing students to put their talents to use, benefit their communities, and further their educations. Teachers can use this method of teaching to help children understand the information that they must learn in order to pass their present grade, while helping the students become contributing members of society. Democratic learning also gives students the opportunity to show local and state business people that they are learning from things other than "the test." Involving these businesses allows them to see firsthand where their money is going, as well as how the students are using the skills that they learn. The use of local businesses could greatly affect high-stakes testing in the future as businesspeople see that students can learn through ways other than testing. As a result, the community is able to see changes made in their communities by the youth, which may greatly affect the way that some community members view youth. Another importance to democratic learning is the ability for community members to engage in what is going on within the classroom. Since there are many controversies over what a teacher does in a classroom, this will provide community members the opportunity to see or be involved in the activities that both the teachers and students are involved in on a daily basis.

IMPLICATIONS FOR THE FUTURE OF EDUCATION

Whether such modifications to the curriculum are referred to as democratic pedagogy or democratic learning, these approaches should be utilized by schools as curricular supports that increase students' involvement with local communities and improve the philanthropic experience of youth through investment in independent project-based models. Democratic learning provides students opportunities for active involvement in the democratic processes of the school and community, at a time when state departments of education are mandating community involvement and dedication. Democratic pedagogies afford all students the opportunity to learn as educators are challenged to meet individual expectations in demonstrating mastery of state academic standards (doing justice to the philosophy behind President Bush's No Child Left Behind, rather than just creating an unachievable unfounded mandate). It is believed that such transitions might afford a variety of schools the opportunity to meet the demands of accountability by allowing alternative performances to serve as evidence of stability and consistent educational strength.

The impact of the classroom meaning-making process and the roles that student empowerment and student-centered pedagogical practices play in changing the nature of the classroom have implications for the metacognition and actualization of students. If teachers are to help learners become competent and critical thinkers, they must be aware of how theories of cognition and brain development can assist them in maximizing the potential of their pedagogy. Teachers can help students learn more effectively if educators create opportunities for students to relate the curriculum to their personal lives, provide an environment that reveals multiple meanings of material, and allow students to see the dynamic nature of information.

Chapter Nine

Enhancing Creativity:
Learning for the Twenty-First Century

Michael Slavkin and Jonathan Plucker

Chapter 8 described an approach to creativity enhancement that is being applied and evaluated with students at a number of nontraditional and innovative schools. The model is largely based on the belief that creativity suffers in light of the preponderance of myths and stereotypes about learning (for example, that learning is an end product and not a process). Such a mechanistic view limits the potential of classrooms and students. Creativity appears to be an important component of problem solving and other higher cognitive abilities. This chapter, based on a presentation originally made by Dr. Jonathan Plucker at the Fifth Biennial Wallace National Research Symposium on Talent Development on May 19, 2000, debunks some of the myths surrounding creativity (much as I have done in previous chapters with respect to learning), reveals some effective problem-solving tasks, and discusses how teachers and parents can help students to improve their creativity.

One of the key desires of parents and teachers is to foster successful growth in their children. Oftentimes, a primary facet of this is the child's ability to be creative, especially in younger years. Parents and teachers are excited by the child's ability to share information in new ways or to comment on a situation and provide his or her unique perspective. Creativity to many is often narrowly viewed as the artwork that kids produce or their ability to paint well. Creativity is far more than artwork, a unique way of saying something, or a song or poem. If children of all ages are to be successful and prosper, innovative thinking and behaving must be present; in fact, if learning is to be considered an individualized process, as stated throughout this text, then it is imperative that children be granted opportunities to develop their divergent thinking skills (e.g., thinking outside of the box).

Creativity appears to be an important component of problem-solving and other cognitive abilities, healthy social and emotional well-being, and scholastic and adult success. Yet the study of creativity is not nearly as simple as one would expect. Teachers and parents who may have attempted to enhance the abilities of their children in the past might have come across some efforts that are ironically lacking in originality. The approach reviewed in this chapter is a form of creativity enhancement that has been found to be successful in assisting youth in recognizing their creativity and tapping into their innovative potential. The model is largely based on the belief that creativity suffers in light of the preponderance of myths and stereotypes about creativity that collectively strangle most research and educational efforts. In this chapter, we will briefly describe the program's goals, analyze the empirical support or lack thereof for the most damaging of the stereotypes, and close with some strategies that can assist educators in supporting the true development of creativity in their children.

CREATIVITY: THE PROMISE AND THE PROBLEM

The importance of creativity to a wide range of human endeavors is well documented. Psychologists and educators have extolled the virtues of creativity regarding the intellectual, educational, and development of intellect and talent in children (Guilford, 1950; Reis and Renzulli, 1991; Torrance, 1962). The concept of building on strengths as opposed to remediating weaknesses has wide appeal: the business sector has identified creativity as an engine of economic and technical development, both in modern and developing countries (Akarakiri, 1998; Amabile, 1998; King, 1998; Kurtzberg, 1998; Retuned, 1999; Robinson and Stern, 1997; Singh, 1977; Stevens and Burley, 1999). Applications of creativity research to technology—and vice versa—also are beginning to pick up steam (Clements, 1995; Kappel and Rubenstein, 1999). Most citizens in our society would agree that in order for the generations that follow us to be productive and competitive, they must be able to think about their world in a variety of ways using a variety of perspectives—creativity is critical to such thinking!

As children develop and their thinking becomes more heterogeneous, it becomes more important for the environments with which they interact to afford opportunities for such differentiated thinking. Teachers may want to ask students questions for which there is more than one response, questions that inquire about their values, beliefs, or experiences. Such opportunities for free thinking, divergent thinking, brainstorming, or creative processing can assist children in making unique connections between prior knowledge and unsolved problems.

The Promise

In addition to these rather traditional perspectives on the benefits of creativity, professionals from diverse specialties have noted its importance. In the last few years, creativity's contributions have been noted in areas as diverse as workplace leadership (Tierney, Farmer, and Graen, 1999), adult vocational and life success (Torrance, 1972a and 1981), healthy psychological functioning, coping, and emotional growth (King and Pope, 1999; Russ, 1998; Zelinger, 1990), maintenance of healthy, loving relationships (Livingston, 1999), and more effective therapeutic treatments (Kendall et al., 1998). Parents and educators, reacting to recent concerns over youth violence, have called for explorations of the role creativity can play in reducing violence and promoting conflict resolution (Kovac, 1998; Plucker, 2000; Webb, 1995). These suggestions range from the use of humor to defuse potentially violent situations (Jurcova, 1998) to learning more effective conflict-resolution strategies (Webb, 1995).

These are but a few of the areas in which creativity is being applied, but they provide a sense of the extraordinary breadth of applications that teachers and parents may pursue. There appears to be no shortage of areas in which creativity can be applied constructively to improve people's lives—and, more importantly, areas in which people can use creativity to improve their own lives.

The Problem

Although the potential applications of creativity are well documented, observers over the past fifty years have noted that this potential is rarely fulfilled. Classrooms generally do not appear to be creativity-fostering places, primarily due to the challenges for accountability that teachers face and traditional classroom organization. Students lack creative outlets because many in our schools still hold to the tenet that "learning is a mechanistic experience"—input/output or stimulus/response models emphasize that there is one right response for each question; thus, divergent thinking is irrelevant (Furman, 1998; Torrance, 1968). Further, many classrooms lack meaningful curriculum differentiation—teachers don't recognize the heterogeneous nature of learners, and if all learners are the same, then all students should come up with similar products and ideas (Archambault et al., 1994; Westberg et al., 1993). Finally, classrooms are designed to follow a set curriculum. As stated in the chapter on service-learning, few teachers have the opportunity in these times of standards-based practices to move beyond the textbooks, and they tend to follow the pedagogical patterns developed for them. Such a lack of originality in classroom-based enhancement efforts weakens the possibility that students will be granted the chance to think abstractly or creatively (Plucker and Beghetto, in press).

As previous chapters have discussed, we know much about how children think and what they need in their home and school environments to learn. And yet, adults often fail to provide environmental setups that can nurture the development of creative abilities. How often do we hear that students in schools are expected to meet accountability standards solely by producing the "right" answer on a multiple-choice test? Do you have memories of being told to "color within the lines," to work by yourself and not to seek help from others, or stick to the way that the book tells you to do something? Such statements and actions are devastating to students who need the opportunity to manipulate their environment, work by interacting with others, and think about problems in multiple ways.

The problems exist beyond the walls of our classrooms. Creativity is too often associated with negative assumptions and characteristics held by researchers, practitioners, and laypeople. As a result, people who study problem solving, cognitive flexibility, or functional fixedness would never dare utter the "C word," yet they are in essence investigating aspects of creativity. This situation mirrors R. J. Sternberg and T. I. Lubart's recent observation, "Creativity is important to society, but it traditionally has been one of psychology's orphans" (1999, 4).

Sternberg and Lubart proceeded to identify six roadblocks to the study of creativity: (1) its mystic and spiritual origins, (2) the negative effects of the numerous pop psychology and commercialized approaches, (3) its early work being conducted in relative isolation from mainstream psychology, (4) elusive or trivial definitions as to what constitutes creativity, (5) negative effects of viewing creativity as an extraordinary phenomenon, and (6) narrow, unidisciplinary approaches. J. A. Plucker and R. A. Beghetto have described a similar set of roadblocks to the lack of creative approaches to enhancement efforts: emphasis on eminent rather than everyday creativity, overemphasis on the role of divergent thinking as part of the creative process, and the insularity of theory and research (Plucker and Beghetto, in press). The literature generally supports the existence and negative effects of these roadblocks (see Sternberg and Lubart, 1996; Treffinger, Isaksen, and Dorval, 1996); however, these lists are not without controversy, and perhaps as a result, little effort is expended to remove these roadblocks.

With regard to studying and enhancing creativity, the authors of this chapter believe that the numerous roadblocks have led to an additional, more immediate problem. More than any other factors, the preponderance of myths and stereotypes about creativity produces an atmosphere that severely restricts the ability to study and apply creativity. The following sections analyze some of the most damaging myths and propose a future direction that may begin to remedy the situation.

DEFINING CREATIVITY

Like weeding dandelions, removing the roadblocks to creativity may help temporarily, but the myths will quickly reemerge unless the taproot is pulled from the soil. As R. L. Williams recently noted, "higher-order cognitive constructs have much surface appeal, [but] their utility is tied to the clarity and fidelity of their definitions and assessment procedures" (1999, 411). The importance of a standard definition was called to our attention as we recently reflected on the state of the field. One senior colleague, after attending a talk by Jonathan Plucker, contacted him later to share her impressions. She said, essentially, "It amazes me that the field still doesn't have a standard definition of creativity." She has a strong point—A. J. Cropley (1999b), H. B. Parkhurst (1999), R. J. Sternberg (1988), C. W. Taylor (1988), and many others have pointed out the numerous definitions currently in existence.

We believe that there is a standard definition, albeit one that is embraced only tentatively and implicitly by the majority of creativity researchers. Elaborate theories of creativity, full-blown empirical creativity studies, ambitious creativity program implementations, and prescriptive recommendations regarding creativity are put forth prior to considering seriously and defining clearly the construct on which these activities are based. Without an agreed-upon definition of the construct, creativity's potential contributions to learning will remain limited. Of course, others have shared similar concerns over the decades (e.g., Yamamoto, 1965), but the situation stubbornly remains the same.

A common definition can be found or inferred from a wide range of studies, including those from the fields of educational, counseling, organizational, social, and personality psychology: creativity involves the production of original, useful products, as determined by the various constituents in a particular field or domain. This is essentially the same definition offered by A. J. Cropley (1999a), R. J. Sternberg and T. I. Lubart (1999), D. F. Halpern (1996), and H. B. Parkhurst (1999), among others, and the idea of novel, useful products is implicit in the product assessment work of S. P. Besemer and K. O'Quin (1986) and S. M. Reis and J. S. Renzulli (1991). In addition, implicit theories of creativity include themes of originality and utility (Runco and Bahleda, 1986; Runco, Johnson, and Bear, 1993; Sternberg, 1985). The major advantage of this definition is that it corrodes the foundation of many of the myths and stereotypes surrounding creativity.

THE MYTHS AND STEREOTYPES

Many if not all of the following myths and stereotypes are widespread both in practice and in the research literature (Isaksen, 1987; Treffinger, Isaksen, and Dorval, 1996). Common themes that run throughout the eight myths are their pervasiveness, even among creativity scholars, and their exclusionary undertones (i.e., their role in reinforcing who is not creative).

People Are Born Creative or Uncreative

The myth that people either have or do not have creativity, with no capacity for enhancement, is one of the most pervasive and stubborn myths surrounding creativity (Treffinger, Isaksen, and Dorval, 1996). Decades of research on positive training and educational effects and, lately, environmental techniques for fostering creativity strongly refute this myth (e.g., Amabile, 1983 and 1996; Fontenot, 1993; Hennessey and Amabile, 1988; Osborn, 1963; Parnes, 1962; Pyryt, 1999; Sternberg and Lubart, 1992; Torrance, 1962, 1972a, and 1987; Westberg, 1996).

This myth probably originates from the mystification of creativity cited by Sternberg and Lubart (1999) and D. J. Treffinger et al. (1996) and the traditional accent on eminent (i.e., "Big C") creativity. Big C creativity involves the study of clearly eminent creators, which has had a significant, positive impact on our understanding of creativity. But Big C creativity also may have a negative side effect by furthering the idea that creativity is only possessed by a blessed few—an idea that is quite controversial and often criticized (Halpern, 1996; Osborn, 1963; Plucker and Beghetto, in press; Sternberg and Lubart, 1999). Although few researchers would claim to believe in a "Big C versus little c" distinction in creativity, this stereotype is very widespread in practice, especially among teachers.

This myth is most likely to be heard in playgroups and parent interactions around the country. It is a commonly articulated statement that one child, often the youngest in a brood, has phenomenal creative talents, while their other siblings lack in innovation. In fact, most teachers and parents who attempt to support divergent thinking and innovation in their kids often are the first to state that creativity is something that is nurtured by the environment (Sound familiar? If not, be sure to go back and review chapter 2 about how kids develop and chapter 3 about the impact of environment on development). Once more, these same supporters of creativity are quick to suggest that creativity can be found in more than just the arts and music.

Creativity Is Limited to the Arts and Music

People frequently relegate creativity to strictly artistic and musical domains. Decades of research in a broad range of domains too voluminous to cite in this paper, provide ample evidence that creativity is not "artistic specific." A related and more problematic concern is the belief that creativity is domain or task specific (e.g., Baer, 1994 and 1998). This conclusion is not without controversy (Plucker, 1998 and 1999) and ignores domain-general aspects such as personality characteristics and dispositions that favor creative production (e.g., Amabile, 1996; Sheldon, 1995). Specificity's potential side effects include functional fixedness, the general loss of flexible thought that severely restricts creativity. And claims of domain specificity overlook the substantial contributions of individuals and groups that have crossed disciplinary boundaries to make major creative contributions in other fields. Furthermore, P. D. Stokes (1999) has produced evidence that domain specificity, at least among women, may be learned, supporting the environmental hypothesis. Domain specificity certainly exists at times in people's lives, but this is probably due more to economic necessities than the nature of creativity. Specificity should not be viewed as inevitable or as necessarily desirable.

As music and arts programs are being forced to close in schools throughout the country due to funding cuts, teachers and parents are desperate to find alternative avenues to assist their kids in nurturing creativity. The simplest route to supporting such an endeavor comes with identifying how creativity can be discovered in areas beyond music and art. Further, do adults recognize how the arts and music can be introduced as facets of other core subject areas, such as through thematic learning? Creativity must be recognized as a phenomenon that can support innovation in such subjects as social studies, science, and language arts—and music and the arts can supplement such subjects by nurturing recognition of the interconnectedness of knowledge and the importance of how ideas from various areas of study can nurture understanding in disparate knowledge bases.

Creativity Is Intertwined with Negative Aspects of Psychology and Society

The "lone nut" stereotype of creativity, that of the strange, creative loner with a dark side, is surprisingly widespread. S. G. Isaksen described this stereotype as the belief that "you must be *mad*, weird, neurotic or at least unusual" to be considered creative (1987, 2, emphasis in original). Numerous studies have been published on the relationship between creativity and drug use, criminality, and mental illness, with many presupposing a strong link between these deviant behaviors and conditions and creativity (e.g., Brower, 1999; Hershman and Lieb, 1998; Ludwig, 1996; Steptoe, 1998).

Little of this research, however, provides conclusive evidence of strong, generalizable relationships (Plucker and Dana, 1998a and 1999; Waddell, 1998). For example, T. Norlander (1999), among many others, has provided evidence that alcohol enhances some skills that may lead to creativity, but hurts many others. Most importantly, these deficits appear most strikingly in secondary processes (e.g., preparation, communication). Therefore, alcohol may lower inhibitions, enhancing opportunities for creative thought, but it may lower one's problem-solving and communicative abilities, producing a net deficit in creative productivity (Plucker and Dana, 1999). This is not to say that creativity cannot emerge from negative circumstances, although the evidence suggests that the context of the negativity is important: Parental conflict may be positively related to later adult creativity (Koestner, Walker, and Fichman, 1999), but family alcohol abuse may not be (Noble, Runco, and Ozkaragoz, 1993; Plucker and Dana, 1998b).

In Isaksen's (1987) opinion, this stereotype emanates from the belief that creativity is essentially novelty. Novelty can be viewed as a form of deviance; therefore, anyone who is deviant in one sense may be likely to exhibit other forms of deviance. However, as many researchers have concluded, this is not necessarily the case (e.g., Neihart, 1998; Plucker and Runco, 1999). Again, the focus on Big C creativity also encourages this myth—nearly all studies that show strong relationships between creativity and a "dark side" are based on case studies of eminently creative people. Even if a strong, positive correlation were found between creativity and criminality, mental illness, or drug abuse among eminent creators, this would not inform our daily efforts to improve most people's lives with creativity.

This myth is especially damaging because it clouds and otherwise distorts the real issues. Many people focus on the fact that alcohol use may cause creativity, but better questions are probably how stereotypes about creativity may lead creative individuals to drug use or how creativity can be used to combat alcoholism. And what of the evidence that some forms of deviance, such as eccentricity, may be a matter of personal choice (Weeks and James, 1995)? If nothing else, the negative perspective of creativity creates an image in teachers' and parents' minds that makes positive applications of creativity very difficult. The more that divergence is misinterpreted as deviance, the less likely it is to be seen as important by parents and teachers.

Creativity Is a Fuzzy, Soft Construct

In courses and at professional conferences, we are always astonished at the degree to which people see the stereotypical creative person, if not as a dangerous loner, then as a barefooted hippie running around a commune rubbing crystals on his or her forehead. This stereotype leads many to think of creativity as "soft psychology," even though many of them study related constructs. The evidence in support of this stereotype is very thin, with research strongly suggesting that creativity is not a "fuzzy" or "soft" construct. For example, recent volumes on creative cognition have strong, well-defined themes that address creativity in a serious manner (Smith, Ward, and Finke, 1995; Ward, Smith, and Vaid, 1997).

Commercialized training programs, many with weak theoretical and empirical foundations, and antireductionist perspectives by many individuals (i.e., a desire to cloak creativity in a mystical aura) factor into this perception, but misinterpretation of lists of creative personality characteristics and behaviors may be an additional cause of this myth. Traits such as "gets lost in a problem," "sensation seeking," "open to the irrational," "impulsive," "uninhibited," and "nonconforming" can easily lead to the stereotype of the creative beatnik, although a more pragmatic profile can be drawn from the same lists: capable of concentrating, strives for distant goals, asks many questions, goes beyond assigned tasks, self-organized, flexible in ideas and thought (all drawn from G. A. Davis's [1999] comprehensive list).

Ironically, many of these characteristics were identified during studies of college students and successful professionals in a wide variety of fields (e.g., Barron, 1969; Davis and Subkoviak, 1978; Domino, 1970; MacKinnon, 1961), groups that are as far from the stereotypical image as one can hope to get. Davis wisely cautions that "not all traits will apply to all creative persons" (1999, 79), which the research strongly supports. For example, although idealism is often included in lists of creative personality traits, G. Yurtsever (1998) provides evidence of a lack of positive correlation between creativity and idealism. Again, the various roadblocks suggested by Sternberg and Lubart (1999) and other authors appear to be at work.

Preservice teachers are quick to want to evaluate their future students by looking at how "creatively" they perform some activity or assignment. Their notion of creativity often follows the "fuzzy" concept of a characteristic that equates to "the child thinking or doing something differently than I originally demonstrated in a lesson." Few teachers recognize the importance of clarifying what outcomes are valid and what outcomes are just trash (teachers and parents must come to understand that creative works move beyond just doing a project in a different form than it has been done before.) As stated previously, the mere fact that an idea is different doesn't necessarily make it equal to or even better than one that mimics an expectation that has been previously set up. Teachers and parents should help foster growth in particular areas by providing freedom within boundaries, not allowing any old thing to work.

Constraints Inhibit Creativity

Oftentimes, teachers and parents believe that in order to improve the creative potential of their children, few constraints should be provided. This myth tends to suggest that creative thinking is nothing more than brainstorming: all ideas that are offered are accepted, and all ideas are of equal importance and value. In fact, this is not the case. If creative potential is to be fostered, it must be fostered with some limitations.

An example of this can be seen in Destination Imagination (DI), a program that provides students of all ages the opportunity to think divergently to solve complex problems. DI invites teams of individuals to think through a problem over a number of months and then represent their unique "solutions" during a public presentation. While creativity is encouraged, it is supported within some boundaries. For example, one group of students was challenged to create a "Leaning Tower of Pasta" that could hold as much weight as possible. Although students were allowed to use any type of pasta or glue, they were unable to use adhesive epoxies and were penalized for weight (thus, they needed to find the strongest structure with the minimal weight load of pasta). Students created different structures with differing results—although all of them met the requirements of the problem, not all responses were equal (some held heavier loads of weight with little damage to the structure, others crumbled under the load!). In any event, not all responses were deemed equal (the limitation of "right-wrong" or concrete thinking). While educators want to ask important questions of children, they should ask questions that allow for differing answers.

You Must Be Relatively Young

This myth commonly manifests itself as a belief that people need to be of a certain age, usually young to in mid-adulthood, to make significant creative contributions. This is somewhat supported by the historiometric research first undertaken in a systematic research program by H. C. Lehman (1953). D. K. Simonton (1999), whose exhaustive work typifies contemporary research in this area, recently summarized the work on age and creativity by noting that creative productivity increases in midlife and tapers off in old age. He cautioned that "age" should be conceptualized as "length of time actively engaged in a creative domain, or career age, rather than in terms of strict chronological age" (Simonton, 1999, 122). These trends vary by individual (i.e., certain people defy the trends) and by the domain in which the creator is working.

These trends and variations are important as they suggest that age need not be viewed as a creative straightjacket. Age brings experience; as long as it is tempered with a tolerance for ambiguity and avoidance of functional fixedness, age should not necessarily have a negative effect on creativity. On the other side of the developmental spectrum, the work of Renzulli (1994) and his colleagues provides evidence that young children can exhibit remarkable degrees of real-world creative productivity. Any observable age effect may be dictated more by self-limitations and constraints imposed by the field or domain in question, rather than by the deleterious impact of youth or old age on creative capabilities.

So often we are entrenched in the idea that creative types tend to be younger, and teachers and parents may focus on the creative abilities of primary students, but by intermediate grades, middle school, or high school, such characteristics are all but ignored. While these creative potentials may go underground during times when there is limited support for such endeavors (as is often the case during middle and high school), environmental constraints are likely to have a stronger influence on the weakening of creative output in students, not their age or pubertal changes. Thus, the windows of opportunity discussed in chapter 2 do not close on creativity around the intermediate grades—it is still open, but largely ignored!

Creativity Is Enhanced within a Group

This myth is particularly evident in applications within the business world, where group creative activities are assumed to be more productive than individual efforts. As with the other myths, research provides a more balanced picture of the relative roles of individuals versus groups during creative activity. Brainstorming research generally provides evidence that traditional idea generation in groups results in a less creative pool of ideas than if people are allowed to brainstorm ideas individually and pool them later in the process (Diehle and Stroebe, 1986; Finke, Ward, and Smith, 1992). Several authors have recently cautioned against overlooking the role of the individual within a group or larger organization (Dacey and Lennon, 1998; Kurtzberg, 1998; Williams and Yang, 1999).

This misperception is relatively new and evolved as a reaction to the perceived overemphasis on the individual in earlier creativity research. The pendulum needs to swing back toward the middle, allowing parents and educators to balance the needs and abilities of individuals with the goals of groups. Further, parents and teachers should support opportunities for children to work with one another on projects and brainstorming ventures. By supporting time for reflection in groups, adults help to model the importance of interaction in forming ideas and nurturing innovative concepts. Reflectivity is a key component of successful divergent thinking, and our schools and communities can foster such growth by providing environments that support questioning, broader thinking, and exploration of concepts.

You Shouldn't Market Your Creativity

"You've sold out!" is one of the most hurtful accusations that can be leveled at a budding creative individual. "Creativity for creativity's sake" is the mantra of this philosophical position, which the speaker had better believe—stopping one's creative efforts too early generally results in an audience of only one. The bias against salespersonship is largely responsible for the almost total absence of marketing (broadly defined) in many enhancement efforts. The exceptions are the Schoolwide Enrichment Model (Reis and Renzulli, 1991; Renzulli, 1994), which encourages students to present their creative products to a wide variety of audiences as part of the creative process, and the Creative Problem Solving model (Treffinger, Isaksen, and Dorval, 1996), which includes a component called "planning for action."

Howard Gardner (1993), in his investigation of the creative lives of seven eminent individuals, found that one strong common characteristic was the well-honed ability to promote their creativity and the creativity of their followers. Failing to market creativity also may lead a person to develop a thin skin toward criticism. In general, avoidance of pragmatic steps in the creative process adds to the perception of creativity as being "soft" and makes creativity enhancement efforts look like play. While play has creative value (Russ, 1993), the resulting misperception, in concert with the other myths and stereotypes, is highly damaging.

PRELIMINARY RESULTS
OF TEACHING CREATIVITY

We are actively gathering and analyzing data to determine the strengths and weaknesses of this approach to enhancing creativity. Creativity work has been offered to students as young as children in primary grades and as advanced as college-level seniors. Most the data has been gathered using open-ended survey questions administered before and after courses of instruction and interviews conducted during or shortly after the creativity activities.

Initial data analysis suggests that the myths and stereotypes that plague creativity also inhibit students' opportunities to increase their innovation. Students' responses to creativity exercises revealed three patterns: (1) deconstructing the myths surrounding creativity takes hands-on work to help students experiment with alternatives, (2) the coursework is difficult for students, but "not because it is hard," (3) and improvements in students' creativity and innovation are not necessarily immediate.

Deconstructing the Myths Surrounding Creativity
Takes Hands-On Work to Help Students
Experiment with Alternatives

The stereotypes commonly identified by both practitioners and researchers (Isaksen, 1987; Treffinger, Isaksen, and Dorval, 1996) were also pervasive in the beliefs of students. Their exclusionary undertones (i.e., their role in reinforcing who is not creative) dominated the first weeks of the coursework with such statements as, "I am not a creative individual," "You have to be born creative," "You can't increase creativity through experience," "You only are creative if you are an artist or a musician," and so forth. Students needed to reconstruct their own implicit definitions of creativity through hands-on activities, interviews, experimentation, and play in order to see their own potential and innovativeness. By providing them with several weeks initially to organize these new and personalized perceptions of their own creativity, students were more likely throughout coursework to practice thinking innovatively in their daily lives and in their fields of interest.

The Coursework Is Difficult for Students, but Not Because It Is Hard

In both preliminary and postcreativity exercise surveys, students indicated that being creative is a difficult enterprise. An overwhelming majority of students shared that the coursework gave them greater insight into themselves and their abilities to tap into unappreciated and underutilized aspects of self. This newfound growth in parts of the personality that was previously unused carried over into other classes, into the workplace, and into their personal relationships (also see King and Pope, 1999; Livingston, 1999; Russ, 1993; Stokes, 1999). Even more interesting, students suggested that involvement in the class improved their leadership abilities (also see Tierney, Farmer, and Graen, 1999). Students at advanced levels also shared that this class had been among the only classes they had taken in college in which they knew everyone, were able to learn from each other, and were given the opportunity to form cohesive groups—almost like a community (also see Bowman and Boone, 1998; Malekoff, 1987).

Improvements to Students' Creativity and Innovation Are Not Necessarily Immediate

A few students are not ready to think in different ways, to challenge their beliefs and worldviews. These students become very frustrated. Students who had seen themselves as creative prior to the class began to see others sharing similar abilities in other areas, which caused them to question just how strong their creativity was. Other students (including one of the instructors for the creativity exercises and authors of this chapter) had been told by teachers and family members that they were not creative and had to overcome the myths surrounding their own ineptitude at being original and innovative. However, by the end of the course, each of these students appeared to benefit from the creativity exercises, showing greater self-efficacy and improved ability to identify and express the creativity within him- or herself.

APPLICATIONS FOR TEACHERS

Despite the current emphasis on high-stakes testing and meeting academic standards, teachers should continue to challenge themselves to reflect on how they can infuse creativity into their coursework. Pedagogical practices at all levels of schooling expect that standards will be met. However, teachers should be careful not to devalue the need to meet such standards through challenging, engaging, and innovative approaches.

Teachers should remember to provide a variety of experiences and situations for learning. By providing multiple environments for students to learn in (see chapter 3), teachers can ensure that students who have different creative characteristics can each share their strengths in the ways that they are creative. All people are creative, but few adults consider the ways that they can provide opportunities for all students to show how they are creative. This is especially critical if teachers are to avoid the myth that only art and music are outlets for demonstrating innovation. By providing them with multiple forums for creativity, students find unique outlets and avoid domain- and task-specific expression (which also helps to ensure that in future activities, they will be able to adapt what they have learned in the classroom).

Also, teachers and parents must remember that creativity should be emphasized, but not at the expense of maintaining standards and high expectations. Creativity doesn't mean that any old idea will cut it (a point we hope you have recognized by this point!). Creative experiences are to be aligned with state curricular standards. Teachers can use the standards as boundaries that can guide and direct student products, showing them what is required, but not mandating the exact form that the assignment is to demonstrate. Flexibility within limits is always an effective model to employ.

Whether students are young or are exiting college, students of all ages should work on divergent thinking strategies as preparation for their roles in professional fields and as community citizens. Though the example activities that follow are designed for primary and intermediate grades, it is hoped that both teachers and parents will recognize their utility for older youths and can modify them to make them developmentally appropriate.

APPLICATIONS FOR PARENTS

The applications for parents are very similar to those for teachers. Parents should attempt to provide their children with opportunities to think about problems from a variety of perspectives. It isn't enough that kids come up with the so-called right response. Children should also be expected to know why they think what they do and how such information might relate to other problems or challenges they have faced in the past. Teaching such reflectivity can ensure that "situational specificity" (only being able to think inside the box) does not occur. Learning how to apply similar problem-solving techniques to a variety of challenges can be a valuable skill.

Parents also can think about the greater strengths of their children and attempt to support improving their abilities in other creative outlets. For example, if children show a unique strength in naturalistic areas (see chapter 4), parents may want to assist by allowing them to create a garden of various herbs and plants. However, it would also be important that their innovative skills be exercised in another area. The children's naturalistic knowledge could be shared in a service project where they teach gardening techniques to an assisted-living community and create a sense garden. In this way, youths can demonstrate their knowledge, but with a unique strategy, one that emphasizes interpersonal abilities as well as naturalistic abilities (and, isn't it great that we can align our knowledge about multiple intelligences, service-learning, and creativity!).

The creativity exercises shared below have been organized around various themes, which should help both parents and teachers to think about the numerous ways that innovation and divergent thinking can be supported in everyday exercises.

CREATIVITY EXERCISES

Art Activities

These activities can also be paired with some reflective writings about the experience and the patterns created.

- *Shaving cream finger paint.* Using a can of shaving cream and some food coloring or tempura paint, spray shaving cream on a flat surface and allow your child to swirl the shaving cream and food coloring until it has the desired pattern of colors. Gently lay a piece of paper on the surface of the shaving cream, then peel back for an image of the pattern. Allow to dry, then imagine what objects the patterns can be.
- *Salad spinner art.* Remove the bottom of a salad spinner. Lay a white paper plate in the salad spinner. Drop several drops of food coloring on the plate in separate areas. Place the top on the salad spinner, and spin for fifteen to twenty seconds. Pull the plate out and allow it to dry.
- *Feather duster painting.* Gather several colors of tempura paints or watercolors. For younger children, pull off several feathers from the feather duster; for older children, keep the duster intact. Place different colors on different feathers, and lightly dust the item of choice. Have your child think about the various items that can be feather decorated: paper, sheets, tee-shirts, the walls of a bedroom, even a sheet of poster board that can be framed as a work of art.
- *Cool crayon art.* This activity is one that should be done only with older children and should not be attempted without close adult supervision. Take any broken crayons or candles that can be found and organize them in a small glass container with a lid. Heat over a low flame in a pan with water until the wax separates. Do not stir! Allow the wax to cool, then remove it in hardened form from the glass. Your child will have a colorful crayon, and can learn a good lesson about recycling.
- *Cool crayon art 2.* This activity is one that should be done only with older children and should not be attempted without close adult supervision. Take any broken crayons or candles that can be found. Place a candle under a baking sheet to provide a low source of heat. Put a sheet of paper on top of the baking sheet and color thickly on the paper. The heat will melt the wax into the paper and allow for some unique patterns.

Divergent Thinking Activities

The following activities are wonderful for use when parents and teachers need "filler" exercises (e.g., in the car, when waiting in lines, or at the beginning of class for board work). Children of all ages enjoy the activities and, as they get older, can come up with their own strategies and questions.

- *The let's pretend game.* Ask your child to pretend he or she is a common object, then ask questions about it. For example, with a toddler, a parent might ask him to pretend he is a lion, then ask what lions sounds like, what lions eat, and where lions live. All answers are right with this form of questioning! As children develop, items can become more abstract, such as questioning them about what it would be like to be a car and what feelings cars have.
- *The question game.* Thinking involves more than just memorizing information, and adults should provide more questions than answers. Ask questions to which there may not be one answer, or perhaps questions that do not have a clear solution. For example, ask your child what item she would most want to bring if she were trapped on a desert island. Questions can be followed up by having the child ask you a similar question or having them ask entirely different questions.
- *What if?* The What if? game is simple: ask your child a question that has no right response and discuss it. For example, what if dinosaurs never became extinct, what if we didn't have names, or what if everyone was the same?
- *Riddles and divergent thinking questions.* Kids of all ages love riddles, and more than anything, they want to try to guess the right response. Part of the excitement comes from the process—remember not to give in too quickly and allow for thinking time! Teachers can provide a riddle in the morning and then give the answer before lunch or at the end of the day. Parents too should allow enough thinking time so answers can percolate. Riddles can easily be accessed online or at any local bookstore, or you can have your kids make them up.

Bodily-Kinesthetic Creativity Exercises

One of the most frequently ignored areas of intelligence is bodily-kinesthetic. Children who are active and learn by doing can show their innovation through some of the activities listed below.

- *Beanbag toss.* Purchase some beanbags, or create your own with some zipping plastic bags and dried lentils. Allow your child to create a game using the bags. Some suggestions to get you started are (1) to use cups to play an indoor game of beanbag toss golf, (2) to create a target out of paper with a hole in the center (questions can be written next to each hole that children can ask the adult if they get a bag through the hole, and (3) to have a game of beanbag bowling with empty plastic soda bottles. Shapes, colors, or numbers also can be put on sheets of poster board, and adults can ask children about objects as the bags land on the items (e.g., if a bag landed on a green spot, a parent could ask his or her child to think of three items the child knows of that are green, or three bags could be thrown to land on numbers, and those numbers could be added together to work on additive abilities).
- *Relay races.* Relay races can be used in a variety of settings with a number of different ages. I taught number sequencing by placing the numbers one to thirty on felt pieces and had my students run from number to number in the appropriate order as fast as they could. A parent or teacher could create other races using different actions and bases (e.g., jumping to the tree, skipping to the chair, rolling to the grass, laughing and twirling back to the start).
- *Physical memory.* Parents and teachers can assist children in recognizing patterns and sequencing by creating activities that can be repeated (almost like playing H-O-R-S-E with a basketball). Kids can create their own sequences and then have adults repeat them (e.g., run from the door to the front board, do five jumping jacks, twirl in a circle, skip to the window, touch your toes and clap three times, twirl in a circle again, and hop back to the door).
- *Find the object.* Identify an object in your immediate environment. Point out a common characteristic and then allow your child to ask questions (in twenty-questions fashion). For example, say, "I am thinking of an object that runs fast," and then allow your child to ask questions that would direct him or her toward the object. Answers that support the characteristic can be considered "right," but can then be redirected by saying, "That is right, but I am thinking of another object."
- *Charades.* The educational strengths of this game are often overlooked; charades feels like a game, but it allows children of all ages to think ab-

stractly about everyday events, items, and people. Teach the rules, but be innovative about the themes that you use (e.g., movies and songs are wonderful, but also act out places, people in your neighborhood, or your child's favorite book). Allow your child the chance to practice alone or with a friend.

This is a far from exhaustive list. For further great ideas, check out Trish Kuffner's *The Toddler's Busy Book* (1999). Other helpful resources can be found at www.destinationimagination.com and www.oddessey-ofthemind.org.

Chapter Ten

Where Do We Go Now?
(Not Conclusions,
Further Opportunities)

The book's conclusion will rest on the notion that teachers and parents who have read its pages will begin to consider altering their practices. This final chapter serves as a call to arms, challenging them to begin taking the steps needed to remodel their communities, schools, and homes to create stronger learning opportunities for their children.

OVERVIEW

Despite all that is known about education and despite all the implications that authentic instruction has for the ways children learn, there are some in education and outside its boundaries who challenge the notion that teachers and students define what they learn. While the term *standards-based practice* once suggested that teachers in all schools throughout the United States might have general expectations that defined what topics were covered and what skills taught, it now is a classic buzzword for accountability mandates, high-stakes testing, and business-driven agendas in education. While most teachers would agree that schools today need standards, consensus is not so forthcoming about the methods we should use to reach global standards. If authentic practices are to have a place in twenty-first–century classrooms, it is critical that teachers, parents, and community members better recognize that standards-based practices can be organized into hands-on, project-based, authentic styles of teaching and learning.

The term *standards-based practice* is frequently used to describe the movement in education that challenges teachers to cover specific content areas. It also has been used to refer to what all students should know and do. Standards-based practice can be defined as a scheme for improving academic achievement based on the idea that children need the opportunity to participate in meaningful educational experiences. Standardized testing and high-stakes testing have been implemented as a form of standards-based practice to assess the standards that have been set and whether or not they are being achieved. Although this is one end result of the standards-based-practice movement (and not originally one that was supported by most in educational-assessment circles), there is more than one way of viewing this term. Some educators challenge that standards need to be set for more than just curriculum content areas; they need to be set for other important areas such as school environment and a student's "opportunity to learn" (Falk, 2002).

Other educators challenge that lifelong standards are critical to children's learning. While academic standards cover the information that students will need to advance to the next grade, lifelong standards cover skills that students will need in the workplace, for example, how to make decisions or work effectively with others. Regardless of what side of the fence you might sit on, the ultimate goal of this practice is to help all children reach the expectations set for them by their communities.

STANDARDS-BASED PRACTICE:
THE HISTORY BEHIND THE MOVEMENT

"The educational foundations of our society are presently being eroded by a rising tide of mediocrity that threatens our very future as a nation and a people. . . . We have, in effect, been committing an act of unthinking, unilateral education disarmament" (Kluth and Straut, 2001). Such was the general tone of the 1983 report *A Nation at Risk* published by the U.S. Department of Education. In the decades following this publication, government has largely vilified the public schools for their poor performance and the underachievement of students, placing schools under increasing pressure to demonstrate student achievement. Further, this document has largely led to a general lack of support for public education in the United States, despite the general strength of our schools. Whereas in the past American schools had been challenged to demonstrate student achievement through grades and performances on assignments, increasingly, states are moving toward a system of accountability that mandates high test scores as indicators of achievement. Despite the protests of most experts in assessment and education, school systems throughout the country are being challenged to "teach to a test" in an effort to boost scores and regain public confidence.

To regain public confidence in what the experts feel is important, it is vital to understand all of the aspects of a standards-based classroom. Standards-based practice is a very broad topic. It is key to first understand what standards-based practice is and then to understand how to form a powerful curriculum around it. The history of the standards movement and the positives and negatives of it are also areas of importance. Lastly, standards-based practice affects all stakeholders in education. This information, therefore, is important to teachers and parents. Teachers and parents must be active participants in educational policy, and the standards-based practice movement is one of those policies.

The standards movement evolved as a result of many developments. According to Hadderman (2003), some of these developments include former president George H. W. Bush's six national educational goals for 1989. He created these goals when he called the nation's governors to an education meeting held in Charlottesville, Virginia, in September of that year (Marzano and Kendall, 1996). These goals were about changing the subject matter that was being taught in schools and finding different ways of assessing students. To put these goals into effect, the National Education Goal Panel and the National Council on Education Standards and Testing were established in 1990. These two groups were tasked with choosing the subject matter to be taught, the assessments to be used, and the standards of performance to be set. Congress enacted the Goals 2000: Educate America Act in 1994 (Hadderman, 2003).

Although all of these developments lead to the standards-based movement and despite the drive to have a general expectation nationally of what students should be able to do, there are still no national standards (at least none that have been mandated) in use. However, forty-nine states (all except Iowa) have implemented some form of content standards. Because the standards movement has been linked to high-stakes testing, educators have viewed a generally benign area of education as a negative development.

The term *standards-based* has been used to describe many different things. According to R. Brandt (1997), the term has at least five different definitions, but two principal definitions have been suggested. First, standards-based practices are those practices that are "to be taught and learned," what many people think of as content standards. Content standards guide the curriculum to be taught and are typically divided by grade level (Vars and Beane, 2000). One example of a content standard can be found for the state of Indiana. In the third grade students are expected to be able to "[r]epresent the concept of multiplication as repeated addition" in the subject of math (Indiana's Academic Standards). Based on this standard, a third-grade teacher would create a lesson plan that teaches this concept, or she would incorporate this concept into a unit she is teaching.

According to the second definition, a standards-based practice is "instruction that is clearly focused on what students are supposed to learn" (Brandt, 2003a and 2003b). The instruction in a classroom would be focused on achieving the standards. Both the teacher and the students would know these standards beforehand. While many teachers are supportive of a system that defines what specific knowledge and skills students should hold at particular points in their academic careers, there is one stumbling block when it comes to focusing on accomplishing the standards: it is possible to have a classroom that is not developmentally appropriate (in that all learners aren't all going to learn in the same way, at the same time, and in the same format). Brandt also goes on to say that a standards-based classroom expects all students to learn and uses tests to measure that learning. These tests are then typically used as accountability for the school, teachers, and students. He adds that the federal and state governments feel that the achievement of the standards is so important that they offer incentives to high achievers (Brandt, 2003a). Although most teachers agree they should be held accountable for student mastery of these standards, many teachers feel that assessing this mastery through one standardized test is not adequate.

While the push for standards-based practices has moved forward from its inception under former president Bush, the practice has been criticized in four broad ways: challenges abound due to (a) resource and equity issues, (b) standards-based practices' relationship to already failed reforms, (c) objectionable content in the standards, and (d) the number of standards covered. Some people feel that by learning only the state standards students will miss out on learning important things that the standards don't cover. Further, some critics suggest that a reform practice similar to standards-based practices has already been tried and failed, so why should we think this reform will succeed? Educators have linked standards-based practices to the efficiency movement that lasted from 1913 to the 1930s. This movement specified in detail what people were to learn and the conclusions that they were to come up with. According to experts, school administrators eventually realized that this did not work, and they say this will happen with standards-based practice as well.

Some educators also are critical of the content presented in the standards and have pointed out that, for instance, a few history standards have ignored important figures such as George Washington and Robert E. Lee. Other critics say that the standards are not strong enough and students will be losing knowledge instead of gaining knowledge.

Finally, some teachers challenge that there are too many standards to be taught in each grade. A study done by Mid-continent Research for Education and Learning (McREL) found that it would take twenty-two years of schooling to cover all the standards (Kendall and Marzano, 1998). Experts say that there is no way teachers can possibly cover all the standards students are required to learn. Time constraints force teachers to "teach to the test," which takes away from the other information they might have taught. According to a survey done by *Education Week*, "Two-thirds of teachers (67 percent) report that the new statewide standards have led to teaching that focuses too much on tests." Teachers feel that the demand of standards-based practices have taken away learning time from subject areas that aren't part of high-stakes assessments, such as art and music.

While the standards-based movement often refers to the cognitive skills to be covered, some education stakeholders are pushing for standards that are based more on life skills. These life skills are more important to the students than the absorption of facts and information. One suggestion for including these life skills is to teach the standards using integrated units (Vars and Beane, 2000).

EFFECT ON STUDENT LEARNING

The standards-based movement affects student learning significantly because it defines what teachers are required to cover in their classrooms.

Therefore, the standards must be created with the students in mind. According to E. Hebert (2001), it is very important to include students in the process of standards development. By giving students ownership of their education, we enable them to play a significant role in what we are challenging them to learn. They also are more likely to learn the material because it will be meaningful to them.

The way that the standards are implemented affects the implications they have for student learning and achievement. If standards are only implemented by teachers who are "teaching to the test," then the resulting effects will most likely be negative. On the contrary, if the standards only serve as a guideline and a framework for creating an exciting curriculum, then the standards will likely have a very positive effect on student learning and achievement. As such, it is very important that the standards not force a teacher to create a curriculum that only benefits some of her students. The standards must be flexible and easily adaptable to individual classrooms and students (Kluth and Straut, 2001).

HOW TEACHERS ARE AFFECTED BY STANDARDS

The standards affect more than students. Some of the primary school stakeholders affected by the introduction of standards have been the teachers. In an attempt to understand these effects, a study interviewed many new teachers to gauge their reactions to the standards mandated by the Commonwealth of Massachusetts. The study found that the standards were provided as a framework for them to use, but without a standardized curriculum to follow. It also found that if a curriculum was provided, it did not follow the state standards. The last problem was the breadth of the standards. The teachers felt that there was too much to cover within the context and duration of one grade (Kauffman et al., 2002).

Overall, most teachers like standards-based practices. Teachers feel that standards-based practices have created more communication between teachers. They collaborate on how to mold curriculums to the standards and how to provide remediation for students who need it. Most teachers think that state standards have made their curriculums more demanding, and this in turn has raised expectations of their students. However, concerns arise with the emphasis on state standards and their connection with high-stakes testing. Teachers feel that because of standards-based practices, their performances as educators are measured solely by their students' performances on standardized tests. While standardized tests can be used to effectively gauge whether students have achieved some of the curricular expectations organized for them, normative tests do not demonstrate teacher effectiveness (Kendall et al., 1998).

Further, because of the issues that exist within standardized testing in general, this method is not by itself a reliable assessment of student potential. According to A. Kohn (2000), inaccuracies are actually built into the tests, which makes them an even less accurate measure of student mastery of the standards. One of the main problems with standardized testing is that the tests do not take into account all of the factors that influence a classroom of children. Teachers and administrators cannot control most of these factors. Kohn goes on to state that low scores are often due to social and economic factors. It is impossible to consider a standardized test reliable and valid when there are so many uncontrollable factors. For example, many students come into a new classroom without the prior knowledge needed from the previous school year. Since most standardized tests are administered in the fall, new teachers do not have an opportunity to instruct their students adequately in the standards so that they will be able to demonstrate their knowledge (Kohn, 2000).

In light of what has already been discussed, most teachers do not feel that students should judged by how well they do on a state standardized test. Rather, grades and individual assessment should be reviewed when considering letting students move up to the next grade level. By looking at numerous assessments, teachers, community members, and parents can better recognize the level of ability of students.

There is still hope for the standards-based practice movement if some significant changes are made to the method of assessing its effects. While the current results in the state of Indiana are not positive, they could be changed if were to include more standards for different areas. Rather than developing a one-size-fits-all view of standards, we must see them as guides for teachers to follow in creating a rich classroom environment (Kluth and Straut, 2001).

For example, while trying to implement state content standards, we should make an effort to implement standards that relate to a student's "opportunity to learn" and "professional practice." These standards would monitor the quality of the school environment and ensure that all students have access to classroom resources such as technology and first-rate textbooks. If there is disparity in the number of fiscal resources designated to schools, then there will be a disparity in the levels of student achievement. Developing new standards around the number of resources allocated to all schools could significantly improve academic achievement and, thereby, increase the validity of the accountability programs being implemented.

If a school is graded based solely on its performance on one standardized test, then all schools should be allocated funds to equalize students' ability to achieve. Students should not be punished for low test scores when their classroom environment greatly differs from another school's classroom environment.

EXAMPLE OF THE STRENGTHS
OF AN AUTHENTIC PRACTICE

The following lesson shows how creative and inviting a standards-based lesson can be. Mr. Smith who is a social studies teacher decided to create a lesson plan that was based on the standards he was teaching. Mr. Smith designed several centers that focused on an aspect of World War II and had activities for students to engage in. One activity involved students' writing in online journals about the Holocaust, while another center involved students mapping the progress of the war based on listening to actual radio broadcasts recorded during World War II. By recognizing how these activities met standards for the social studies, language arts, and technology, Mr. Smith could ensure that his students were learning at grade level. Further, he would be able to assist students in recognizing how his information from social studies had a relationship with what they were learning in a language arts class, as well as the technology skills they knew from school and from their experiences outside the classroom.

IMPLICATIONS FOR STUDENT LEARNING

Student learning is greatly affected by the standards-based practice movement. In fact, this movement affects student learning at all levels of the educational system. One way that standards affect student learning is by requiring all students to be at the same level at one time, rather than affording them the chance to learn at their own pace. Instead of DAP, teachers are forced to implement standards that may not be at the same level as all of their students. For example, if a third grader is reading at the first-grade level, but has improved from a kindergarten level, he is still not meeting the standards for the third grade. Therefore, the standards have not had a positive effect on this third grader. Although the third grader is making progress, he is still not mastering the standards at the third-grade level. This is difficult for both the teacher and the student because the teacher is expected to implement the standards, and yet not all of her students are at the same level of instruction (Laguardia et al., 2002).

Further, students are expected to demonstrate mastery of standards, but often only through one form of presentation. This type of presentation is typically a standardized test. Standardized tests are not a valid way to evaluate the mastery of the standards because they are designed to compare one student with another. Therefore, it is important that the mastery of the standards be assessed through multiple indicators. The teacher should use criterion-referenced assessments such as rubrics, portfolios, and checklists to indicate the mastery of standards. According to C. A. Mertler, the purpose of criterion-referenced assessment methods is to "[c]ompare a student's performance to some preestablished criteria or objectives." He goes on to state that they are sometimes called "mastery tests" (2003).

Finally, the standards-based movement was originally designed to support students' demonstrations of mastery of a core battery of knowledge and skills. Such a system would require that students reveal these skills through a system that demonstrates their ability to apply the information, and oftentimes implications abound that such behaviors occur in real-world contexts. However, despite the common practice of measuring mastery using criterion-based assessments aligned with the standards (projects, performances, portfolios, presentations, essays), accountability mandates have bastardized this process, aligning standards with high-stakes assessments. Oftentimes, states have failed to identify whether the assessments they use actually meet academic standards.

Some neglect to share with parents and community members that mastery cannot be indicated on a standardized test. Rather than taking a snapshot of student achievement using a multiple-choice test, educators should be looking at how students develop across time and whether they are evidencing improvement in core areas (criterion-referenced assessments, not normative standardized tests). While President Bush's No Child Left Behind policy is a step forward, challenging all students to meet state standards, it fails to address the fact that benchmarks on normative tests are not effective evaluations of mastery.

PARENTAL INVOLVEMENT

It is important that parents support and understand the standards and how they affect their children. Parents must be informed about the decisions and standards that affect their children so that they can play an active role in the learning process. It is important to invite parents to play this active role so that they realize that their children's education is not just of concern to teachers and administrators. How can parents become more involved with their children's learning and the standards that are being developed? They can help their children meet the standards by understanding what those standards are and how to achieve them (Cunningham, 2003).

Parents also need to be aware that high-stakes testing is separate from, but involved in, the standards-based movement because policy makers have taken the lead from businesses and corporations in using the test as a system of accountability (businesses fail to understand that we are not in the business of "making children" in the way they make products; therefore, most educators find the mindset that equates accountability with a per capita ratio of test scores bizarre).

Systems of accountability need to take into account all of the variables involved in student learning. Parents need to realize that although the standards are a positive thing for guiding the curriculums of their children's classroom, the stigma that surrounds standardized testing makes standards seem like a negative development. If parents were aware of the difference between a standards-based classroom and the standardized testing being implemented, they could take an active role in creating a more adequate form of assessing the achievement of the standards.

In August 2001 the Business Roundtable took a poll to see how parents felt about standards-based learning. This poll showed that parents think that by raising standards our nation is heading in the right direction. Parents feel that students should have to pass a national reading and math test before being passed to the next grade, regardless of what grades they might have gotten in their class. The majority of parents feel that students should have to pass a test to graduate from high school. The poll showed that only 2 percent of parents wanted to abandon using standards altogether. Teachers need to work with parents to help them understand what their children need to learn. If parents are aware of the standards their children are learning, then they can create an active learning environment at home. Standards-based practices allow teachers to work one on one with the parents (Kendall et al., 1998).

AUTHENTIC ASSESSMENT: USING STANDARDS FOR THEIR INTENDED PURPOSE

In a standards-based classroom, the most important achievement is the mastery of the standards. It is clear that teachers must properly assess their students in order to know if they have mastered the standards. However, the most difficult problem with educational assessment in a standards-based classroom is that it inhibits the use of DAP, brain-based learning, service-learning, and PBL (as well as most of the authentic practices that are discussed in education today). Since the main form of assessment related to the standards is a standardized test, this greatly diminishes the use of the more effective forms of assessment. This is seen as the major drawback of the standards movement.

Standards should show the knowledge students have at the end of an academic term, not how well they did on a normative test as compared with a person who lives two hundred miles away from them. Using norm-referenced tests can limit the ways in which students can be assessed. When they assess students by how well they meet the standards, teachers should be using a criterion-referenced assessment, because criterion-referenced assessment compares a student's performance to recognized criteria or objectives. Teachers can assess standards by using essay tests that are centered on the standards. Teachers should use portfolios or informal assessments to assess standards-based practices because this allows teachers to see how students have learned over a certain period.

FUTURE IMPLICATIONS

A standards-based practice classroom can still be an active learning environment, and we plan on our classrooms becoming communities of learners, committed to learning the most important life skills. Teachers know what their students need, but it is critical that we call upon parents and community members to understand what authentic practices are. Only when communities unite against the oppression of a standardized curriculum governed by high-stakes tests will the system reorganize. While twenty-first-century education is doing much to support the growth of students, even more can be done to ensure that the environments with which our children interact are as positive and powerful for their learning as possible. For further information about the strength of American public schools in relation to American home schools, private schools, or foreign schools, see P. Sacks's (1999) *Standardized Minds*, or access the Nation's Report Card at http://nces.ed.gov/nationsreportcard.

Appendix A

Problem-Based Learning Examples

MATH MYSTERY: AN EXAMPLE OF A MIDDLE SCHOOL PROBLEM-BASED LEARNING SCENARIO

Oh, no! One of my valued monkeys has been kidnapped from my classroom. There is a ransom note where he usually sits, and there is a footprint by the door. Who would do such a thing?

Overview

The crime scene will be set up in my classroom. (I will even have it set up before homeroom to peak curiosity. Students will have to wait two whole periods to find out what was behind the yellow taped door.) The ransom note is constructed from pieces of cutout newspaper and magazine letters, taped to a piece of Harwood stationery. The kidnapper's fingerprint has been captured in the tape. There is a footprint on the back of some papers that have fallen to the floor near the door. These are the only two clues we have to use.

The police liaison officer will be solicited to help me create some videos showing how police preserve a crime scene, map the clues, and process the evidence to help narrow down the suspects. The students will start by creating a sketch of the scene, with measurements of the clues to fixed points within the room. They will then create a scale map of the room. (The ransom note would indicate an inside job.) Students will gather staff and faculty fingerprints, classify and compare the prints to the partial print, thus narrowing down the list of suspects to compare with the second clue. Students will create scatter plots to see the relationship of their classmates' shoe sizes to their heights to predict the height (or range of possible heights) of the suspect. Then, they will be sent out to take pictures of the suspects holding an object or standing next to one of the classmates. Using proportions, they will measure the object or classmate in real life, and the measurements from the photos to determine the suspects' heights. The height will narrow down the list of suspects once again.

At this point, there should be no more than four suspects. In order to narrow down the list to one suspect, we must revisit the fingerprints and prove that there are at least ten points of commonality between the kidnapper's print and the suspects' prints. The fingerprints will be blown up to about 400 percent. Students will have to mark points of interest (loops, whorls, arches, scars, etc.). They will also have to calculate the distance from the center of the print and the angle at which it lies from the center. At each transition in studying evidence, students will be allowed to discuss or present their ideas for "whodunit." Students will turn in their final report, with all the evidence and a reflection about their CSI experience and the math they had to use. With luck, we can assemble the final four suspects in the auditorium and confront the kidnapper as an entire grade level to bring closure. I will also ask the kidnapper to provide the reason that the monkey was kidnapped in the first place.

Overall, the kids will be excited by the mystery. It's different, realistic, and feeds their natural curiosity and love of mystery. I hope I can get the liaison officer to stay all day. If he can't, perhaps he can help me find some fellow officers who could come in and help students process the crime scene. I would have him help me with the videos if I can't get live police officers involved.

My goals for the project are:

1. To provide students with a real-life situation that involves the use of mathematics.
2. To involve all of my students in a fun activity.

My objectives are:

1. After instruction, students will be able to construct a scale map of the classroom, as evidenced by their ability to create a detailed, accurate map of the classroom (complete with clues) to scale.

2. After instruction, students will be able to organize data, as evidenced by their ability to sort and classify fingerprints by common characteristics.

3. After instruction, students will be able to predict an outcome, as evidenced by their ability to graph shoe size and height in a scatter plot and use the trend line to determine the average height for a given shoe size.

4. After instruction, students will be able to measure heights indirectly, as evidenced by their ability to use ratio and proportion to measure the heights of objects in photographs.

5. After instruction, students will be able to analyze data, as evidenced by their ability to measure line segments and angles of various forms and concur that there are exactly two matching forms.

6. After instruction, students will be able to synthesize data, as evidenced by their ability to organize the processes and observations involved in the mystery in a written reflection about their mathematical experiences.

7. After instruction, students will be able to critique the work and participation of their group members and themselves, as evidenced by the completion of self-evaluation and group-evaluation forms.

Alignment of Goals, Objectives, and Standards

Standards Assessment: M = math, A = algebra I, SC = science
   Goal 1: To provide students with a real-life situation that involves the use of mathematics.

1. After instruction, students will be able to construct a scale map of the classroom, as evidenced by their ability to create a detailed, accurate map of the classroom (complete with clues) to scale.
   M8.5.3 Solve problems involving scale factors, area, and volume using ratio and proportion.
   M8.6.2 Identify different methods of selecting samples, analyzing the strengths and weaknesses of each method and the possible bias in a sample or display.
   M8.7.1 Analyze problems by identifying relationships, telling relevant from irrelevant information, identifying missing information, sequencing and prioritizing information, and observing patterns.
   M8.7.6 Express solutions clearly and logically by using the appropriate mathematical terms and notation. Support solutions with evidence in both verbal and symbolic work.

M8.7.11 Decide whether a solution is reasonable in the context of the original situation.

A1.9.1 Use a variety of problem-solving strategies, such as drawing a diagram, making a chart, doing guess-and-check, solving a simpler problem, writing an equation, and working backwards.

A1.9.2 Decide whether a solution is reasonable in the context of the original situation.

SC8.1.4 Explain why accurate record keeping, openness, and replication are essential for maintaining an investigator's credibility with other scientists and society.

SC8.2.1 Estimate distances and travel times from maps and the actual size of objects from scale drawings.

SC 8.2.2 Determine in what unit, such as seconds, meters, grams, and the like, an answer should be expressed based on the units of the inputs to the calculation.

SC8.2.7 Participate in group discussions on scientific topics by restating or summarizing accurately what others have said, asking for clarification or elaboration and expressing alternative positions.

SC8.2.8 Use tables, charts, and graphs in making arguments and claims in, for example, oral and written presentations about lab or fieldwork.

SC8.5.5 Illustrate that it takes two numbers to locate a point on a map or any other two-dimensional surface.

2. After instruction, students will be able to organize data, as evidenced by their ability to sort and classify fingerprints by common characteristics.

M8.6.1 Identify claims based on statistical data and, in simple cases, evaluate the reasonableness of the claims. Design a study to investigate the claim.

M8.6.2 Identify different methods of selecting samples, analyzing the strengths and weaknesses of each method and the possible bias in a sample or display.

M8.7.1 Analyze problems by identifying relationships, telling relevant from irrelevant information, identifying missing information, sequencing and prioritizing information, and observing patterns.

M8.7.3 Decide when and how to divide a problem into simpler parts.

M8.7.6 Express solutions clearly and logically by using the appropriate mathematical terms and notation. Support solutions with evidence in both verbal and symbolic work.

M8.7.11 Decide whether a solution is reasonable in the context of the original situation.

A1.9.1 Use a variety of problem-solving strategies, such as drawing a diagram, making a chart, doing guess-and-check, solving a simpler problem, writing an equation, and working backwards.

A1.9.2 Decide whether a solution is reasonable in the context of the original situation.

SC8.2.7 Participate in group discussions on scientific topics by restating or summarizing accurately what others have said, asking for clarification or elaboration, and expressing alternative positions.

SC8.2.8 Use tables, charts, and graphs in making arguments and claims in, for example, oral and written presentations about lab or fieldwork.

SC8.2.9 Explain why arguments are invalid if based on very small samples of data, biased samples, or samples for which there was no control sample.

SC8.2.10 Identify and criticize the reasoning in arguments in which fact and opinion are intermingled or the conclusions do not follow logically from the evidence given, an analogy is not apt, no mention is made of whether the control group is very much like the experimental group, or all members of a group are implied to have nearly identical characteristics that differ from those of other groups.

3. After instruction, students will be able to predict an outcome, as evidenced by their ability to graph shoe size and height in a scatter plot and use the trend line to determine the height for a given shoe size.

M8.3.7 Demonstrate an understanding of rate as a measure of one quantity with respect to another quantity.

M8.3.8 Demonstrate an understanding of the relationships among tables, equations, verbal expressions, and graphs of linear functions.

M8.6.1 Identify claims based on statistical data and, in simple cases, evaluate the reasonableness of the claims. Design a study to investigate the claim.

M8.6.2 Identify different methods of selecting samples, analyzing the strengths and weaknesses of each method and the possible bias in a sample or display.

M8.6.5 Represent two-variable data with a scatter plot on the coordinate plane and describe how the data points are distributed. If the pattern appears to be linear, draw a line that appears to fit the data best and write the equation of that line.

M8.7.1 Analyze problems by identifying relationships, telling relevant from irrelevant information, identifying missing information, sequencing and prioritizing information, and observing patterns.

M8.7.5 Make and test conjectures using inductive reasoning.

M8.7.6 Express solutions clearly and logically by using the appropriate mathematical terms and notation. Support solutions with evidence in both verbal and symbolic work.

M8.7.11 Decide whether a solution is reasonable in the context of the original situation.

A1.3.1 Sketch a reasonable graph for a given relationship.

A1.3.2 Interpret a graph representing a given situation.

A1.3.4 Find the domain and range of a relation.

A1.9.1 Use a variety of problem-solving strategies, such as drawing a diagram, making a chart, doing guess-and-check, solving a simpler problem, writing an equation, and working backwards.

A1.9.2 Decide whether a solution is reasonable in the context of the original situation.

A1.9.7 Identify the hypothesis and conclusion in a logical deduction.

SC8.2.7 Participate in group discussions on scientific topics by restating or summarizing accurately what others have said, asking for clarification or elaboration and expressing alternative positions.

SC8.2.8 Use tables, charts, and graphs in making arguments and claims in, for example, oral and written presentations about lab or fieldwork.

SC8.2.9 Explain why arguments are invalid if based on very small samples of data, biased samples, or samples for which there was no control sample.

SC8.2.10 Identify and criticize the reasoning in arguments in which fact and opinion are intermingled or the conclusions do not follow logically from the evidence given, an analogy is not apt, no mention is made of whether the control group is very much like the experimental group, or all members of a group are implied to have nearly identical characteristics that differ from those of other groups.

SC8.5.3 Demonstrate that mathematical statements can be used to describe how one quantity changes when another changes.

SC8.5.4 Illustrate how graphs can show a variety of possible relationships between two variables.

SC8.5.5 Illustrate that it takes two numbers to locate a point on a map or any other two-dimensional surface.

4. After instruction, students will be able to measure heights indirectly, as evidenced by their ability to use ratio and proportion to measure the heights of objects in photographs.

M8.2.1 Add, subtract, multiply, and divide rational numbers (integers, fractions, and terminating decimals) in multistep problems.

M8.5.1 Convert common measurements for length, area, volume, weight, capacity, and time to equivalent measurements within the same system.

M8.6.2 Identify different methods of selecting samples, analyzing the strengths and weaknesses of each method and the possible bias in a sample or display.

M8.7.1 Analyze problems by identifying relationships, telling relevant from irrelevant information, identifying missing information, sequencing and prioritizing information, and observing patterns.

M8.7.3 Decide when and how to divide a problem into simpler parts.

M8.7.5 Make and test conjectures using inductive reasoning.

M8.7.6 Express solutions clearly and logically by using the appropriate mathematical terms and notation. Support solutions with evidence in both verbal and symbolic work.

M8.7.9 Use graphing to estimate solutions and check the estimates with analytic approaches.

M8.7.11 Decide whether a solution is reasonable in the context of the original situation.

A1.1.5 Use dimensional (unit) analysis to organize conversions and computations.

A1.9.1 Use a variety of problem-solving strategies, such as drawing a diagram, making a chart, doing guess-and-check, solving a simpler problem, writing an equation, and working backwards.

A1.9.2 Decide whether a solution is reasonable in the context of the original situation.

SC8.2.3 Use proportional reasoning to solve problems.

SC8.2.4 Use technological devices, such as calculators and computers, to perform calculations.

SC8.2.7 Participate in group discussions on scientific topics by restating or summarizing accurately what others have said, asking for clarification or elaboration, and expressing alternative positions.

SC8.2.8 Use tables, charts, and graphs in making arguments and claims in, for example, oral and written presentations about lab or fieldwork.

5. After instruction, students will be able to analyze data, as evidenced by their ability to measure line segments and angles of various forms and concur that there are exactly two matching forms.

M8.4.2 Perform simple constructions, such as bisectors of segments and angles, copies of segments and angles, and perpendicular segments. Describe and justify the constructions.

M8.6.1 Identify claims based on statistical data and, in simple cases, evaluate the reasonableness of the claims. Design a study to investigate the claim.

M8.7.1 Analyze problems by identifying relationships, telling relevant from irrelevant information, identifying missing information, sequencing and prioritizing information, and observing patterns.

M8.7.3 Decide when and how to divide a problem into simpler parts.

M8.7.6 Express solutions clearly and logically by using the appropriate mathematical terms and notation. Support solutions with evidence in both verbal and symbolic work.

M8.7.11 Decide whether a solution is reasonable in the context of the original situation.

A1.9.1 Use a variety of problem-solving strategies, such as drawing a diagram, making a chart, doing guess-and-check, solving a simpler problem, writing an equation, and working backwards.

A1.9.2 Decide whether a solution is reasonable in the context of the original situation.

A1.9.7 Identify the hypothesis and conclusion in a logical deduction.

A1.9.8 Use counterexamples to show that statements are false, recognizing that a single counterexample is sufficient to prove a general statement false.

SC8.2.6 Write clear, step-by-step instructions (procedural summaries) for conducting investigations, operating something, or following a procedure.

SC8.2.7 Participate in group discussions on scientific topics by restating or summarizing accurately what others have said, asking for clarification or elaboration and expressing alternative positions.

SC8.2.8 Use tables, charts, and graphs in making arguments and claims in, for example, oral and written presentations about lab or fieldwork.

SC8.2.10 Identify and criticize the reasoning in arguments in which fact and opinion are intermingled or the conclusions do not follow logically from the evidence given, an analogy is not apt, no mention is made of whether the control group is very much like the experimental group, or all members of a group are implied to have nearly identical characteristics that differ from those of other groups.

SC8.5.6 Explain that a single example can never prove that something is always true, but it can prove that something is not always true.

Goal 2: To involve all my students in a fun activity.

6. After instruction, students will be able to synthesize data, as evidenced by their ability to organize the processes and observations involved in the mystery in a written reflection about their mathematical experiences.

   LA8.4.1 Discuss ideas for writing, keep a list or notebook of ideas, and use graphic organizers to plan writing.

   LA8.4.2 Create compositions that have a clear message, a coherent thesis (a statement of position on the topic), and a clear and well-supported conclusion.

LA8.4.3 Support theses or conclusions with analogies (comparisons), paraphrases, quotations, opinions from experts, and similar devices.

LA8.5.4 Write persuasive compositions that do the following:
- Include a well-defined thesis that makes a clear and knowledgeable appeal
- Present detailed evidence, examples, and reasoning to support effective arguments and emotional appeals
- Provide details, reasons, and examples, arranging them effectively by anticipating and answering reader concerns and counterarguments

LA8.5.6 Write using precise word choices to make writing interesting and exact.

LA8.5.7 Write for different purposes and to a specific audience or person, adjusting tone and style as necessary.

LA8.6.4 Edit written manuscripts to ensure that correct grammar is used.

LA8.6.5 Use correct punctuation.

LA8.6.6 Use correct capitalization.

LA8.6.7 Use correct spelling conventions.

SC8.2.6 Write clear, step-by-step instructions (procedural summaries) for conducting investigations, operating something, or following a procedure

7. After instruction, students will be able to critique the work and participation of their group members and themselves, as evidenced by completion of self-evaluation and group-evaluation forms.

LA8.5.4 Write persuasive compositions that do the following:
- Include a well-defined thesis that makes a clear and knowledgeable appeal
- Present detailed evidence, examples, and reasoning to support effective arguments and emotional appeals
- Provide details, reasons, and examples, arranging them effectively by anticipating and answering reader concerns and counterarguments

LA8.5.7 Write for different purposes and to a specific audience or person, adjusting tone and style as necessary.

LA8.6.4 Edit written manuscripts to ensure that correct grammar is used.

LA8.6.5 Use correct punctuation.

LA8.6.6 Use correct capitalization.

LA8.6.7 Use correct spelling conventions.

Alignment to Schlechty's Ten Design Qualities

(1) *Content and substance*—The unit aligns with thirty-eight eighth-grade standards (math—15, language arts—10, science—13) and eight algebra I standards.

(2) *Organization of knowledge*—The information and knowledge are arranged in a logical order, increasing in difficulty as the unit progresses.

(3) *Product focus*—The work is designed to engage the students.

(4) *Clear and compelling product standards*—The students will be given rubrics in advance, so that they will know what is expected and what will be graded.

(5) *Protection from adverse consequences for initial failures*—The unit is designed for students to make guesses and change their opinions based on new evidence. Participation grades will accrue throughout the project, but the final grade will not be assessed until the very end.

(6) *Affirmation of performance*—A bulletin board will be set up outside the classroom, displaying student work and hypotheses throughout the project. The entire school will have access to the bulletin board to view the students' progress.

(7) *Affiliation*—The unit is designed for students to work in cooperative groups.

(8) *Novelty and variety*—The lessons incorporate new activities in which the students will most likely never have had experience. Also, this will be the first time the entire eighth-grade class has worked together on a project in which each individual group's results are important to the entire group.

(9) *Choice*—Students will have the choice of with whom they will work in their small groups. Student groups will have a choice as to the teachers with whom they would like to focus. Students may also draw upon their experiences to complete the tasks in a variety of ways, so long as they are mathematically sound.

(10) *Authenticity*—Kidnapping, crime scenes, and the skills involved
   are definitely related to the real world. I hope that this unit inspires
   some students to pursue a career as a police officer or crime-scene
   investigator.

LESSON PLAN 1A

"Unveiling the Crime Scene"

Goal 1: To provide students with a real-life situation that involves the use
   of mathematics.
Objective 1: After instruction, students will be able to construct a scale
   map of the classroom, as evidenced by their ability to create a detailed,
   accurate map of the classroom (complete with clues) to scale.
Introduction (five minutes):

1. The crime scene will be in place, with the classroom door blocked
   off with caution tape, before homeroom. (Students won't show up
   for math class for about an hour and a half. During that time, students will build up curiosity and discuss among themselves what
   could possibly have happened in my classroom.)
2. A sign near the door will direct students to another room for the day,
   a temporary classroom.
3. Upon arriving at the classroom, the teacher will look worried, but
   not speak to the students until everyone had arrived.
4. The police liaison officer will appear in the door (or be video taped
   in advance) and describe the circumstances surrounding the crime
   scene. He will also review the procedures for collecting evidence
   and mapping out the crime scene.
5. Students will then discuss the big task of collecting all the evidence
   and brainstorm ideas for how to divide the task so that all the evidence can be gathered and the crime scene sketched within our al-
   lotted thirty minutes. A cameraperson will be chosen to photograph
   the scene. An official sketcher will be chosen to assemble each
   group's data as it's turned in. A small group will be assigned to describe the ransom letter and other pertinent information. The re-

maining groups will be assigned specific areas to be measured, so that each measurement is taken by two groups.

Activity (thirty minutes):
1. Students will arrive on the scene and enter the room carefully, so as not to disturb the evidence.
2. Tasks and supplies will be divided.
3. Students will collect evidence and sketch the scene. (Group tasks include measuring each wall [NSEW] and distances to evidence from at least two fixed points.)
4. At the end of thirty minutes, students gather back at the temporary classroom.

Wrap-up Discussion (ten minutes):
1. The sketch of the crime scene will be taped to the chalkboard.
2. The class will discuss the visual evidence with the photographer to make sure that all important items were captured on film as the photographer points out the locations of the evidence on the sketch.
3. The small groups will present their observations of the ransom note and other items.
4. The class will discuss what supplies will be needed to create a scale map of the crime scene, which will be submitted in the crime report to the police captain (who is a real stickler for accurate maps).
5. In groups, the students will begin to discuss their ideas of whodunit based on the crime scene. Groups are to write up a brief account of the events from class, their particular role in the evidence collection, and some ideas of how we should go about trying to figure out who took the monkey. (There will be daily group reports that will be compiled so that there is a running record of the mystery unit.)

Materials:
1. Caution tape
2. Video tape of officer's instructions
3. Digital camera for photographer
4. Large paper and marker for sketcher
5. Measuring tapes and/or meter sticks
6. Manila envelopes (for storing and organizing daily reports)

Standards Assessment: M = math, A = algebra I, SC = science

M8.6.2 Identify different methods of selecting samples, analyzing the strengths and weaknesses of each method and the possible bias in a sample or display. *This standard will be evidenced as students collect data from the crime scene.*

M8.7.1 Analyze problems by identifying relationships, telling relevant from irrelevant information, identifying missing information, sequencing and prioritizing information, and observing patterns. *This standard will be evidenced as students collect data from the crime scene.*

M8.7.6 Express solutions clearly and logically by using the appropriate mathematical terms and notation. Support solutions with evidence in both verbal and symbolic work. *This standard will be evidenced as students write their reflections for the day.*

A1.9.1 Use a variety of problem-solving strategies, such as drawing a diagram, making a chart, doing guess-and-check, solving a simpler problem, writing an equation, and working backwards. *This standard will be evidenced as students draw a diagram of the crime scene.*

SC8.1.4 Explain why accurate record keeping, openness, and replication are essential for maintaining an investigator's credibility with other scientists and society. *This standard will be evidenced in the discussion of the importance of detailing the crime scene accurately.*

SC 8.2.2 Determine in what unit, such as seconds, meters, grams, and the like, an answer should be expressed based on the units of the inputs to the calculation. *This standard will be evidenced in the discussion regarding how to document the measurements of the crime scene.*

SC8.2.7 Participate in group discussions on scientific topics by restating or summarizing accurately what others have said, asking for clarification or elaboration and expressing alternative positions. *This standard will be evidenced in the group discussions prior to the groups' writing their reflections.*

SC8.2.8 Use tables, charts, and graphs in making arguments and claims in, for example, oral and written presentations about lab or fieldwork. *This standard will be evidenced in the group reflection writing that documents the work for the day.*

SC8.5.5 Illustrate that it takes two numbers to locate a point on a map or any other two-dimensional surface. *This standard will be evidenced in the discussion of the importance of detailing the crime scene accurately.*

Schlechty's WOW

(1) *Content and substance*—The unit aligns with thirty-eight eighth-grade standards (math—15, language arts—10, science—13) and eight algebra I standards.

(2) *Organization of knowledge*—The information and knowledge are arranged in a logical order, increasing in difficulty as the unit progresses.

(3) *Product focus*—The work is designed to engage the students.

(5) *Protection from adverse consequences for initial failures*—The unit is designed for students to make guesses and change their opinions based on new evidence. Participation grades will accrue throughout the project, but the final grade will not be assessed until the very end.

(7) *Affiliation*—The unit is designed for students to work in cooperative groups.

(8) *Novelty and variety*—The lessons incorporate new activities in which the students will most likely never have had experience. Also, this will be the first time the entire eighth-grade class has worked together on a project in which each individual group's results are important to the entire group.

(9) *Choice*—Students will have the choice of with whom they will work in their small groups. Student groups will have a choice as to the teachers with whom they would like to focus. Students may also draw upon their experiences to complete the tasks in a variety of ways, so long as they are mathematically sound.

(10) *Authenticity*—Kidnapping, crime scenes, and the skills involved are definitely related to the real world. I hope that this unit inspires some students to pursue a career as a police officer or crime-scene investigator.

LESSON PLAN 1B

"Documenting the Crime Scene"

Goal 1: To provide students with a real-life situation that involves the use of mathematics.

Objective 1: After instruction, students will be able to construct a scale map of the classroom, as evidenced by the their ability to create a detailed, accurate map of the classroom (complete with clues) to scale.

Introduction (five minutes):

1. The classroom will be cleared for use. Class will resume in the crime scene.
2. The students will debrief by reading or summarizing their reports from the previous day. (This will help anyone who may have been absent, as well as to refresh the students' memories regarding the previous day's class.)
3. Students will share their ideas for how we should go about analyzing the evidence (which I have in plastic evidence bags).

Activity (thirty minutes):

1. The groups will assign members specific tasks: (1) create scale map, (2) analyze ransom note, or (3) analyze footprint.
2. The groups will split up. The (1)s will meet and discuss the what they need to create the scale map, including any specific characteristics of scale maps. The (2)s will meet and discuss the ransom note and what information can be drawn from the note, documenting their meeting. The (3)s will meet and discuss the footprint left at the scene and how we might draw information from the print.
3. After about ten to fifteen minutes, groups will reconvene and share the information that was gathered from their discussions.
4. The groups will determine if there is anything else they need to consider or if there are supplies they need to gather to carry out the mapping task.

Wrap-up Discussion (ten minutes):

1. The class will discuss the mapping needs and assemble a list of supplies needed for the following day.

2. The class will discuss the evidence and a possible list of suspects.
3. The groups will write their reports for the day, including their ideas about whodunit and ways that the evidence can be used or processed to narrow down the list of possible suspects.

Materials:
1. Digital camera for photographer
2. Large paper and marker for sketcher
3. Measuring tapes and/or meter sticks
4. Plastic evidence bags
5. Rulers
6. Grid paper
7. Computer paper
8. Various scale maps for group (1)

Standards Assessment: M = math, A = algebra I, SC = science

M8.6.2 Identify different methods of selecting samples, analyzing the strengths and weaknesses of each method and the possible bias in a sample or display. *This standard will be evidenced as students review the crime scene and analyze the evidence.*

M8.7.1 Analyze problems by identifying relationships, telling relevant from irrelevant information, identifying missing information, sequencing and prioritizing information, and observing patterns. *This standard will be evidenced as students analyze the evidence.*

M8.7.6 Express solutions clearly and logically by using the appropriate mathematical terms and notation. Support solutions with evidence in both verbal and symbolic work. *This standard will be evidenced as students write their reflections for the day.*

A1.9.1 Use a variety of problem-solving strategies, such as drawing a diagram, making a chart, doing guess-and-check, solving a simpler problem, writing an equation, and working backwards. *This standard will be evidenced as students create scale maps of the crime scene.*

SC 8.2.2 Determine in what unit, such as seconds, meters, grams, and the like, an answer should be expressed based on the units of the inputs to the calculation. *This standard will be evidenced as students create scale maps of the crime scene.*

SC8.2.7 Participate in group discussions on scientific topics by restating or summarizing accurately what others have said, asking for clarification or elaboration, and expressing alternative positions. *This standard will be evidenced in the group discussions regarding their piece of evidence as well as prior to the groups' writing their reflections.*

SC8.2.8 Use tables, charts, and graphs in making arguments and claims in, for example, oral and written presentations about lab or field-work. *This standard will be evidenced in the group reflection writing that documents the work for the day.*

Schlechty's WOW

(1) *Content and substance*—The unit aligns with thirty-eight eighth-grade standards (math—15, language arts—10, science—13) and eight algebra I standards.

(2) *Organization of knowledge*—The information and knowledge are arranged in a logical order, increasing in difficulty as the unit progresses.

(3) *Product focus*—The work is designed to engage the students.

(5) *Protection from adverse consequences for initial failures*—The unit is designed for students to make guesses and change their opinions based on new evidence. Participation grades will accrue throughout the project, but the final grade will not be assessed until the very end.

(7) *Affiliation*—The unit is designed for students to work in cooperative groups.

(8) *Novelty and variety*—The lessons incorporate new activities in which the students will most likely never have had experience. Also, this will be the first time the entire eighth grade class has worked together on a project in which each individual groups' results are important to the entire group.

(9) *Choice*—Students will have the choice of with whom they will work in their small groups. Student groups will have a choice as to the teachers with whom they would like to focus. Students may also draw upon their experiences to complete the tasks in a variety of ways, so long as they are mathematically sound.

(10) *Authenticity*—Kidnapping, crime scenes, and the skills involved are definitely related to the real world. I hope that this unit inspires

some students to pursue a career as a police officer or crime-scene investigator.

LESSON PLAN 1C

"Reconstructing the Crime Scene"

Goal 1: To provide students with a real-life situation that involves the use of mathematics.

Objective 1: After instruction, students will be able to construct a scale map of the classroom, as evidenced by the their ability to create a detailed, accurate map of the classroom (complete with clues) to scale.

Introduction (five minutes):

1. The students will debrief by reading or summarizing their reports from the previous day. (This will help anyone who may have been absent as well as refresh the students' memories regarding the previous day's class.)

2. Students will share their ideas for whodunit and ways that the evidence can be used or processed to narrow down the list of possible suspects.

3. The class will discuss the "musts" of a scale map. Together we will construct the exemplary criteria for a rubric.

Activity (thirty minutes):

1. Students will be assigned roles for their participation in the construction of a scale map. The roles are artist(s), supplier, and supervisor. A group-participation sheet will be distributed, explaining the requirements of each role.

2. The supplier gathers the materials needed for the group.

3. The groups work on their scale maps.

Wrap-up Discussion (ten minutes):

1. The class will discuss additional mapping needs and assemble a list of supplies needed for the following day.

2. The groups will write their reports for the day, which should include the criteria that they have met for the scale map and a list of the criteria they still need to meet. There should also be a plan for completion: estimated time needed and any job changes.

Materials:

1. Measuring tapes and/or meter sticks
2. Other supplies deemed necessary by the students (graph paper, computer paper, compass, protractor, etc.)
3. Group-participation or role sheet

Standards Assessment: M = math, A = algebra I, SC = science

M8.5.3 Solve problems involving scale factors, area, and volume using ratio and proportion. *This standard will be evidenced by the students using ratio and proportion to convert classroom measurements to the scaled-down measurements for the map.*

M8.7.1 Analyze problems by identifying relationships, telling relevant from irrelevant information, identifying missing information, sequencing and prioritizing information, and observing patterns. *This standard will be evidenced as students analyze the "musts" for a scale map.*

M8.7.6 Express solutions clearly and logically by using the appropriate mathematical terms and notation. Support solutions with evidence in both verbal and symbolic work. *This standard will be evidenced as students write their reflections for the day.*

M8.7.11 Decide whether a solution is reasonable in the context of the original situation. *This standard will be evidenced as students critique their scale map (using the "musts" determined by the class) in their written reflection for the day.*

A1.9.1 Use a variety of problem-solving strategies, such as drawing a diagram, making a chart, doing guess-and-check, solving a simpler problem, writing an equation, and working backwards. *This standard will be evidenced as students create scale maps of the crime scene.*

A1.9.2 Decide whether a solution is reasonable in the context of the original situation. *This standard will be evidenced as students critique their scale map (using the "musts" determined by the class) in their written reflection for the day.*

SC 8.2.2 Determine in what unit, such as seconds, meters, grams, and the like, an answer should be expressed based on the units of the inputs to the calculation. *This standard will be evidenced as students create scale maps of the crime scene.*

SC8.2.7 Participate in group discussions on scientific topics by restating or summarizing accurately what others have said, asking for clarification or elaboration, and expressing alternative positions. *This standard will be evidenced in the group discussions prior to the groups' writing their reflections.*

SC8.2.8 Use tables, charts, and graphs in making arguments and claims in, for example, oral and written presentations about lab or field-work. *This standard will be evidenced in the group reflection writing that documents the work for the day.*

SC8.5.5 Illustrate that it takes two numbers to locate a point on a map or any other two-dimensional surface. *This standard will be evidenced as students create scale maps of the crime scene, where every piece of evidence has two measurements that determine its location.*

Schlechty's WOW

(1) *Content and substance*—The unit aligns with thirty-eight eighth-grade standards (math—15, language arts—10, science—13) and eight algebra I standards.

(2) *Organization of knowledge*—The information and knowledge are arranged in a logical order, increasing in difficulty as the unit progresses.

(3) *Product focus*—The work is designed to engage the students.

(4) *Clear and compelling product standards*—The students will be given rubrics in advance, so that they will know what is expected and what will be graded.

(5) *Protection from adverse consequences for initial failures*—The unit is designed for students to make guesses and change their opinions based on new evidence. Participation grades will accrue throughout the project, but the final grade will not be assessed until the very end.

(7) *Affiliation*—The unit is designed for students to work in cooperative groups.

(8) *Novelty and variety*—The lessons incorporate new activities in which the students will most likely never have had experience. Also, this will be the first time the entire eighth-grade class has worked together on a project in which each individual groups' results are important to the entire group.

(9) *Choice*—Students will have the choice of with whom they will work in their small groups. Student groups will have a choice as to the teachers with whom they would like to focus. Students may also

draw upon their experiences to complete the tasks in a variety of ways, so long as they are mathematically sound.

(10) *Authenticity*—Kidnapping, crime scenes, and the skills involved are definitely related to the real world. I hope that this unit inspires some students to pursue a career as a police officer or crime-scene investigator.

LESSON PLAN 1D

"Reconstructing the Crime Scene" (continued)

Goal 1: To provide students with a real-life situation that involves the use of mathematics.

Objective 1: After instruction, students will be able to construct a scale map of the classroom, as evidenced by the their ability to create a detailed, accurate map of the classroom (complete with clues) to scale.

Introduction (five minutes):

1. The students will debrief by stating their progress from the previous day. (This will help anyone who may have been absent as well as refresh the students' memories regarding the previous day's class. It will also provide the teacher with an idea of how much time to give students to complete their maps.)

2. The class will view the criteria in the rubric, discussing any changes that need to be made.

Activity (thirty minutes):

1. Students will reassign the roles for their participation. (Note: Students do not have to keep the same job from the previous day.) The group-participation sheet should indicate the distribution of roles.

2. The supplier gathers the materials needed for the group.

3. The groups work on their scale maps.

Wrap-up Discussion (ten minutes):

1. The maps will be displayed in the classroom, and the students will describe the similarities and differences between the maps.

2. Constructive criticism will be allowed for groups to point out rubric criteria that might be missing from the map. Also, students can ask questions regarding anything that seems to be unclear. (Remember, the police captain is a real stickler for accurate details.)
3. The groups will write their reports for the day. The criteria groups still need to meet should be included. There should also be a plan for completion/adaptation (estimated time needed and when and where they will meet).

Materials:
1. Measuring tapes and/or meter sticks
2. Other supplies deemed necessary by the students (graph paper, computer paper, compass, protractor, etc.)
3. Group-participation or role sheet

Standards Assessment: M = math, A = algebra I, SC = science

M8.5.3 Solve problems involving scale factors, area, and volume using ratio and proportion. *This standard will be evidenced by the students using ratio and proportion to convert classroom measurements to the scaled-down measurements for the map.*

M8.7.1 Analyze problems by identifying relationships, telling relevant from irrelevant information, identifying missing information, sequencing and prioritizing information, and observing patterns. *This standard will be evidenced as students analyze the "musts" for a scale map.*

M8.7.6 Express solutions clearly and logically by using the appropriate mathematical terms and notation. Support solutions with evidence in both verbal and symbolic work. *This standard will be evidenced as students write their reflections for the day.*

M8.7.11 Decide whether a solution is reasonable in the context of the original situation. *This standard will be evidenced as students critique their scale map (using the "musts" determined by the class) in their written reflection for the day.*

A1.9.1 Use a variety of problem-solving strategies, such as drawing a diagram, making a chart, doing guess-and-check, solving a simpler problem, writing an equation, and working backwards. *This standard will be evidenced as students create scale maps of the crime scene.*

A1.9.2 Decide whether a solution is reasonable in the context of the original situation. *This standard will be evidenced as students critique their scale map (using the "musts" determined by the class) in their written reflection for the day.*

SC 8.2.2 Determine in what unit, such as seconds, meters, grams, and the like, an answer should be expressed based on the units of the inputs to the calculation. *This standard will be evidenced as students create scale maps of the crime scene.*

SC8.2.7 Participate in group discussions on scientific topics by restating or summarizing accurately what others have said, asking for clarification or elaboration and expressing alternative positions. *This standard will be evidenced in the group discussions prior to the groups' writing their reflections.*

SC8.2.8 Use tables, charts, and graphs in making arguments and claims in, for example, oral and written presentations about lab or fieldwork. *This standard will be evidenced in the group reflection writing that documents the work for the day.*

SC8.5.5 Illustrate that it takes two numbers to locate a point on a map or any other two-dimensional surface. *This standard will be evidenced as students create scale maps of the crime scene, where every piece of evidence has two measurements that determine its location.*

Schlechty's WOW

(1) *Content and substance*—The unit aligns with thirty-eight eighth-grade standards (math—15, language arts—10, science—13) and eight algebra I standards.

(2) *Organization of knowledge*—The information and knowledge are arranged in a logical order, increasing in difficulty as the unit progresses.

(3) *Product focus*—The work is designed to engage the students.

(4) *Clear and compelling product standards*—The students will be given rubrics in advance, so that they will know what is expected and what will be graded.

(5) *Protection from adverse consequences for initial failures*—The unit is designed for students to make guesses and change their opinions based on new evidence. Participation grades will accrue throughout the project, but the final grade will not be assessed until the very end.

(7) *Affiliation*—The unit is designed for students to work in cooperative groups.

(8) *Novelty and variety*—The lessons incorporate new activities in which the students will most likely never have had experience. Also, this will be the first time the entire eighth-grade class has worked together on a project in which each individual groups' results are important to the entire group.

(9) *Choice*—Students will have the choice of with whom they will work in their small groups. Student groups will have a choice as to the teachers with whom they would like to focus. Students may also draw upon their experiences to complete the tasks in a variety of ways, so long as they are mathematically sound.

(10) *Authenticity*—Kidnapping, crime scenes, and the skills involved are definitely related to the real world. I hope that this unit inspires some students to pursue a career as a police officer or crime-scene investigator.

LESSON PLAN 1E

"Evaluating the Scale Maps"

Goal 1: To provide students with a real-life situation that involves the use of mathematics.

Objective 1: After instruction, students will be able to construct a scale map of the classroom, as evidenced by the their ability to create a detailed, accurate map of the classroom (complete with clues) to scale.

Introduction (five minutes):

1. The students will be debriefed that the police captain (who is a real stickler for accurate details) will be evaluating their maps later that day. As a precaution, we will assess each other's maps to make sure they will pass the police captain's inspection.

2. The class will view the criteria in the rubric and discuss ways that we can evaluate each criterion for the map.

3. The teacher will point out that each student will evaluate a different map, using the rubric. Students will also be expected to provide

written responses supporting their evaluation (improvements that can be made, positive comments, etc.).

Activity/Assessment (thirty-five minutes):
1. Students will be grouped so that collaboration can occur. Each group will be provided copies of the maps drawn by the other groups.
2. Students will gather supplies needed to evaluate the maps.
3. Individuals will assess the accuracy of the maps.

Wrap-up Discussion (five minutes):
1. The maps and rubrics will be collected.
2. The groups can discuss if more time is needed to complete the evaluation and when time should be provided.

Materials:
1. Measuring tapes and/or meter sticks
2. Other supplies deemed necessary by the students (graph paper, computer paper, compass, protractor, etc.)
3. Rubrics
4. Copies of group maps

Standards Assessment: M = math, A = algebra I, SC = science
   M8.5.3 Solve problems involving scale factors, area, and volume using ratio and proportion. *This standard will be evidenced by the students using ratio and proportion to validate other groups' maps.*
   M8.7.1 Analyze problems by identifying relationships, telling relevant from irrelevant information, identifying missing information, sequencing and prioritizing information, and observing patterns. *This standard will be evidenced as students analyze the "musts" for scale maps.*
   M8.7.6 Express solutions clearly and logically by using the appropriate mathematical terms and notation. Support solutions with evidence in both verbal and symbolic work. *This standard will be evidenced as students assess the accuracy of each other's scale maps and write critiques.*
   M8.7.11 Decide whether a solution is reasonable in the context of the original situation. *This standard will be evidenced as students assess the accuracy of each other's scale maps and write critiques.*

A1.9.1 Use a variety of problem-solving strategies, such as drawing a diagram, making a chart, doing guess-and-check, solving a simpler problem, writing an equation, and working backwards. *This standard will be evidenced as students decide how to critique the scale map.*

A1.9.2 Decide whether a solution is reasonable in the context of the original situation. *This standard will be evidenced as students assess the accuracy of each other's scale maps and write critiques.*

SC8.2.1 Estimate distances and travel times from maps and the actual size of objects from scale drawings. *This standard will be evidenced as students assess the distances between objects on each other's maps.*

SC 8.2.2 Determine in what unit, such as seconds, meters, grams, and the like, an answer should be expressed based on the units of the inputs to the calculation. *This standard will be evidenced as students assess the units of measurement used in the scale maps.*

SC8.2.7 Participate in group discussions on scientific topics by restating or summarizing accurately what others have said, asking for clarification or elaboration and expressing alternative positions.

SC8.2.8 Use tables, charts, and graphs in making arguments and claims in, for example, oral and written presentations about lab or fieldwork. *This standard will be evidenced in the critiques written about other students' scale maps, validating or disproving the students' work.*

SC8.5.5 Illustrate that it takes two numbers to locate a point on a map or any other two-dimensional surface. *This standard will be evidenced by the students checking for two points of measurement for each object in the scale map.*

Schlechty's WOW

(1) *Content and substance*—The unit aligns with thirty-eight eighth-grade standards (math—15, language arts—10, science—13) and eight algebra I standards.

(2) *Organization of knowledge*—The information and knowledge are arranged in a logical order, increasing in difficulty as the unit progresses.

(3) *Product focus*—The work is designed to engage the students.

(4) *Clear and compelling product standards*—The students will be given rubrics in advance, so that they will know what is expected and what will be graded.

(5) *Protection from adverse consequences for initial failures*—The unit is designed for students to make guesses and change their opinions based on new evidence. Participation grades will accrue throughout the project, but the final grade will not be assessed until the very end.

(7) *Affiliation*—The unit is designed for students to work in cooperative groups.

(8) *Novelty and variety*—The lessons incorporate new activities in which the students will most likely never have had experience. Also, this will be the first time the entire eighth-grade class has worked together on a project in which each individual groups' results are important to the entire group.

(9) *Choice*—Students will have the choice of with whom they will work in their small groups. Student groups will have a choice as to the teachers with whom they would like to focus. Students may also draw upon their experiences to complete the tasks in a variety of ways, so long as they are mathematically sound.

(10) *Authenticity*—Kidnapping, crime scenes, and the skills involved are definitely related to the real world. I hope that this unit inspires some students to pursue a career as a police officer or crime-scene investigator.

LESSON PLAN 1F

"Reflection of Evaluation"

Goal 1: To provide students with a real-life situation that involves the use of mathematics.

Objective 1: After instruction, students will be able to construct a scale map of the classroom, as evidenced by the their ability to create a detailed, accurate map of the classroom (complete with clues) to scale.

Introduction (five minutes):

1. The students will be reminded that the police captain (who is a real stickler for accurate details) will be evaluating their maps later that day.

2. The class will view the criteria in the rubric and clarify ways to evaluate each criterion for the map.

Activity/Assessment (twenty-five minutes):
1. The groups will receive their map peer evaluations.
2. Students will discuss the comments make by the evaluator.
3. Students will write an acceptance (including revisions of map as needed) or a rebuttal (providing evidence that their map is correct and the evaluator is mistaken).

Wrap-up Discussion (fifteen minutes):
1. The maps and rubrics will be collected for final documentation.
2. The groups will be given instructions to create a poster to be displayed in the hallway.
3. Students will hang their posters and mark its location on a copy of the school map.

Materials:
1. Measuring tapes and/or meter sticks
2. Other supplies deemed necessary by the students (graph paper, computer paper, compass, protractor, etc.)
3. Rubrics
4. Clean copies of group maps
5. Construction paper
6. Tape, glue, stapler
7. Photos from the crime scene

Standards Assessment: M = math, A = algebra I, SC = science
M8.5.3 Solve problems involving scale factors, area, and volume using ratio and proportion. *This standard will be evidenced by the students' reflections (approvals or rebuttals) of the critics' evaluations of the math work they showed.*
M8.7.1 Analyze problems by identifying relationships, telling relevant from irrelevant information, identifying missing information, sequencing and prioritizing information, and observing patterns. *This standard will be evidenced by the students' reflections (approvals or rebuttals) of the critics' evaluations of the math work they showed.*

M8.7.6 Express solutions clearly and logically by using the appropriate mathematical terms and notation. Support solutions with evidence in both verbal and symbolic work. *This standard will be evidenced by the students' reflections (approvals or rebuttals) of the critics' evaluations of the math work they showed.*

M8.7.11 Decide whether a solution is reasonable in the context of the original situation. *This standard will be evidenced by the students' reflections (approvals or rebuttals) of the critics' evaluations of the math work they showed.*

A1.9.1 Use a variety of problem-solving strategies, such as drawing a diagram, making a chart, doing guess-and-check, solving a simpler problem, writing an equation, and working backwards. *This standard will be evidenced by the students' reflections (approvals or rebuttals) of the critics' evaluations of the diagram they created.*

A1.9.2 Decide whether a solution is reasonable in the context of the original situation. *This standard will be evidenced by the students' reflections (approvals or rebuttals) of the critics' evaluations of the math work they showed.*

SC8.2.1 Estimate distances and travel times from maps and the actual size of objects from scale drawings. *This standard will be evidenced by the students' reflections (approvals or rebuttals) of the critics' evaluations of the distances in the scale maps.*

SC 8.2.2 Determine in what unit, such as seconds, meters, grams, and the like, an answer should be expressed based on the units of the inputs to the calculation. *This standard will be evidenced by the students' reflections (approvals or rebuttals) of the critics' evaluations of the measurements in the scale maps.*

SC8.2.7 Participate in group discussions on scientific topics by restating or summarizing accurately what others have said, asking for clarification or elaboration and expressing alternative positions. *This standard will be evidenced by the groups' reflections of the critics' evaluations of the math work they showed.*

SC8.2.8 Use tables, charts, and graphs in making arguments and claims in, for example, oral and written presentations about lab or fieldwork. *This standard will be evidenced in the students' use of rubrics to evaluate the scale maps and the arguments used to accept or disprove the critics' results.*

SC8.5.5 Illustrate that it takes two numbers to locate a point on a map or any other two-dimensional surface. *This standard will be evidenced by the students' reflections (approvals or rebuttals) of the critics' evaluations of the measurements in the scale maps.*

Schlechty's WOW

(1) *Content and substance*—The unit aligns with thirty-eight eighth-grade standards (math—15, language arts—10, science—13) and eight algebra I standards.

(2) *Organization of knowledge*—The information and knowledge are arranged in a logical order, increasing in difficulty as the unit progresses.

(3) *Product focus*—The work is designed to engage the students.

(4) *Clear and compelling product standards*—The students will be given rubrics in advance, so that they will know what is expected and what will be graded.

(5) *Protection from adverse consequences for initial failures*—The unit is designed for students to make guesses and change their opinions based on new evidence. Participation grades will accrue throughout the project, but the final grade will not be assessed until the very end.

(6) *Affirmation of performance*—A bulletin board will be set up outside the classroom, displaying student work and hypotheses throughout the project. The entire school will have access to the bulletin board to view the students' progress.

(7) *Affiliation*—The unit is designed for students to work in cooperative groups.

(8) *Novelty and variety*—The lessons incorporate new activities in which the students will most likely never have had experience. Also, this will be the first time the entire eighth-grade class has worked together on a project in which each individual groups' results are important to the entire group.

(9) *Choice*—Students will have the choice of with whom they will work in their small groups. Student groups will have a choice as to the teachers with whom they would like to focus. Students may also draw upon their experiences to complete the tasks in a variety of ways, so long as they are mathematically sound.

(10) *Authenticity*—Kidnapping, crime scenes, and the skills involved are definitely related to the real world. I hope that this unit inspires some students to pursue a career as a police officer or crime-scene investigator.

LESSON PLAN 2A

"Analyzing the Fingerprint"

Goal 1: To provide students with a real-life situation that involves the use of mathematics.

Objective 2: After instruction, students will be able to organize data, as evidenced by their ability to sort and classify fingerprints by common characteristics.

Introduction (five minutes):
1. Look at small version of the kidnapper's fingerprint.
2. Have students describe the print.
3. Take the students to the computer lab.

Activity (twenty-five minutes):
1. The students will go to the Web page at www.thdesigns.biz/WebDesign/Fingerprints/frames_main.html#TypesofRidges.
2. Students will look at the most common characteristics of fingerprints.
3. Students will take notes on the various kinds of characteristics, marking which ones they find in the kidnapper's print. (Students may choose to work with a partner or with their group.)
4. Students will brainstorm a list of possible suspects (faculty and staff at school).

Wrap-up Discussion (fifteen minutes):
1. Student groups will share the characteristics they feel are evident in the kidnapper's fingerprint.
2. The class will compile a list of suspects.
3. The groups will write their reports for the day, which should include the characteristics of the kidnapper's fingerprint, their top five sus-

pects, and a set of rules or procedures for how to collect someone's fingerprint properly.

Materials:
1. Computer lab
2. Multiple (life-size) copies of the kidnapper's fingerprint

Standards Assessment: M = math, A = algebra I, SC = science

M8.6.1 Identify claims based on statistical data and, in simple cases, evaluate the reasonableness of the claims. Design a study to investigate the claim. *This standard will be evidenced by the student plans for collecting fingerprints properly.*

M8.6.2 Identify different methods of selecting samples, analyzing the strengths and weaknesses of each method and the possible bias in a sample or display. *This standard will be evidenced by the various student plans for collecting fingerprints properly.*

M8.7.1 Analyze problems by identifying relationships, telling relevant from irrelevant information, identifying missing information, sequencing and prioritizing information, and observing patterns. *This standard will be evidenced by the students' sharing of important fingerprint characteristics.*

M8.7.3 Decide when and how to divide a problem into simpler parts. *This standard will be evidenced by the various student plans for collecting fingerprints properly.*

A1.9.1 Use a variety of problem-solving strategies, such as drawing a diagram, making a chart, doing guess-and-check, solving a simpler problem, writing an equation, and working backwards. *This standard will be evidenced by the various student plans for collecting fingerprints properly.*

SC8.2.7 Participate in group discussions on scientific topics by restating or summarizing accurately what others have said, asking for clarification or elaboration, and expressing alternative positions. *This standard will be evidenced by the students' sharing of important fingerprint characteristics, prior to the groups writing up their reflections for the day.*

SC8.2.8 Use tables, charts, and graphs in making arguments and claims in, for example, oral and written presentations about lab or field-work. *This standard will be evidenced by the students' sharing of important fingerprint characteristics, prior to the groups writing up their reflections for the day.*

Schlechty's WOW

(1) *Content and substance*—The unit aligns with thirty-eight eighth-grade standards (math—15, language arts—10, science—13) and eight algebra I standards.

(2) *Organization of knowledge*—The information and knowledge are arranged in a logical order, increasing in difficulty as the unit progresses.

(3) *Product focus*—The work is designed to engage the students.

(5) *Protection from adverse consequences for initial failures*—The unit is designed for students to make guesses and change their opinions based on new evidence. Participation grades will accrue throughout the project, but the final grade will not be assessed until the very end.

(6) *Affirmation of performance*—A bulletin board will be set up outside the classroom, displaying student work and hypotheses throughout the project. The entire school will have access to the bulletin board to view the students' progress.

(7) *Affiliation*—The unit is designed for students to work in cooperative groups.

(8) *Novelty and variety*—The lessons incorporate new activities in which the students will most likely never have had experience. Also, this will be the first time the entire eighth-grade class has worked together on a project in which each individual groups' results are important to the entire group.

(9) *Choice*—Students will have the choice of with whom they will work in their small groups. Student groups will have a choice as to the teachers with whom they would like to focus. Students may also draw upon their experiences to complete the tasks in a variety of ways, so long as they are mathematically sound.

(10) *Authenticity*—Kidnapping, crime scenes, and the skills involved are definitely related to the real world. I hope that this unit inspires

some students to pursue a career as a police officer or crime-scene investigator.

LESSON PLAN 2B

"Collecting Fingerprints"

Goal 1: To provide students with a real-life situation that involves the use of mathematics.

Objective 2: After instruction, students will be able to organize data, as evidenced by their ability to sort and classify fingerprints by common characteristics.

Introduction (five minutes):

1. The students will debrief by reading or summarizing their reports from the previous day. This will help anyone who may have been absent as well as to refresh the students' memories regarding the previous day's class.
2. The class will discuss the best ways to collect fingerprints. (Teacher, make sure they decide to print the same finger or thumb, because all digits have similar, but not identical prints.)

Activity (twenty-five minutes):

1. Each group is given a warrant to collect the fingerprint, an index card, and an ink pad.
2. Each person is given a job: (1) read the warrant to the suspect, (2) ink the suspect's finger, (3) carefully place the print on the index card and label it (right or left hand), (4) inform suspect that should his fingerprint eliminate him from the list of suspects, we apologize for any inconvenience; however, if his print does not eliminate him, someone will be back to collect a full set of prints (write down when will be the best time of day to collect the evidence, should the suspect not be eliminated).
3. The group will bring the fingerprint back to the classroom.
4. The group will look at the print for clues, characteristics that may be similar to the kidnapper's print.

Wrap-up Discussion (fifteen minutes):

1. Class will discuss ways to organize the fingerprints (arches, whorls, and loops in a Venn diagram may be one way).
2. Each group will share its suspect and the characteristics of the fingerprint.
3. The groups will write their reports for the day, which should include the characteristics of their suspect's fingerprint, how it compares with the kidnapper's fingerprint, why their suspect could or could not be the kidnapper, and what they think will be the best way to organize the fingerprints.

Materials:

1. Blank index cards with suspects' names written on them
2. Extra blank index cards
3. Six inkpads
4. Warrants

Standards Assessment: M = math, A = algebra I, SC = science

M8.6.1 Identify claims based on statistical data and, in simple cases, evaluate the reasonableness of the claims. Design a study to investigate the claim. *This standard will be evidenced by the students sharing their plans for properly collecting the fingerprints.*

M8.6.2 Identify different methods of selecting samples, analyzing the strengths and weaknesses of each method and the possible bias in a sample or display. *This standard will be evidenced by the class discussions evaluating the various fingerprint collection methods.*

M8.7.1 Analyze problems by identifying relationships, telling relevant from irrelevant information, identifying missing information, sequencing and prioritizing information, and observing patterns. *This standard will be evidenced by the written comparison of their collected fingerprint to the kidnapper's print.*

M8.7.3 Decide when and how to divide a problem into simpler parts. *This standard will be evidenced by the groups' discussions regarding any changes in their fingerprint-collection plan and reviewing all the steps necessary for their plan's completion.*

M8.7.6 Express solutions clearly and logically by using the appropriate mathematical terms and notation. Support solutions with evidence in both verbal and symbolic work. *This standard will be evidenced as students write their reflections for the day.*

A1.9.1 Use a variety of problem-solving strategies, such as drawing a diagram, making a chart, doing guess-and-check, solving a simpler problem, writing an equation, and working backwards. *This standard will be evidenced as students gather fingerprints and discuss the ways to organize the fingerprints.*

SC8.2.7 Participate in group discussions on scientific topics by restating or summarizing accurately what others have said, asking for clarification or elaboration, and expressing alternative positions. *This standard will be evidenced by the groups' discussions regarding the comparisons between their fingerprint and the kidnapper's fingerprint, prior to the groups writing up their reflections for the day.*

SC8.2.8 Use tables, charts, and graphs in making arguments and claims in, for example, oral and written presentations about lab or fieldwork. *This standard will be evidenced by the written reflections from each group regarding their work in class for the day.*

SC8.2.10 Identify and criticize the reasoning in arguments in which fact and opinion are intermingled or the conclusions do not follow logically from the evidence given, an analogy is not apt, no mention is made of whether the control group is very much like the experimental group, or all members of a group are implied to have nearly identical characteristics that differ from those of other groups. *This standard will be evidenced by the elimination of their suspect's fingerprint based on differences between their fingerprint and the kidnapper's print and how their class only collected a few of the fingerprints necessary for comparison.*

Schlechty's WOW

(1) *Content and substance*—The unit aligns with thirty-eight eighth-grade standards (math—15, language arts—10, science—13) and eight algebra I standards.

(2) *Organization of knowledge*—The information and knowledge are arranged in a logical order, increasing in difficulty as the unit progresses.

(3) *Product focus*—The work is designed to engage the students.

(5) *Protection from adverse consequences for initial failures*—The unit is designed for students to make guesses and change their opinions

based on new evidence. Participation grades will accrue throughout the project, but the final grade will not be assessed until the very end.

(6) *Affirmation of performance*—A bulletin board will be set up outside the classroom, displaying student work and hypotheses throughout the project. The entire school will have access to the bulletin board to view the students' progress.

(7) *Affiliation*—The unit is designed for students to work in cooperative groups.

(8) *Novelty and variety*—The lessons incorporate new activities in which the students will most likely never have had experience. Also, this will be the first time the entire eighth-grade class has worked together on a project in which each individual groups' results are important to the entire group.

(9) *Choice*—Students will have the choice of with whom they will work in their small groups. Student groups will have a choice as to the teachers with whom they would like to focus. Students may also draw upon their experiences to complete the tasks in a variety of ways, so long as they are mathematically sound.

(10) *Authenticity*—Kidnapping, crime scenes, and the skills involved are definitely related to the real world. I hope that this unit inspires some students to pursue a career as a police officer or crime-scene investigator.

LESSON PLAN 2C

"Classifying Fingerprints"

Goal 1: To provide students with a real-life situation that involves the use of mathematics.

Objective 2: After instruction, students will be able to organize data, as evidenced by their ability to sort and classify fingerprints by common characteristics.

Introduction (five minutes):

1. The students will debrief by reading or summarizing their reports from the previous day. (This will help anyone who may have been absent as well as refresh the students' memories regarding the previous day's class.)

2. The class will discuss their ideas for ways to organize the finger-prints.
3. The class will discuss the various components needed to create a complete picture of the fingerprint data (i.e., title for organizational tool, clear labels, key or legend, neat writing, use of color, etc.).

Activity (twenty-five minutes):
1. Each group is given a set of fingerprints that were collected the previous day.
2. The groups will decide how to organize the set of fingerprints.
3. Group members will cut apart the fingerprints and use them in an organizational tool of their choice.
4. The teacher will inform the class that anyone within each group may be called upon to describe that group's organizational tool, why the group chose it, and which prints indicate possible suspects.

Wrap-up Discussion (fifteen minutes):
1. Organizational tools are placed on the chalkboard.
2. The teacher will choose a group member to explain his or her group's organizational tool, why the group chose that tool, and which prints in the group's tool represent the possible suspects.
3. The teacher may ask questions pertaining to how students knew that so-and-so was not a suspect. Other questions may include comparisons between the different tools' strengths and weaknesses.
4. A hand count will be taken to establish the class's vote for the "best" type of tool.
5. The groups will write their reports for the day, which should include a sketch of their tools and descriptions of why certain suspects were eliminated based upon their fingerprints' characteristics.

Materials:
1. Set of fingerprints for each group
2. Markers, colored pencils, crayons
3. Colored construction paper
4. Rulers, compasses, protractors
5. White construction paper

Standards Assessment: M = math, A = algebra I, SC = science

M8.6.1 Identify claims based on statistical data and, in simple cases, evaluate the reasonableness of the claims. Design a study to investigate the claim. *This standard will be evidenced by the students sharing their plans for properly collecting the fingerprints.*

M8.6.2 Identify different methods of selecting samples, analyzing the strengths and weaknesses of each method and the possible bias in a sample or display. *This standard will be evidenced by the class discussions evaluating the various fingerprint collection methods.*

M8.7.1 Analyze problems by identifying relationships, telling relevant from irrelevant information, identifying missing information, sequencing and prioritizing information, and observing patterns. *This standard will be evidenced by the written comparison of their collected fingerprint to the kidnapper's print.*

M8.7.3 Decide when and how to divide a problem into simpler parts. *This standard will be evidenced by the groups' discussions regarding any changes in their fingerprint-collection plan and reviewing all the steps necessary for their plan's completion.*

M8.7.6 Express solutions clearly and logically by using the appropriate mathematical terms and notation. Support solutions with evidence in both verbal and symbolic work. *This standard will be evidenced as students write their reflections for the day.*

M8.7.11 Decide whether a solution is reasonable in the context of the original situation. *This standard will be evidenced in the written reflections regarding the possibility that a suspect is the kidnapper based on the characteristics that are common or different between their suspect's print and the kidnapper's.*

A1.9.1 Use a variety of problem-solving strategies, such as drawing a diagram, making a chart, doing guess-and-check, solving a simpler problem, writing an equation, and working backwards. *This standard will be evidenced as students gather fingerprints and discuss the ways to organize the fingerprints.*

SC8.2.7 Participate in group discussions on scientific topics by restating or summarizing accurately what others have said, asking for clarification or elaboration, and expressing alternative positions. *This standard will be evidenced by the groups' discussions regarding the comparisons between their fingerprint and the kidnapper's finger-print, prior to the groups writing up their reflections for the day.*

SC8.2.8 Use tables, charts, and graphs in making arguments and claims in, for example, oral and written presentations about lab or field-work. *This standard will be evidenced by the written reflections from each group regarding their work in class for the day.*

SC8.2.10 Identify and criticize the reasoning in arguments in which fact and opinion are intermingled or the conclusions do not follow logi-cally from the evidence given, an analogy is not apt, no mention is made of whether the control group is very much like the experimen-tal group, or all members of a group are implied to have nearly iden-tical characteristics that differ from those of other groups. *This stan-dard will be evidenced by the elimination of a suspect based on differences between the suspect's fingerprint and the kidnapper's print and how the class only collected a few of the fingerprints nec-essary for comparison.*

A1.9.2 Decide whether a solution is reasonable in the context of the original situation. *This standard will be evidenced in the written re-flections regarding the possibility that the group's suspect is the kid-napper based on the characteristics that are common or different be-tween the suspect's print and the kidnapper's.*

Schlechty's WOW

(1) *Content and substance*—The unit aligns with thirty-eight eighth-grade standards (math—15, language arts—10, science—13) and eight algebra I standards.

(2) *Organization of knowledge*—The information and knowledge are arranged in a logical order, increasing in difficulty as the unit pro-gresses.

(3) *Product focus*—The work is designed to engage the students.

(4) *Clear and compelling product standards*—The students will be given rubrics in advance, so that they will know what is expected and what will be graded.

(5) *Protection from adverse consequences for initial failures*—The unit is designed for students to make guesses and change their opinions based on new evidence. Participation grades will accrue throughout the project, but the final grade will not be assessed until the very end.

(6) *Affirmation of performance*—A bulletin board will be set up outside the classroom, displaying student work and hypotheses throughout the project. The entire school will have access to the bulletin board to view the students' progress.

(7) *Affiliation*—The unit is designed for students to work in cooperative groups.

(8) *Novelty and variety*—The lessons incorporate new activities in which the students will most likely never have had experience. Also, this will be the first time the entire eighth-grade class has worked together on a project in which each individual groups' results are important to the entire group.

(9) *Choice*—Students will have the choice of with whom they will work in their small groups. Student groups will have a choice as to the teachers with whom they would like to focus. Students may also draw upon their experiences to complete the tasks in a variety of ways, so long as they are mathematically sound.

(10) *Authenticity*—Kidnapping, crime scenes, and the skills involved are definitely related to the real world. I hope that this unit inspires some students to pursue a career as a police officer or crime-scene investigator.

LESSON PLAN 2D

"Releasing Findings"

Goal 1: To provide students with a real-life situation that involves the use of mathematics.

Objective 2: After instruction, students will be able to organize data, as evidenced by their ability to sort and classify fingerprints by common characteristics.

Introduction (five minutes):

1. The students will debrief by reading or summarizing their reports from the previous day. This will help anyone who may have been absent as well as refresh the students' memories regarding the previous day's class.

2. The class will view the previous day's vote results regarding the best type of organizational tool.

Activity (twenty-five minutes):
1. Students will be drawn at random to complete various tasks for this class period.
2. Some students will collect full sets of fingerprints. Others will construct a bulletin board representation of the fingerprint results. The rest of the students will hang the organizational tools in the hallway near the previous posters (to keep the school informed of our investigation).

Wrap-up Discussion (fifteen minutes):
1. Individuals will write their reports for the day, which should include a description of each member's contributions to the class for that day. Also, the group will write a press release statement that will be aired on WCAT the next day.

Materials:
1. Tape
2. Stapler
3. The groups' organizational tools
4. Ink pads
5. Fingerprint sheets (full set)
6. Construction paper
7. Markers, colored pencils, crayons

Standards Assessment: M = math, A = algebra I, SC = science
M8.6.1 Identify claims based on statistical data and, in simple cases, evaluate the reasonableness of the claims. Design a study to investigate the claim. *This standard will be evidenced by students participating in the class discussion regarding organizing fingerprints.*
M8.6.2 Identify different methods of selecting samples, analyzing the strengths and weaknesses of each method and the possible bias in a sample or display. *This standard will be evidenced by students participating in the class discussion regarding organizing fingerprints.*
M8.7.1 Analyze problems by identifying relationships, telling relevant from irrelevant information, identifying missing information, sequencing and prioritizing information, and observing patterns. *This*

standard will be evidenced by students discussing their ideas for organizing the fingerprints.

M8.7.3 Decide when and how to divide a problem into simpler parts. *This standard will be evidenced by the discussion at the beginning of class regarding students' duties (i.e., collecting fingerprints, hanging informational posters, updating the mystery bulletin board, and so forth).*

M8.7.6 Express solutions clearly and logically by using the appropriate mathematical terms and notation. Support solutions with evidence in both verbal and symbolic work. *This standard will be evidenced in the written press release reports regarding the processes used to narrow down the list of suspects.*

SC8.2.7 Participate in group discussions on scientific topics by restating or summarizing accurately what others have said, asking for clarification or elaboration, and expressing alternative positions. *This standard will be evidenced by students participating in the class discussion regarding organizing fingerprints.*

SC8.2.8 Use tables, charts, and graphs in making arguments and claims in, for example, oral and written presentations about lab or fieldwork. *This standard will be evidenced in the written press release reports regarding the processes used to narrow down the list of suspects.*

Schlechty's WOW

(1) *Content and substance*—The unit aligns with thirty-eight eighth-grade standards (math—15, language arts—10, science—13) and eight algebra I standards.

(2) *Organization of knowledge*—The information and knowledge are arranged in a logical order, increasing in difficulty as the unit progresses.

(3) *Product focus*—The work is designed to engage the students.

(4) *Clear and compelling product standards*—The students will be given rubrics in advance, so that they will know what is expected and what will be graded.

(5) *Protection from adverse consequences for initial failures*—The unit is designed for students to make guesses and change their opinions based on new evidence. Participation grades will accrue throughout the project, but the final grade will not be assessed until the very end.

(6) *Affirmation of performance*—A bulletin board will be set up outside the classroom, displaying student work and hypotheses throughout the project. The entire school will have access to the bulletin board to view the students' progress.

(7) *Affiliation*—The unit is designed for students to work in cooperative groups.

(8) *Novelty and variety*—The lessons incorporate new activities in which the students will most likely never have had experience. Also, this will be the first time the entire eighth-grade class has worked together on a project in which each individual groups' results are important to the entire group.

(9) *Choice*—Students will have the choice of with whom they will work in their small groups. Student groups will have a choice as to the teachers with whom they would like to focus. Students may also draw upon their experiences to complete the tasks in a variety of ways, so long as they are mathematically sound.

(10) *Authenticity*—Kidnapping, crime scenes, and the skills involved are definitely related to the real world. I hope that this unit inspires some students to pursue a career as a police officer or crime-scene investigator.

LESSON PLAN 3A

"Analyzing the Shoe Print"

Goal 1: To provide students with a real-life situation that involves the use of mathematics.

Objective 3: After instruction, students will be able to predict an outcome, as evidenced by their ability to graph shoe size and height in a scatter plot and use the trend line to determine the height for a given shoe size.

Introduction (five minutes):

1. The class will discuss the narrowed-down list of suspects and how that group was determined using the fingerprints.

2. The class will look at the shoe print left behind at the scene and discuss the information we can gather from looking at the shoe print. What do we not know, but want to find out?

3. The class will discuss some ways that we may be able to use the shoe print to figure out who is the kidnapper. (If we can figure out the shoe size, then we might be able to determine the kidnapper's height.) Can we use the same plot for males and females? Are shoe sizes consistent between the sexes? (No—make two scatter plots, or use two different colored marks on one scatter plot.)

Activity (twenty-five minutes):
1. The pieces of paper for the scatter plots will be on the chalkboard.
2. The class will decide which things are necessary for a scatter plot. (What is the smallest size shoe in the school? The largest? What should the scale be on the scatter plot? What interval should be used? What should the title be? How should the axes be labeled? What unit of measurement should be used to measure the length of the shoe?)
3. The scatter plots will compare shoe size to length of shoe. Have individual volunteers create different parts of the scatter plot.
4. Assign each group to measure their members' shoe lengths. Record data in a chart along with shoe size.
5. Students place a footprint sticker on the appropriate scatter plot to indicate their shoe size versus their shoe length.
6. Students copy the scatter plot data into a smaller group-sized version of the scatter plot (for their records).

Wrap-up Discussion (fifteen minutes):
1. Once all of the stickers are in place, discuss the information you have from this sample size. Discuss the shoe-size ranges. Is our sample size large enough to determine an accurate range? What can we do to get a more accurate range?
2. The groups will write their reports for the day, which should include a chart (name, shoe size, shoe length), the ranges of shoe sizes from the scatter plots, and a plan for what we should do with the information we have learned from the scatter plots.

Materials:
1. Two large white papers
2. Footprint stickers

3. Rulers, meter sticks
4. Group-sized scatter plot outline

Standards Assessment: M = math, A = algebra I, SC = science

M8.3.7 Demonstrate an understanding of rate as a measure of one quantity with respect to another quantity. *This standard will be evidenced as students compare shoe print length to shoe size.*

M8.3.8 Demonstrate an understanding of the relationships among tables, equations, verbal expressions, and graphs of linear functions. *This standard will be evidenced as students create tables of the relations between shoe print length and shoe size and determine a trend line from a scatter plot of the data.*

M8.6.1 Identify claims based on statistical data and, in simple cases, evaluate the reasonableness of the claims. Design a study to investigate the claim. *This standard will be evidenced as students analyze the results of the scatter plot, look for a range of possible shoe sizes, and determine a plan for using the range of data to narrow down the list of suspects.*

M8.6.2 Identify different methods of selecting samples, analyzing the strengths and weaknesses of each method and the possible bias in a sample or display. *This standard will be evidenced in the class discussion regarding our class data as a small sample and the weaknesses of such a small sample.*

M8.6.5 Represent two-variable data with a scatter plot on the coordinate plane and describe how the data points are distributed. If the pattern appears to be linear, draw a line that appears to fit the data best and write the equation of that line. *This standard will be evidenced by the scatter plot that is created from the relationships between one's shoe size and the length of the shoe print and the possible trend line that could represent the data.*

M8.7.1 Analyze problems by identifying relationships, telling relevant from irrelevant information, identifying missing information, sequencing and prioritizing information, and observing patterns. *This standard will be evidenced as the students analyze the results of the scatter plot and determine if there is a pattern or trend in the data.*

M8.7.5 Make and test conjectures using inductive reasoning. *This standard will be evidenced as the students make a guess as to the range of possible shoe sizes of the kidnapper and how they will use this range to narrow down the list of suspects.*

M8.7.6 Express solutions clearly and logically by using the appropriate mathematical terms and notation. Support solutions with evidence in both verbal and symbolic work. *This standard will be evidenced within the written reflections of the students regarding their activities that day.*

M8.7.11 Decide whether a solution is reasonable in the context of the original situation. *This standard will be evidenced in the class discussion regarding the reasonableness of the scatter plot based on the small sample.*

A1.3.1 Sketch a reasonable graph for a given relationship. *This standard will be evidenced as the students graph the relationship between shoe size and shoe length in a scatter plot.*

A1.3.2 Interpret a graph representing a given situation. *This standard will be evidenced in the discussion about the scatter plot and the range of shoe sizes possible for the kidnapper.*

A1.3.4 Find the domain and range of a relation. *This standard will be evidenced in the discussion about the scatter plot and the range of shoe sizes possible for the kidnapper.*

A1.9.1 Use a variety of problem-solving strategies, such as drawing a diagram, making a chart, doing guess-and-check, solving a simpler problem, writing an equation, and working backwards. *This standard will be evidenced by the scatter plot that is created from the relationships between one's shoe size and the length of the shoe print and the possible trend line that could represent the data.*

A1.9.7 Identify the hypothesis and conclusion in a logical deduction. *This standard will be evidenced in the written reflections that the students will write at the end of the period regarding their thoughts about the range of shoe sizes determined by our graph is sufficient or too small.*

SC8.2.7 Participate in group discussions on scientific topics by restating or summarizing accurately what others have said, asking for clarification or elaboration, and expressing alternative positions. *This standard will be evidenced by the class discussion regarding the information that can be gathered from the scatter plots.*

SC8.2.8 Use tables, charts, and graphs in making arguments and claims in, for example, oral and written presentations about lab or fieldwork. *This standard will be evidenced by the graphs and the written comments in the students' reflections.*

SC8.2.10 Identify and criticize the reasoning in arguments in which fact and opinion are intermingled or the conclusions do not follow logically from the evidence given, an analogy is not apt, no mention is made of whether the control group is very much like the experimental group, or all members of a group are implied to have nearly identical characteristics that differ from those of other groups. *This standard will be evidenced by the class discussions and in the written reflections.*

SC8.5.3 Demonstrate that mathematical statements can be used to describe how one quantity changes when another changes. *This standard will be evidenced in the class discussion about how as the shoe size increases, so does the shoe length.*

SC8.5.4 Illustrate how graphs can show a variety of possible relationships between two variables. *This standard will be evidenced by the class discussion and written reflections regarding the information that can be deduced from the scatter plot.*

SC8.5.5 Illustrate that it takes two numbers to locate a point on a map or any other two-dimensional surface. *This standard will be evidenced by the plotting of points on a scatter plot using two numbers (shoe size and shoe length).*

Schlechty's WOW

(1) *Content and substance*—The unit aligns with thirty-eight eighth-grade standards (math—15, language arts—10, science—13) and eight algebra I standards.

(2) *Organization of knowledge*—The information and knowledge are arranged in a logical order, increasing in difficulty as the unit progresses.

(3) *Product focus*—The work is designed to engage the students.

(4) *Clear and compelling product standards*—The students will be given rubrics in advance, so that they will know what is expected and what will be graded.

(5) *Protection from adverse consequences for initial failures*—The unit is designed for students to make guesses and change their opinions based on new evidence. Participation grades will accrue throughout the project, but the final grade will not be assessed until the very end.

(7) *Affiliation*—The unit is designed for students to work in cooperative groups.

(8) *Novelty and variety*—The lessons incorporate new activities in which the students will most likely never have had experience. Also, this will be the first time the entire eighth-grade class has worked together on a project in which each individual groups' results are important to the entire group.

(9) *Choice*—Students will have the choice of with whom they will work in their small groups. Student groups will have a choice as to the teachers with whom they would like to focus. Students may also draw upon their experiences to complete the tasks in a variety of ways, so long as they are mathematically sound.

(10) *Authenticity*—Kidnapping, crime scenes, and the skills involved are definitely related to the real world. I hope that this unit inspires some students to pursue a career as a police officer or crime-scene investigator.

LESSON PLAN 3B

"Shoe Size vs. Height"

Goal 1: To provide students with a real-life situation that involves the use of mathematics.

Objective 3: After instruction, students will be able to predict an outcome, as evidenced by their ability to graph shoe size and height in a scatter plot and use the trend line to determine the height for a given shoe size.

Introduction (ten minutes):

1. Students will view the scatter plots from the various classes.
2. Students will discuss the various scatter plots and compare them. Do all show the same range of shoe sizes? Are the results the same?
3. Each group will plot the other four sample sets of data onto their scatter plots (one for males, one for females) and discuss the ranges of shoe sizes that our kidnapper may wear. Discuss the differences between the class-sized sample size versus the eighth-grade sample size.
4. The groups will share how the shoe-size range may help narrow down who the kidnapper might be. How will the range be used? Can

we determine anything else about the kidnapper from the range (compare sizes to heights)?

Activity (twenty minutes):
1. The pieces of paper for the scatter plots will be on the chalkboard.
2. The class will decide what things are necessary for a scatter plot. (How tall is the shortest person in the school? The tallest? What should the scale be on the scatter plot? What interval should be used? What should the title be? How should the axes be labeled? What unit of measurement should be used to measure the heights of people in our class?)
3. The scatter plots will compare shoe size to height. Have individual volunteers create different parts of the scatter plot.
4. Direct each group to measure its members' heights. Record data in a chart along with shoe size.
5. Students place a footprint sticker on the appropriate scatter plot to indicate their shoe size versus their shoe length.
6. Students copy the scatter plot data into a smaller, group-sized version of the scatter plot (for their records).

Wrap-up Discussion (fifteen minutes):
1. Once all the stickers are in place, discuss the information you have from this sample size. Discuss the shoe-size ranges and the height ranges. Are the ranges helpful in narrowing down the list of suspects?
2. The groups will write their reports for the day, which should include a chart (name, shoe size, height), the ranges of heights from the scatter plots, and a plan for how we should compare the suspects' heights to the data range determined by our scatter plots.

Materials:
1. Two large white papers
2. Footprint stickers
3. Rulers, meter sticks

Standards Assessment: M = math, A = algebra I, SC = science
M8.3.7 Demonstrate an understanding of rate as a measure of one quantity with respect to another quantity. *This standard will be evidenced as students compare height to shoe size.*

M8.3.8 Demonstrate an understanding of the relationships among tables, equations, verbal expressions, and graphs of linear functions. *This standard will be evidenced as students create tables of the relations between height and shoe size and determine a trend line from a scatter plot of the data.*

M8.6.1 Identify claims based on statistical data and, in simple cases, evaluate the reasonableness of the claims. Design a study to investigate the claim. *This standard will be evidenced as students analyze the results of the scatter plot, look for a range of possible shoe sizes, and determine a plan for using the range of data to narrow down the list of suspects.*

M8.6.2 Identify different methods of selecting samples, analyzing the strengths and weaknesses of each method and the possible bias in a sample or display. *This standard will be evidenced in the class discussion regarding our class data as a small sample and the weaknesses of such a small sample.*

M8.6.5 Represent two-variable data with a scatter plot on the coordinate plane and describe how the data points are distributed. If the pattern appears to be linear, draw a line that appears to fit the data best and write the equation of that line. *This standard will be evidenced by the scatter plot that is created from the relationships between one's shoe size and height and the possible trend line that could represent the data.*

M8.7.1 Analyze problems by identifying relationships, telling relevant from irrelevant information, identifying missing information, sequencing and prioritizing information, and observing patterns. *This standard will be evidenced as the students analyze the results of the scatter plot and determine if there is a pattern or trend in the data.*

M8.7.5 Make and test conjectures using inductive reasoning. *This standard will be evidenced as the students make a guess as to the range of possible heights of the kidnapper and use this range to narrow down the list of suspects.*

M8.7.6 Express solutions clearly and logically by using the appropriate mathematical terms and notation. Support solutions with evidence in both verbal and symbolic work. *This standard will be evidenced within the written reflections of the students regarding their activities that day.*

M8.7.11 Decide whether a solution is reasonable in the context of the original situation. *This standard will be evidenced in the class discussion regarding the reasonableness of the scatter plot based on the small sample.*

A1.3.1 Sketch a reasonable graph for a given relationship. *This standard will be evidenced as the students graph the relationship between shoe size and height in a scatter plot.*

A1.3.2 Interpret a graph representing a given situation. *This standard will be evidenced in the discussion about the scatter plot and the range of heights possible for the kidnapper.*

A1.3.4 Find the domain and range of a relation. *This standard will be evidenced in the discussion about the scatter plot and the range of heights possible for the kidnapper.*

A1.9.1 Use a variety of problem-solving strategies, such as drawing a diagram, making a chart, doing guess-and-check, solving a simpler problem, writing an equation, and working backwards. *This standard will be evidenced by the scatter plot that is created from the relationships between one's shoe size and height and the possible trend line that could represent the data.*

A1.9.7 Identify the hypothesis and conclusion in a logical deduction. *This standard will be evidenced in the written reflections that the students will write at the end of the period regarding their thoughts about whether the range of heights determined by our graph is sufficient or too small.*

SC8.2.7 Participate in group discussions on scientific topics by restating or summarizing accurately what others have said, asking for clarification or elaboration, and expressing alternative positions. *This standard will be evidenced by the class discussion regarding the information that can be gathered from the scatter plots.*

SC8.2.8 Use tables, charts, and graphs in making arguments and claims in, for example, oral and written presentations about lab or fieldwork. *This standard will be evidenced by the graphs and the written comments in the students' reflections.*

SC8.2.10 Identify and criticize the reasoning in arguments in which fact and opinion are intermingled or the conclusions do not follow logically from the evidence given, an analogy is not apt, no mention is made of whether the control group is very much like the experimental group, or all members of a group are implied to have nearly identical characteristics that differ from those of other groups. *This standard will be evidenced by the class discussions and the written reflections.*

SC8.5.3 Demonstrate that mathematical statements can be used to describe how one quantity changes when another changes. *This standard will be evidenced in the class discussion regarding how as the shoe size increases, so does the height.*

SC8.5.4 Illustrate how graphs can show a variety of possible relationships between two variables. *This standard will be evidenced by the class discussion and written reflections regarding the information that can be deduced from the scatter plot.*

SC8.5.5 Illustrate that it takes two numbers to locate a point on a map or any other two-dimensional surface. *This standard will be evidenced by the plotting of points on a scatter plot using two numbers (shoe size and height).*

Schlechty's WOW

(1) *Content and substance*—The unit aligns with thirty-eight eighth-grade standards (math—15, language arts—10, science—13) and eight algebra I standards.

(2) *Organization of knowledge*—The information and knowledge are arranged in a logical order, increasing in difficulty as the unit progresses.

(3) *Product focus*—The work is designed to engage the students.

(4) *Clear and compelling product standards*—The students will be given rubrics in advance, so that they will know what is expected and what will be graded.

(5) *Protection from adverse consequences for initial failures*—The unit is designed for students to make guesses and change their opinions based on new evidence. Participation grades will accrue throughout the project, but the final grade will not be assessed until the very end.

(7) *Affiliation*—The unit is designed for students to work in cooperative groups.

(8) *Novelty and variety*—The lessons incorporate new activities in which the students will most likely never have had experience. Also,

this will be the first time the entire eighth-grade class has worked together on a project in which each individual groups' results are important to the entire group.

(9) *Choice*—Students will have the choice of with whom they will work in their small groups. Student groups will have a choice as to the teachers with whom they would like to focus. Students may also draw upon their experiences to complete the tasks in a variety of ways, so long as they are mathematically sound.

(10) *Authenticity*—Kidnapping, crime scenes, and the skills involved are definitely related to the real world. I hope that this unit inspires some students to pursue a career as a police officer or crime-scene investigator.

LESSON PLAN 4A

"Devising a Plan"

Goal 1: To provide students with a real-life situation that involves the use of mathematics.

Objective 4: After instruction, students will be able to measure heights indirectly, as evidenced by their ability to use ratio and proportion to measure heights of objects in photographs.

Introduction (five minutes):
1. The groups will review their reports from the previous day.
2. The groups will discuss their plans for how we should compare the suspects' heights to the data range determined by our scatter plots.

Activity (twenty-five minutes):
1. The groups will brainstorm ideas for collecting data regarding suspects' heights.
2. Group members will number off (1), (2), (3), and (4).
3. All the (1)s will gather and share their ideas for how to determine the suspects heights. Same for the (2)s, (3)s, and (4)s.
4. After about five minutes, groups will reconvene and share any new ideas with their members.
5. Students will be asked to choose one method they think will work the best.

6. The groups will share their methods with the class; the teacher records the methods on the overhead. Students discuss the pros and cons of each method.

Wrap-up Discussion (fifteen minutes):
1. The teacher places some rules on the students: (1) the suspect cannot be asked his or her height, and (2) the suspect's height cannot be measured with his or her knowledge.
2. The groups will determine a method to use to determine the suspects' heights.
3. The groups will write their reports for the day, which should include a plan for how they will go about determining the heights of the suspects.

Materials:
1. Overhead transparencies and marker

Standards Assessment: M = math, A = algebra I, SC = science
M8.6.2 Identify different methods of selecting samples, analyzing the strengths and weaknesses of each method and the possible bias in a sample or display. *This standard will be evidenced in the class and group discussions regarding how to gather suspects' heights indirectly.*
M8.7.1 Analyze problems by identifying relationships, telling relevant from irrelevant information, identifying missing information, sequencing and prioritizing information, and observing patterns. *This standard will be evidenced in the class and group discussions regarding how to gather suspects' heights indirectly.*
M8.7.3 Decide when and how to divide a problem into simpler parts. *This standard will be evidenced in the class and group discussions regarding how to gather suspects' heights indirectly.*
M8.7.5 Make and test conjectures using inductive reasoning. *This standard will be evidenced in the class and group discussions regarding how to gather suspects' heights indirectly.*
M8.7.6 Express solutions clearly and logically by using the appropriate mathematical terms and notation. Support solutions with evidence in both verbal and symbolic work. *This standard will be evidenced in the students' written reflections for the day.*

A1.9.1 Use a variety of problem-solving strategies, such as drawing a diagram, making a chart, doing guess-and-check, solving a simpler problem, writing an equation, and working backwards. *This standard will be evidenced in the class and group discussions regarding how to gather suspects' heights indirectly.*

SC8.2.7 Participate in group discussions on scientific topics by restating or summarizing accurately what others have said, asking for clarification or elaboration, and expressing alternative positions. *This standard will be evidenced in the class and group discussions regarding how to gather suspects' heights indirectly.*

SC8.2.8 Use tables, charts, and graphs in making arguments and claims in, for example, oral and written presentations about lab or fieldwork. *This standard will be evidenced in the class and group discussions regarding how to gather suspects' heights indirectly.*

Schlechty's WOW

(1) *Content and substance*—The unit aligns with thirty-eight eighth-grade standards (math—15, language arts—10, science—13) and eight algebra I standards.

(2) *Organization of knowledge*—The information and knowledge are arranged in a logical order, increasing in difficulty as the unit progresses.

(3) *Product focus*—The work is designed to engage the students.

(4) *Clear and compelling product standards*—The students will be given rubrics in advance, so that they will know what is expected and what will be graded.

(5) *Protection from adverse consequences for initial failures*—The unit is designed for students to make guesses and change their opinions based on new evidence. Participation grades will accrue throughout the project, but the final grade will not be assessed until the very end.

(6) *Affirmation of performance*—A bulletin board will be set up outside the classroom, displaying student work and hypotheses throughout the project. The entire school will have access to the bulletin board to view the students' progress.

(7) *Affiliation*—The unit is designed for students to work in cooperative groups.

(8) *Novelty and variety*—The lessons incorporate new activities in which the students will most likely never have had experience. Also, this will be the first time the entire eighth-grade class has worked together on a project in which each individual groups' results are important to the entire group.

(9) *Choice*—Students will have the choice of with whom they will work in their small groups. Student groups will have a choice as to the teachers with whom they would like to focus. Students may also draw upon their experiences to complete the tasks in a variety of ways, so long as they are mathematically sound.

(10) *Authenticity*—Kidnapping, crime scenes, and the skills involved are definitely related to the real world. I hope that this unit inspires some students to pursue a career as a police officer or crime-scene investigator.

LESSON PLAN 4B

"Carrying Out a Plan"

Goal 1: To provide students with a real-life situation that involves the use of mathematics.

Objective 4: After instruction, students will be able to measure heights indirectly, as evidenced by their ability to use ratio and proportion to measure the heights of objects in photographs.

Introduction (fifteen minutes):

1. The groups will share their methods for determining the suspects' heights.
2. The different methods will be field tested before the students actually go out and gather more evidence.

Activity (fifteen minutes):

1. The groups will decide if their method works or if they would like to try a different method.
2. The groups will present their proofs (or disproofs) of their mathematical work to the class.

3. The groups will be sent out to collect a picture of their suspects (each group will do one) with something measurable, as well as to collect other evidence deemed necessary in their plan.
4. Students will begin analyzing the evidence they have collected.

Wrap-up Discussion (fifteen minutes):
1. The groups will write their reports for the day, which should include a description of their activities (as carried out according to their plans) and the mathematical deductions taken to determine their suspect's height.
2. Students will display their scatter plots next to the posters in the school, indicating the range of possible heights for the kidnapper.

Standards Assessment: M = math, A = algebra I, SC = science
   M8.2.1 Add, subtract, multiply, and divide rational numbers (integers, fractions, and terminating decimals) in multistep problems. *This standard will be evidenced when students prove to the class that their method of indirect measurement will work.*
   M8.5.1 Convert common measurements for length, area, volume, weight, capacity, and time to equivalent measurements within the same system. *This standard will be evidenced when students convert measurements when using their method of indirect measurement.*
   M8.6.2 Identify different methods of selecting samples, analyzing the strengths and weaknesses of each method and the possible bias in a sample or display. *This standard will be evidenced as students critique each other's methods for indirect measurement.*
   M8.7.1 Analyze problems by identifying relationships, telling relevant from irrelevant information, identifying missing information, sequencing and prioritizing information, and observing patterns. *This standard will be evidenced as students critique each other's methods for indirect measurement, as well as when each group presents its own method for indirect measurement.*
   M8.7.3 Decide when and how to divide a problem into simpler parts. *This standard will be evidenced when the groups present their methods for indirect measurement.*

M8.7.5 Make and test conjectures using inductive reasoning. *This standard will be evidenced as students make conjectures as to how they can measure something indirectly and then use mathematics to test their conjectures in class.*

M8.7.6 Express solutions clearly and logically by using the appropriate mathematical terms and notation. Support solutions with evidence in both verbal and symbolic work. *This standard will be evidenced when students prove to the class that their method of indirect measurement will work, as well as in their written reflections for the day.*

M8.7.11 Decide whether a solution is reasonable in the context of the original situation. *This standard will be evidenced as students critique each other's methods for indirect measurement.*

A1.1.5 Use dimensional (unit) analysis to organize conversions and computations. *This standard will be evidenced in students' math computations using rates and ratios to determine heights indirectly.*

A1.9.1 Use a variety of problem-solving strategies, such as drawing a diagram, making a chart, doing guess-and-check, solving a simpler problem, writing an equation, and working backwards. *This standard will be evidenced by the diagrams drawn and other problem-solving techniques used by the groups to determine the height of an object via indirect measurement.*

A1.9.2 Decide whether a solution is reasonable in the context of the original situation. *This standard will be evidenced as students critique each other's methods for indirect measurement.*

SC8.2.3 Use proportional reasoning to solve problems. *This standard will be evidenced in students' math computations using rates and ratios to determine heights indirectly.*

SC8.2.4 Use technological devices, such as calculators and computers, to perform calculations. *This standard will be evidenced as students use calculators (and computers if they are requested to do so) to aid them in performing calculations for determining indirect measurements.*

SC8.2.7 Participate in group discussions on scientific topics by restating or summarizing accurately what others have said, asking for clarification or elaboration, and expressing alternative positions. *This standard will be evidenced as students critique each other's methods for indirect measurement.*

SC8.2.8 Use tables, charts, and graphs in making arguments and claims in, for example, oral and written presentations about lab or field-work. *This standard will be evidenced in the class and group discussions regarding how to gather suspects' heights indirectly, as well as in the written reflections.*

Schlechty's WOW

(1) *Content and substance*—The unit aligns with thirty-eight eighth-grade standards (math—15, language arts—10, science—13) and eight algebra I standards.

(2) *Organization of knowledge*—The information and knowledge are arranged in a logical order, increasing in difficulty as the unit progresses.

(3) *Product focus*—The work is designed to engage the students.

(4) *Clear and compelling product standards*—The students will be given rubrics in advance, so that they will know what is expected and what will be graded.

(5) *Protection from adverse consequences for initial failures*—The unit is designed for students to make guesses and change their opinions based on new evidence. Participation grades will accrue throughout the project, but the final grade will not be assessed until the very end.

(6) *Affirmation of performance*—A bulletin board will be set up outside the classroom, displaying student work and hypotheses throughout the project. The entire school will have access to the bulletin board to view the students' progress.

(7) *Affiliation*—The unit is designed for students to work in cooperative groups.

(8) *Novelty and variety*—The lessons incorporate new activities in which the students will most likely never have had experience. Also, this will be the first time the entire eighth-grade class has worked together on a project in which each individual groups' results are important to the entire group.

(9) *Choice*—Students will have the choice of with whom they will work in their small groups. Student groups will have a choice as to the teachers with whom they would like to focus. Students may also draw upon their experiences to complete the tasks in a variety of ways, so long as they are mathematically sound.

(10) *Authenticity*—Kidnapping, crime scenes, and the skills involved are definitely related to the real world. I hope that this unit inspires some students to pursue a career as a police officer or crime-scene investigator.

LESSON PLAN 4C

"Critiquing the Plans"

Goal 1: To provide students with a real-life situation that involves the use of mathematics.

Objective 4: After instruction, students will be able to measure heights indirectly, as evidenced by their ability to use ratio and proportion to measure the heights of objects in photographs.

Introduction (five minutes):

1. Students will be informed that today we will be critiquing each other's mathematical efforts to determine the suspects' heights.
2. The teacher will go over the polite way to state problems that may occur within the presentations. (Write some polite phrases on the chalkboard or overhead.)
3. The teacher will emphasize the importance of accurate heights so we don't eliminate the kidnapper or accuse an innocent person.

Activity (twenty-five minutes):

1. A group will present its work, briefly describing its actions from the previous day and the height that it has determined for their suspect.
2. The class will critique the methods used, looking for possible errors. (Does the height seem reasonable? Did the group forget to convert measurements? Did the group convert measurements incorrectly?)
3. Each group will present its work.

Wrap-up Discussion (fifteen minutes):

1. The groups will write their reports for the day, which should include a reflection of the various methods used in class, any errors that

were made along the way, how they were corrected, and a list of the heights determined for the suspects.

Materials:
1. Overhead
2. Student photos

Standards Assessment: M = math, A = algebra I, SC = science

M8.2.1 Add, subtract, multiply, and divide rational numbers (integers, fractions, and terminating decimals) in multistep problems. *This standard will be evidenced when students prove to the class that their method of indirect measurement will work.*

M8.5.1 Convert common measurements for length, area, volume, weight, capacity, and time to equivalent measurements within the same system. *This standard will be evidenced when students convert measurements when using their method of indirect measurement.*

M8.6.2 Identify different methods of selecting samples, analyzing the strengths and weaknesses of each method and the possible bias in a sample or display. *This standard will be evidenced as students critique each other's methods for indirect measurement.*

M8.7.1 Analyze problems by identifying relationships, telling relevant from irrelevant information, identifying missing information, sequencing and prioritizing information, and observing patterns. *This standard will be evidenced as students critique each other's methods for indirect measurement, as well as when each group presents its own method for indirect measurement.*

M8.7.3 Decide when and how to divide a problem into simpler parts. *This standard will be evidenced when the groups present their methods for indirect measurement.*

M8.7.5 Make and test conjectures using inductive reasoning. *This standard will be evidenced as students make conjectures as to how they can measure something indirectly and then use mathematics to test their conjectures in class.*

M8.7.6 Express solutions clearly and logically by using the appropriate mathematical terms and notation. Support solutions with evidence in both verbal and symbolic work. *This standard will be evidenced when students prove to the class that their method of indirect measurement will work, as well as in their written reflections for the day.*

M8.7.11 Decide whether a solution is reasonable in the context of the original situation. *This standard will be evidenced as students critique each other's methods for indirect measurement.*

A1.1.5 Use dimensional (unit) analysis to organize conversions and computations. *This standard will be evidenced in students' math computations using rates and ratios to determine heights indirectly.*

A1.9.1 Use a variety of problem-solving strategies, such as drawing a diagram, making a chart, doing guess-and-check, solving a simpler problem, writing an equation, and working backwards. *This standard will be evidenced by the diagrams drawn and other problem-solving techniques used by the groups to determine the height of an object via indirect measurement.*

A1.9.2 Decide whether a solution is reasonable in the context of the original situation. *This standard will be evidenced as students critique each other's methods for indirect measurement.*

SC8.2.3 Use proportional reasoning to solve problems. *This standard will be evidenced in students' math computations using rates and ratios to determine heights indirectly.*

SC8.2.4 Use technological devices, such as calculators and computers, to perform calculations. *This standard will be evidenced as students use calculators (and computers if they are requested to do so) to aid them in performing calculations for determining indirect measurements.*

SC8.2.7 Participate in group discussions on scientific topics by restating or summarizing accurately what others have said, asking for clarification or elaboration, and expressing alternative positions. *This standard will be evidenced as students critique each other's methods for indirect measurement.*

SC8.2.8 Use tables, charts, and graphs in making arguments and claims in, for example, oral and written presentations about lab or fieldwork. *This standard will be evidenced in the class and group discussions regarding how to gather suspects' heights indirectly, as well as in the written reflections.*

Schlechty's WOW

(1) *Content and substance*—The unit aligns with thirty-eight eighth-grade standards (math—15, language arts—10, science—13) and eight algebra I standards.

(2) *Organization of knowledge*—The information and knowledge are arranged in a logical order, increasing in difficulty as the unit progresses.

(3) *Product focus*—The work is designed to engage the students.

(4) *Clear and compelling product standards*—The students will be given rubrics in advance, so that they will know what is expected and what will be graded.

(5) *Protection from adverse consequences for initial failures*—The unit is designed for students to make guesses and change their opinions based on new evidence. Participation grades will accrue throughout the project, but the final grade will not be assessed until the very end.

(6) *Affirmation of performance*—A bulletin board will be set up outside the classroom, displaying student work and hypotheses throughout the project. The entire school will have access to the bulletin board to view the students' progress.

(7) *Affiliation*—The unit is designed for students to work in cooperative groups.

(8) *Novelty and variety*—The lessons incorporate new activities in which the students will most likely never have had experience. Also, this will be the first time the entire eighth-grade class has worked together on a project in which each individual groups' results are important to the entire group.

(9) *Choice*—Students will have the choice of with whom they will work in their small groups. Student groups will have a choice as to the teachers with whom they would like to focus. Students may also draw upon their experiences to complete the tasks in a variety of ways, so long as they are mathematically sound.

(10) *Authenticity*—Kidnapping, crime scenes, and the skills involved are definitely related to the real world. I hope that this unit inspires some students to pursue a career as a police officer or crime-scene investigator.

LESSON PLAN 4D

"Reviewing the Data"

Goal 1: To provide students with a real-life situation that involves the use of mathematics.

Objective 4: After instruction, students will be able to measure heights indirectly, as evidenced by their ability to use ratio and proportion to measure the heights of objects in photographs.

Introduction (ten minutes):

1. The class will look at the pictures taken by all of the classes and the heights of the suspects.
2. The class will organize the pictures (and data) and double-check to make sure that the heights seem reasonable as compared with the pictures and with their own experiences with the suspects.

Activity (twenty minutes):

1. Students will decide which suspects should remain under investigation and which suspects should be eliminated.
2. Students will support their ideas with the gathered evidence.
3. Students will compile a final list of suspects to be further scrutinized.

Wrap-up Discussion (fifteen minutes):

1. The groups will write their reports for the day, which should include a reflection on the elimination process used by the class and which suspects are still on the list.
2. The groups will write a press release of the new information to be broadcast on WCAT.

Materials:

1. Student photos

Standards Assessment: M = math, A = algebra I, SC = science

M8.6.2 Identify different methods of selecting samples, analyzing the strengths and weaknesses of each method and the possible bias in a sample or display. *This standard will be evidenced as students critique each other's work using indirect measurement to determine their suspects' heights.*

M8.7.1 Analyze problems by identifying relationships, telling relevant from irrelevant information, identifying missing information, sequencing and prioritizing information, and observing patterns. *This standard will be evidenced as students critique each other's work to determine their suspects' heights, as well as when each group presents its work for the class.*

M8.7.5 Make and test conjectures using inductive reasoning. *This standard will be evidenced as students critique the testing of conjectures made by other groups.*

M8.7.6 Express solutions clearly and logically by using the appropriate mathematical terms and notation. Support solutions with evidence in both verbal and symbolic work. *This standard will be evidenced when students prove to the class that their method of indirect measurement works, as well as in their written reflections for the day.*

M8.7.11 Decide whether a solution is reasonable in the context of the original situation. *This standard will be evidenced when the students critique each other's work.*

A1.9.2 Decide whether a solution is reasonable in the context of the original situation. *This standard will be evidenced when the students critique each other's work.*

SC8.2.7 Participate in group discussions on scientific topics by restating or summarizing accurately what others have said, asking for clarification or elaboration, and expressing alternative positions. *This standard will be evidenced when the students critique each other's work.*

SC8.2.8 Use tables, charts, and graphs in making arguments and claims in, for example, oral and written presentations about lab or fieldwork. *This standard will be evidenced when the students critique each other's work, as well as in their written reflections for the day.*

Schlechty's WOW

(1) *Content and substance*—The unit aligns with thirty-eight eighth-grade standards (math—15, language arts—10, science—13) and eight algebra I standards.

(2) *Organization of knowledge*—The information and knowledge are arranged in a logical order, increasing in difficulty as the unit progresses.

(3) *Product focus*—The work is designed to engage the students.

(4) *Clear and compelling product standards*—The students will be given rubrics in advance, so that they will know what is expected and what will be graded.

(5) *Protection of adverse consequences for initial failures*—The unit is designed for students to make guesses and change their opinions based on new evidence. Participation grades will accrue throughout the project, but the final grade will not be assessed until the very end.

(6) *Affirmation of performance*—A bulletin board will be set up outside the classroom, displaying student work and hypotheses throughout the project. The entire school will have access to the bulletin board to view the students' progress.

(7) *Affiliation*—The unit is designed for students to work in cooperative groups.

(8) *Novelty and variety*—The lessons incorporate new activities in which the students will most likely never have had experience. Also, this will be the first time the entire eighth-grade class has worked together on a project in which each individual groups' results are important to the entire group.

(9) *Choice*—Students will have the choice of with whom they will work in their small groups. Student groups will have a choice as to the teachers with whom they would like to focus. Students may also draw upon their experiences to complete the tasks in a variety of ways, so long as they are mathematically sound.

(10) *Authenticity*—Kidnapping, crime scenes, and the skills involved are definitely related to the real world. I hope that this unit inspires some students to pursue a career as a police officer or crime-scene investigator.

LESSON PLAN 5A

"Fingerprint Analysis"

Goal 1: To provide students with a real-life situation that involves the use of mathematics.

Objective 5: After instruction, students will be able to analyze data, as evidenced by their ability to measure line segments and angles of various forms and concur that there are exactly two matching forms.

Introduction (ten minutes):
1. Review press releases created by the students.
2. Discuss the narrowed-down list of suspects and their fingerprints.

Activity (twenty minutes):
1. Introduce the ten points of commonality and how they are used to distinguish between fingerprints. It takes ten points of commonality in order to positively identify two different fingerprints as coming from the same person.
2. On the overhead, place a transparency of the kidnapper's fingerprint. Highlight different areas that seem to be distinct, things that we will be looking at trying to match.
3. Place another transparency on the overhead, this time of the teacher's fingerprints, and prove or disprove that the teacher is the kidnapper by comparing the attributes or characteristics of the two prints.
4. The teacher will model how to match the characteristics using distance and angle measurements.

Wrap-up Discussion (fifteen minutes):
1. The class will discuss the procedure. What can we do to make the comparisons easier?
2. The groups will discuss what they need to compare fingerprints. The groups will write a reflection discussing their material needs for comparing fingerprints, as well as how their group will divide the fingerprints for comparisons.

Materials:
1. Transparency of kidnapper's fingerprint
2. Transparency of teacher's fingerprints
3. Overhead (clear) ruler (mm)
4. Overhead (clear) protractor

Standards Assessment: M = math, A = algebra I, SC = science
M8.6.1 Identify claims based on statistical data and, in simple cases, evaluate the reasonableness of the claims. Design a study to investigate the claim. *This standard will be evidenced as the students participate in the group discussions regarding the comparison of the*

teacher's fingerprint with the kidnapper's fingerprint, as well as in the groups' reflections containing their plans for dividing the tasks for the next day.

M8.7.1 Analyze problems by identifying relationships, telling relevant from irrelevant information, identifying missing information, sequencing and prioritizing information, and observing patterns. *This standard will be evidenced as the students participate in the group discussions regarding the comparison of the teacher's fingerprint with the kidnapper's fingerprint, finding the unique characteristics of the kidnapper's fingerprint, and determining the common patterns (if any) with the teacher's fingerprint.*

M8.7.3 Decide when and how to divide a problem into simpler parts. *This standard will be evidenced in the group reflections as students decide how to divide the tasks for the next day.*

M8.7.6 Express solutions clearly and logically by using the appropriate mathematical terms and notations. Support solutions with evidence in both verbal and symbolic work. *This standard will be evidenced in the group reflections as students decide how to divide the tasks for the next day.*

M8.7.11 Decide whether a solution is reasonable in the context of the original situation. *This standard will be evidenced as the students participate in the group discussions regarding the comparison of the teacher's fingerprint with the kidnapper's fingerprint, finding the unique characteristics of the kidnapper's fingerprint, and determining the common patterns (if any) with the teacher's fingerprint.*

A1.9.1 Use a variety of problem-solving strategies, such as drawing a diagram, making a chart, doing guess-and-check, solving a simpler problem, writing an equation, and working backwards. *This standard will be evidenced as the students participate in the group discussions regarding the comparison of the teacher's fingerprint with the kidnapper's fingerprint, finding the unique characteristics of the kidnapper's fingerprint, and determining the common patterns (if any) with the teacher's fingerprint.*

A1.9.2 Decide whether a solution is reasonable in the context of the original situation. *This standard will be evidenced as the students participate in the group discussions regarding the comparison of the teacher's fingerprint with the kidnapper's fingerprint, finding the unique characteristics of the kidnapper's fingerprint, and determining the common patterns (if any) with the teacher's fingerprint.*

A1.9.8 Use counterexamples to show that statements are false, recognizing that a single counterexample is sufficient to prove a general statement false. *This standard will be evidenced as the students participate in the group discussions regarding the comparison of the teacher's fingerprint with the kidnapper's fingerprint, finding the unique characteristics of the kidnapper's fingerprint, and determining that one obvious difference between the prints is enough to rule that the print is not the kidnapper's.*

SC8.2.6 Write clear, step-by-step instructions (procedural summaries) for conducting investigations, operating something, or following a procedure. *This standard will be evidenced in the group reflections as students decide how to divide the tasks for the next day.*

SC8.2.7 Participate in group discussions on scientific topics by restating or summarizing accurately what others have said, asking for clarification or elaboration, and expressing alternative positions. *This standard will be evidenced as the students participate in the class and group discussions regarding the comparison of the teacher's fingerprint with the kidnapper's fingerprint, as well as in the groups' written reflections for the next day.*

SC8.2.8 Use tables, charts, and graphs in making arguments and claims in, for example, oral and written presentations about lab or fieldwork. *This standard will be evidenced in the group reflections as students decide how to divide the tasks for the next day.*

SC8.5.6 Explain that a single example can never prove that something is always true, but it can prove that something is not always true. *This standard will be evidenced as the students participate in the group discussions regarding the comparison of the teacher's fingerprint with the kidnapper's fingerprint, finding the unique characteristics of the kidnapper's fingerprint, and determining that one obvious difference between the prints is enough to rule that the print is not the kidnapper's.*

Schlechty's WOW

(1) *Content and substance*—The unit aligns with thirty-eight eighth-grade standards (math—15, language arts—10, science—13) and eight algebra I standards.

(2) *Organization of knowledge*—The information and knowledge are arranged in a logical order, increasing in difficulty as the unit progresses.

(3) *Product focus*—The work is designed to engage the students.

(4) *Clear and compelling product standards*—The students will be given rubrics in advance, so that they will know what is expected and what will be graded.

(5) *Protection from adverse consequences for initial failures*—The unit is designed for students to make guesses and change their opinions based on new evidence. Participation grades will accrue throughout the project, but the final grade will not be assessed until the very end.

(6) *Affirmation of performance*—A bulletin board will be set up outside the classroom, displaying student work and hypotheses throughout the project. The entire school will have access to the bulletin board to view the students' progress.

(7) *Affiliation*—The unit is designed for students to work in cooperative groups.

(8) *Novelty and variety*—The lessons incorporate new activities in which the students will most likely never have had experience. Also, this will be the first time the entire eighth-grade class has worked together on a project in which each individual groups' results are important to the entire group.

(9) *Choice*—Students will have the choice of with whom they will work in their small groups. Student groups will have a choice as to the teachers with whom they would like to focus. Students may also draw upon their experiences to complete the tasks in a variety of ways, so long as they are mathematically sound.

(10) *Authenticity*—Kidnapping, crime scenes, and the skills involved are definitely related to the real world. I hope that this unit inspires some students to pursue a career as a police officer or crime-scene investigator.

LESSON PLAN 5B

"Fingerprint Analysis, cont." (may take two days)

Goal 1: To provide students with a real-life situation that involves the use of mathematics.

Objective 5: After instruction, students will be able to analyze data, as evidenced by their ability to measure line segments and the angles of various forms and concur that there are exactly two matching forms.

Introduction (ten minutes):

1. The groups will share their plans and material needs for fingerprint classification.
2. The teacher will inform students that each group will receive the same number of fingerprints (which will depend on the number of suspects still on the list). The groups will have to write down their plans (on the given form) and have them authorized for use by the teacher before they will be allowed to gather their supplies.

Activity (twenty minutes):

1. The groups will write their plans (on the given form).
2. The teacher will authorize (or decline, with clarifications outlined) the plans and sign the appropriate location on the form.
3. Students will gather supplies (protractor, metric ruler, envelope of fingerprints, and plan).
4. Students will begin to compare the suspects' fingerprints with the kidnapper's, according to their plan.

Wrap-up Discussion (fifteen minutes):

1. The groups will discuss and write their reflections for the day, which should include a description of the fingerprints that have been (or are in the process of being) compared with the kidnapper's fingerprint, which fingerprints have been eliminated and why, and any changes to their plan that have occurred (or will have to occur the following day).

Materials:
1. Protractors
2. Metric rulers
3. Kidnapper's fingerprints
4. Suspects' fingerprints (prenumbered and randomized) in envelopes
5. Group plan form for comparing fingerprints

Standards Assessment: M = math, A = algebra I, SC = science
    M8.6.1 Identify claims based on statistical data and, in simple cases, evaluate the reasonableness of the claims. Design a study to investigate the claim. *This standard will be evidenced as the students participate in the group discussions regarding the comparison of the suspects' fingerprints with the kidnapper's fingerprint, as well as in the groups' reflections containing their plans for dividing the tasks for the next day.*

    M8.7.1 Analyze problems by identifying relationships, telling relevant from irrelevant information, identifying missing information, sequencing and prioritizing information, and observing patterns. *This standard will be evidenced as the students participate in the group discussions regarding the comparison of the suspects' fingerprints with the kidnapper's fingerprint, finding the unique characteristics of the kidnapper's fingerprint, and determining the common patterns (if any) with the suspects' fingerprints.*

    M8.7.3 Decide when and how to divide a problem into simpler parts. *This standard will be evidenced in the group reflections as students decide how to divide the tasks for the next day.*

    M8.7.6 Express solutions clearly and logically by using the appropriate mathematical terms and notation. Support solutions with evidence in both verbal and symbolic work. *This standard will be evidenced in the group reflections as students decide how to divide the tasks for the next day, as well as in the reflection for the day.*

    M8.7.11 Decide whether a solution is reasonable in the context of the original situation. *This standard will be evidenced as the students participate in the group discussions regarding the comparison of the suspects' fingerprints with the kidnapper's fingerprint, finding the unique characteristics of the kidnapper's fingerprint, and determining the common patterns (if any) with the suspects' fingerprints.*

A1.9.1 Use a variety of problem-solving strategies, such as drawing a diagram, making a chart, doing guess-and-check, solving a simpler problem, writing an equation, and working backwards. *This standard will be evidenced as the students participate in the group discussions regarding the comparison of the suspects' fingerprints with the kidnapper's fingerprint, finding the unique characteristics of the kidnapper's fingerprint, and determining the common patterns (if any) with the suspects' fingerprints.*

A1.9.2 Decide whether a solution is reasonable in the context of the original situation. *This standard will be evidenced as the students participate in the group discussions regarding the comparison of the suspects' fingerprints with the kidnapper's fingerprint, finding the unique characteristics of the kidnapper's fingerprint, and determining the common patterns (if any) with the suspects' fingerprints.*

A1.9.8 Use counterexamples to show that statements are false, recognizing that a single counterexample is sufficient to prove a general statement false. *This standard will be evidenced as the students participate in the group discussions regarding the comparison of the suspects' fingerprints with the kidnapper's fingerprint, finding the unique characteristics of the kidnapper's fingerprint, and determining that one obvious difference between the prints is enough to rule that the print is not the kidnapper's.*

SC8.2.6 Write clear, step-by-step instructions (procedural summaries) for conducting investigations, operating something, or following a procedure. *This standard will be evidenced in the group reflections as students decide how to divide the tasks for the next day, as well as in their reflections for the day.*

SC8.2.7 Participate in group discussions on scientific topics by restating or summarizing accurately what others have said, asking for clarification or elaboration, and expressing alternative positions. *This standard will be evidenced as the students participate in the class and group discussions regarding the comparison of the suspects' fingerprints with the kidnapper's fingerprint, as well as in the groups' written reflections for the next day.*

SC8.2.8 Use tables, charts, and graphs in making arguments and claims in, for example, oral and written presentations about lab or fieldwork. *This standard will be evidenced in the group reflections as students decide how to divide the tasks for the next day, as well as in the group reflections for the day.*

SC8.5.6 Explain that a single example can never prove that something is always true, but it can prove that something is not always true. *This standard will be evidenced as the students participate in the group discussions regarding the comparison of the suspects' fingerprints with the kidnapper's fingerprint, finding the unique characteristics of the kidnapper's fingerprint, and determining that one obvious difference between the prints is enough to rule that the print is not the kidnapper's.*

Schlechty's WOW

(1) *Content and substance*—The unit aligns with thirty-eight eighth-grade standards (math—15, language arts—10, science—13) and eight algebra I standards.

(2) *Organization of knowledge*—The information and knowledge are arranged in a logical order, increasing in difficulty as the unit progresses.

(3) *Product focus*—The work is designed to engage the students.

(4) *Clear and compelling product standards*—The students will be given rubrics in advance, so that they will know what is expected and what will be graded.

(5) *Protection from adverse consequences for initial failures*—The unit is designed for students to make guesses and change their opinions based on new evidence. Participation grades will accrue throughout the project, but the final grade will not be assessed until the very end.

(6) *Affirmation of performance*—A bulletin board will be set up outside the classroom, displaying student work and hypotheses throughout the project. The entire school will have access to the bulletin board to view the students' progress.

(7) *Affiliation*—The unit is designed for students to work in cooperative groups.

(8) *Novelty and variety*—The lessons incorporate new activities in which the students will most likely never have had experience. Also, this will be the first time the entire eighth-grade class has worked together on a project in which each individual groups' results are important to the entire group.

(9) *Choice*—Students will have the choice of with whom they will work in their small groups. Student groups will have a choice as to the teachers with whom they would like to focus. Students may also draw upon their experiences to complete the tasks in a variety of ways, so long as they are mathematically sound.

(10) *Authenticity*—Kidnapping, crime scenes, and the skills involved are definitely related to the real world. I hope that this unit inspires some students to pursue a career as a police officer or crime-scene investigator.

LESSON PLAN 6A

"Report Format"

Goal 2: To involve all of my students in a fun activity.

Objective 6: After instruction, students will be able to synthesize data, as evidenced by their ability to organize the processes and observations involved in the mystery in a written reflection of their mathematical experiences.

Introduction (ten minutes):

1. Students will synthesize the data gathered from all the groups.
2. The class will discuss who they think is the kidnapper and why (what evidence supports their claim).

Activity (twenty minutes):

1. Students are given a tic-tac-toe chart, from which they are to complete the task in the center square, along with two other tasks that complete a tic-tac-toe. Rubrics for each activity will be available so students can understand the criteria on which they will be graded.
2. Students will submit their choices the following class day.
3. The center square asks for a written report or reflection on the entire mystery process and experience.
4. The groups will be given an outline format to use as a guide for their report or reflection.
5. Student groups will discuss the parts of the outline, noting what parts of the processes and experiences can be used to support the various parts of the outline.

Wrap-up Discussion (fifteen minutes):
1. Students will be informed that we will be working in conjunction
   with the English teacher to write the paper, but that we will organize the notes we need before she will begin the writing
   process.
2. Students will be given time in class (and copies of the rubrics) for
   the other two activities from their tic-tac-toe choices. Remind
   students that their tic-tac-toe choices are due the following class
   day.

Materials:
1. Tic-tac-toe choices
2. Rubrics for tic-tac-toe choices
3. Report or reflection outline

Standards Assessment: LA = language arts
   LA8.4.1 Discuss ideas for writing, keep a list or notebook of ideas, and
   use graphic organizers to plan writing. *This standard will be evidenced by the students' daily written reflections, and the use of an
   outline to organize their ideas for the final paper.*
   LA8.4.3 Support theses or conclusions with analogies (comparisons),
   paraphrases, quotations, opinions from experts, and similar devices.
   *This standard will be evidenced by the use of paraphrases of the
   group reflections used in their final papers.*
   LA8.5.7 Write for different purposes and to a specific audience or person, adjusting tone and style as necessary. *This standard will be evidenced in the different writing styles used in the group reflections
   and the final paper.*

Schlechty's WOW
   (1) *Content and substance*—The unit aligns with thirty-eight eighth-
   grade standards (math—15, language arts—10, science—13) and
   eight algebra I standards.
   (2) *Organization of knowledge*—The information and knowledge are
   arranged in a logical order, increasing in difficulty as the unit progresses.
   (3) *Product focus*—The work is designed to engage the students.

(4) *Clear and compelling product standards*—The students will be given rubrics in advance, so that they will know what is expected and what will be graded.

(5) *Protection from adverse consequences for initial failures*—The unit is designed for students to make guesses and change their opinions based on new evidence. Participation grades will accrue throughout the project, but the final grade will not be assessed until the very end.

(6) *Affirmation of performance*—A bulletin board will be set up outside the classroom, displaying student work and hypotheses throughout the project. The entire school will have access to the bulletin board to view the students' progress.

(7) *Affiliation*—The unit is designed for students to work in cooperative groups.

(8) *Novelty and variety*—The lessons incorporate new activities in which the students will most likely never have had experience. Also, this will be the first time the entire eighth-grade class has worked together on a project in which each individual groups' results are important to the entire group.

(9) *Choice*—Students will have the choice of with whom they will work in their small groups. Student groups will have a choice as to the teachers with whom they would like to focus. Students may also draw upon their experiences to complete the tasks in a variety of ways, so long as they are mathematically sound.

(10) *Authenticity*—Kidnapping, crime scenes, and the skills involved are definitely related to the real world. I hope that this unit inspires some students to pursue a career as a police officer or crime-scene investigator.

LESSON PLAN 6B

"Report Organization"

Goal 2: To involve all of my students in a fun activity.

Objective 6: After instruction, students will be able to synthesize data, as evidenced by their ability to organize the processes and observations involved in the mystery in a written reflection of their mathematical experiences.

Introduction (ten minutes):
1. Students will turn in their tic-tac-toe choice sheets.
2. Students will brainstorm ideas about what to include in their papers by creating a web of details on the chalkboard.
3. The teacher will review plagiarism and model how to paraphrase an idea.

Activity (twenty minutes):
1. The teacher will distribute supplies for student note cards (the English teacher will determine which supplies will be needed).
2. Students will browse their group reflections for information they would like to write about in their final paper.
3. Students will write information in their outline format, citing the reflection that can be used at a later date.
4. Student will take notes on their note cards.

Wrap-up Discussion (fifteen minutes):
1. Distribute the individual rubrics to each student (as determined by their tic-tac-toe choice sheet) and review the criteria for the final paper.
2. Discuss any questions or concerns regarding the other rubrics.

Materials:
1. 60 copies of each rubric
2. 130 copies of the report rubric
3. Note card supplies (determined by the English teacher)

Standards Assessment: LA = language arts
LA8.4.1 Discuss ideas for writing, keep a list or notebook of ideas, and use graphic organizers to plan writing. *This standard will be evidenced by the students' daily written reflections and the use of an outline to organize their ideas for the final paper.*
LA8.4.3 Support theses or conclusions with analogies (comparisons), paraphrases, quotations, opinions from experts, and similar devices.

This standard will be evidenced by the use of paraphrases of the group reflections used in their final papers.

LA8.5.7 Write for different purposes and to a specific audience or person, adjusting tone and style as necessary. *This standard will be evidenced in the different writing styles used in the group reflections and the final paper.*

Schlechty's WOW

(1) *Content and substance*—The unit aligns with thirty-eight eighth-grade standards (math—15, language arts—10, science—13) and eight algebra I standards.

(2) *Organization of knowledge*—The information and knowledge are arranged in a logical order, increasing in difficulty as the unit progresses.

(3) *Product focus*—The work is designed to engage the students.

(4) *Clear and compelling product standards*—The students will be given rubrics in advance, so that they will know what is expected and what will be graded.

(5) *Protection from adverse consequences for initial failures*—The unit is designed for students to make guesses and change their opinions based on new evidence. Participation grades will accrue throughout the project, but the final grade will not be assessed until the very end.

(6) *Affirmation from performance*—A bulletin board will be set up outside the classroom, displaying student work and hypotheses throughout the project. The entire school will have access to the bulletin board to view the students' progress.

(7) *Affiliation*—The unit is designed for students to work in cooperative groups.

(8) *Novelty and variety*—The lessons incorporate new activities in which the students will most likely never have had experience. Also, this will be the first time the entire eighth-grade class has worked together on a project in which each individual groups' results are important to the entire group.

(9) *Choice*—Students will have the choice of with whom they will work in their small groups. Student groups will have a choice as to the teachers with whom they would like to focus. Students may also

draw upon their experiences to complete the tasks in a variety of ways, so long as they are mathematically sound.

(10) *Authenticity*—Kidnapping, crime scenes, and the skills involved are definitely related to the real world. I hope that this unit inspires some students to pursue a career as a police officer or crime-scene investigator.

LESSON PLAN 6C

"Writing the Report" (This may take several days)

Goal 2: To involve all of my students in a fun activity.

Objective 6: After instruction, students will be able to synthesize data, as evidenced by their ability to organize the processes and observations involved in the mystery in a written reflection of their mathematical experiences.

Introduction (ten minutes):
1. Students will be able to ask questions about their note cards.
2. The teacher and students will review the rubric criteria.

Activity (twenty minutes):
1. Students will finish organizing their note cards.
2. Students will write their rough draft.
3. Students will peer-edit each other's papers.
4. Students will write or type their final papers.

Wrap-up Discussion (fifteen minutes):
1. The rubric criteria will be reviewed and posted.

Standards Assessment: LA = language arts, SC = science

LA8.4.1 Discuss ideas for writing, keep a list or notebook of ideas, and use graphic organizers to plan writing. *This standard will be evidenced by the students' daily written reflections and the use of an outline to organize their ideas for the final paper.*

LA8.4.2 Create compositions that have a clear message, a coherent thesis (a statement of position on the topic), and a clear and well-supported conclusion. *This standard will be evidenced by students' papers that contain a thesis statement regarding the mystery unit and a well-supported conclusion that summarizes all the key points in the body of the report.*

LA8.4.3 Support theses or conclusions with analogies (comparisons), paraphrases, quotations, opinions from experts, and similar devices. *This standard will be evidenced by the use of paraphrases of the group reflections used in their final papers.*

LA8.5.6 Write using precise word choices to make writing interesting and exact. *This will be evidenced by the precise word choices used in the final paper.*

LA8.5.7 Write for different purposes and to a specific audience or person, adjusting tone and style as necessary. *This standard will be evidenced in the different writing styles used in the group reflections and the final paper.*

LA8.6.4 Edit written manuscripts to ensure that correct grammar is used. *This standard will be evidenced in the peer-editing process before the composition of the final paper.*

LA8.6.5 Use correct punctuation. *This standard will be evidenced by the use of correct punctuation in the final paper.*

LA8.6.6 Use correct capitalization. *This standard will be evidenced by the use of correct capitalization in the final paper.*

LA8.6.7 Use correct spelling conventions. *This standard will be evidenced by the use of correct spelling conventions in the final paper.*

SC8.2.6 Write clear, step-by-step instructions (procedural summaries) for conducting investigations, operating something, or following a procedure. *This standard will be evidenced by the use of clear instructions as illustrated in the final paper.*

Schlechty's WOW

(1) *Content and substance*—The unit aligns with thirty-eight eighth-grade standards (math—15, language arts—10, science—13) and eight algebra I standards.

(2) *Organization of knowledge*—The information and knowledge are arranged in a logical order, increasing in difficulty as the unit progresses.

(3) *Product focus*—The work is designed to engage the students.

(4) *Clear and compelling product standards*—The students will be given rubrics in advance, so that they will know what is expected and what will be graded.

(5) *Protection from adverse consequences for initial failures*—The unit is designed for students to make guesses and change their opinions based on new evidence. Participation grades will accrue throughout the project, but the final grade will not be assessed until the very end.

(6) *Affirmation of performance*—A bulletin board will be set up outside the classroom, displaying student work and hypotheses throughout the project. The entire school will have access to the bulletin board to view the students' progress.

(7) *Affiliation*—The unit is designed for students to work in cooperative groups.

(8) *Novelty and variety*—The lessons incorporate new activities in which the students will most likely never have had experience. Also, this will be the first time the entire eighth-grade class has worked together on a project in which each individual groups' results are important to the entire group.

(9) *Choice*—Students will have the choice of with whom they will work in their small groups. Student groups will have a choice as to the teachers with whom they would like to focus. Students may also draw upon their experiences to complete the tasks in a variety of ways, so long as they are mathematically sound.

(10) *Authenticity*—Kidnapping, crime scenes, and the skills involved are definitely related to the real world. I hope that this unit inspires some students to pursue a career as a police officer or crime-scene investigator.

LESSON PLAN 7A

"Presenting the Report" (This may take several days)

Goal 2: To involve all of my students in a fun activity.

Objective 7: After instruction, students will be able to critique the work and participation of their group members and themselves, as evidenced by completion of self-evaluation and group-evaluation forms.

Introduction (five minutes):
1. Students will be asked to choose one of the two nonreport activities from their tic-tac-toe choice sheets.
2. Students will be told to present their project, according to the oral presentation part of their rubric (according their activity).

Activity (twenty-five minutes):
1. Students will present their project, in accordance with the oral presentation part of their rubric.
2. Students will be asked to peer-evaluate the oral presentation.
3. Students will be informed that the projects will be on display in order for them to complete the other portion of the rubric.

Wrap-up Discussion (fifteen minutes):
1. Students will finish the peer-evaluations of the projects.
2. Students will turn in their peer-evaluations.

Materials:
1. Copies of rubrics for all presentations

Standards Assessment: LA = language arts, SC = science
LA8.4.1 Discuss ideas for writing, keep a list or notebook of ideas, and use graphic organizers to plan writing. *This standard will be evidenced by the students' daily written reflections and the use of an outline to organize their ideas for the final paper.*
LA8.4.2 Create compositions that have a clear message, a coherent thesis (a statement of position on the topic), and a clear and well-supported conclusion. *This standard will be evidenced by students' papers that contain a thesis statement regarding the mystery unit and a well-supported conclusion that summarizes all the key points in the body of the report.*
LA8.4.3 Support theses or conclusions with analogies (comparisons), paraphrases, quotations, opinions from experts, and similar devices. *This standard will be evidenced by the use of paraphrases of the group reflections used in their final papers.*
LA8.5.6 Write using precise word choices to make writing interesting and exact. *This will be evidenced by the precise word choices used in the final paper.*

LA8.5.7 Write for different purposes and to a specific audience or person, adjusting tone and style as necessary. *This standard will be evidenced in the different writing styles used in the group reflections and the final paper.*

LA8.6.4 Edit written manuscripts to ensure that correct grammar is used. *This standard will be evidenced in the peer-editing process before the composition of the final paper.*

LA8.6.5 Use correct punctuation. *This standard will be evidenced by the use of correct punctuation in the final paper.*

LA8.6.6 Use correct capitalization. *This standard will be evidenced by the use of correct capitalization in the final paper.*

LA8.6.7 Use correct spelling conventions. *This standard will be evidenced by the use of correct spelling conventions in the final paper.*

SC8.2.6 Write clear, step-by-step instructions (procedural summaries) for conducting investigations, operating something, or following a procedure. *This standard will be evidenced by the use of clear instructions as illustrated in the final paper.*

Schlechty's WOW

(1) *Content and substance*—The unit aligns with thirty-eight eighth-grade standards (math—15, language arts—10, science—13) and eight algebra I standards.

(2) *Organization of knowledge*—The information and knowledge are arranged in a logical order, increasing in difficulty as the unit progresses.

(3) *Product focus*—The work is designed to engage the students.

(4) *Clear and compelling product standards*—The students will be given rubrics in advance, so that they will know what is expected and what will be graded.

(5) *Protection from adverse consequences for initial failures*—The unit is designed for students to make guesses and change their opinions based on new evidence. Participation grades will accrue throughout the project, but the final grade will not be assessed until the very end.

(6) *Affirmation of performance*—A bulletin board will be set up outside the classroom, displaying student work and hypotheses throughout

the project. The entire school will have access to the bulletin board to view the students' progress.

(7) *Affiliation*—The unit is designed for students to work in cooperative groups.

(8) *Novelty and variety*—The lessons incorporate new activities in which the students will most likely never have had experience. Also, this will be the first time the entire eighth-grade class has worked together on a project in which each individual groups' results are important to the entire group.

(9) *Choice*—Students will have the choice of with whom they will work in their small groups. Student groups will have a choice as to the teachers with whom they would like to focus. Students may also draw upon their experiences to complete the tasks in a variety of ways, so long as they are mathematically sound.

(10) *Authenticity*—Kidnapping, crime scenes, and the skills involved are definitely related to the real world. I hope that this unit inspires some students to pursue a career as a police officer or crime-scene investigator.

MAKING A MAP

Category	4	3	2	1
Neatness of color and lines	All straight lines are ruler drawn, all errors have been neatly corrected, and all features are colored completely	All straight lines are ruler drawn, most errors have been neatly corrected, and most features are colored completely	Most straight lines are ruler drawn, most errors have been neatly corrected, and most features are colored completely	Many lines, corrections of errors, and/or features are not neatly done
Spelling/ capitalization	95–100 percent of words on the map are spelled and capitalized correctly	85–94 percent of words on the map are spelled and capitalized correctly	75–84 percent of words on the map are spelled and capitalized correctly	Less than 75 percent of words on the map are spelled and capitalized correctly
Labels— accuracy	At least 90 percent of the items are labeled and located correctly	80–89 percent of the items are labeled and located correctly	70–79 percent of the items are labeled and located correctly	Less than 70 percent of the items are labeled and located correctly

Scale	All features on the map are drawn to scale, and the scale used is clearly indicated on the map	Most features on the map are drawn to scale, and the scale used is clearly indicated on the map	Many features on the map are not drawn to scale, even though a scale is clearly indicated on the map	Many features of the map are not drawn to scale and/or there is no scale marker on the map
Map legend/key	The legend is easy to find and contains a complete set of symbols, including a compass rose	The legend contains a complete set of symbols, including a compass rose	The legend contains an almost complete set of symbols, including a compass rose	The legend is absent or lacks several symbols
Title	The title tells the purpose/content of the map, is clearly distinguishable as the title (e.g., larger letters, underlined, etc.), and is printed at the top of the map	The title tells the purpose/content of the map and is printed at the top of the map	The title tells the purpose/content of the map, but is not located at the top of the map	The purpose/content of the map is not clear from the title

REPORT

Category	4	3	2	1
Introduction (organization)	The introduction is inviting, states the main topic, and previews the structure of the paper	The introduction clearly states the main topic and previews the structure of the paper but is not particularly inviting to the reader	The introduction states the main topic but does not adequately preview the structure of the paper, nor is it particularly inviting to the reader	There is no clear introduction of the main topic or structure of the paper
Flow and rhythm (sentence fluency)	All sentences sound natural and are easy on the ear when read aloud; each sentence is clear and has an obvious emphasis	Almost all sentences sound natural and are easy on the ear when read aloud, but one or two are stiff and awkward or difficult to understand	Most sentences sound natural and are easy on the ear when read aloud, but several are stiff and awkward or are difficult to understand	The sentences are difficult to read aloud because they sound awkward, are distractingly repetitive, or difficult to understand
Sequencing (organization)	Details are placed in a logical order, and the way they are presented effectively keeps the interest of the reader	Details are placed in a logical order, but the way in which they are presented/introduced sometimes makes the writing less interesting	Some details are not presented in a logical or expected order, and this distracts the reader	Many details are not in a logical or expected order, and there is little sense that the writing is organized

Transitions (organization)	A variety of thoughtful transitions are used that clearly show how ideas are connected	Transitions clearly show how ideas are connected, but there is little variety	Some transitions work well, but connections between other ideas are fuzzy	The transitions between ideas are unclear or nonexistent
Accuracy of facts (content)	All supportive facts are reported accurately	Almost all supportive facts are reported accurately	Most supportive facts are reported accurately	No facts are reported, or most are inaccurately reported
Grammar and spelling (conventions)	The writer makes no errors in grammar or spelling that distract the reader from the content	The writer makes one or two errors in grammar or spelling that distract the reader from the content	The writer makes three or four errors in grammar or spelling that distract the reader from the content	The writer makes more than four errors in grammar or spelling that distract the reader from the content
Penmanship (conventions)	The paper is neatly written or typed with no distracting corrections	The paper is neatly written or typed with one or two distracting corrections (e.g., dark cross-outs, bumpy white-out, words written over)	The writing is generally readable, but the reader has to exert quite a bit of effort to figure out some of the words	Many words are unreadable, or there are several distracting corrections
Conclusion (organization)	The conclusion is strong and leaves readers with the feeling that they understand what the writer is "getting at"	The conclusion is recognizable and ties up almost all the loose ends	The conclusion is recognizable, but does not tie up several loose ends	There is no clear conclusion; the paper just ends

INTERVIEW

Category	4	3	2	1
Setting up the interview	The student introduced himself, explained why he wanted to interview the person, and asked permission to set up a time for an interview	The student introduced himself and asked permission to set up a time for the interview, but needed a reminder to explain why he wanted to do the interview	The student asked permission to set up a time for the interview, but needed reminders to introduce himself and to tell why he wanted to interview the person	The student needed assistance in all aspects of setting up the interview
Politeness	The student never interrupted or hurried the person being interviewed and thanked him or her for being willing to be interviewed	The student rarely interrupted or hurried the person being interviewed and thanked him or her for being willing to be interviewed	The student rarely interrupted or hurried the person being interviewed, but forgot to thank the person	Several times, the student interrupted or hurried the person being interviewed and forgot to thank the person
Preparation	Before the interview, the student prepared several in-depth and factual questions to ask	Before the interview, the student prepared a couple of in-depth questions and several factual questions to ask	Before the interview, the student prepared several factual questions to ask	The student did not prepare any questions before the interview

Formatting and editing	The student edited and organized the transcript in a way that made the information clear and interesting	The student edited and organized the transcript in a way that made the information clear	The student edited and organized the transcript, but the information was not as clear or as interesting as it could have been	The student did not edit or organize the transcript
Note taking	The interviewer took occasional notes during the interview, but usually maintained focus on the person rather than the notes, which were added to immediately after the interview so facts were not lost	The interviewer took occasional notes during the interview, but usually maintained focus on the person rather than the notes; no additional notes were taken	The interviewer took notes during the interview, but did so in a way that interrupted the flow of the interview; additional notes may or may not have been taken	The interviewer took no notes during or after the interview
Follow-up questions	The student listened carefully to the person being interviewed and asked several relevant follow-up questions based on what the person said	The student listened carefully to the person being interviewed and asked a couple of relevant follow-up questions based on what the person said	The student asked a couple of follow-up questions based on what he thought the person had said	The student did not ask any follow-up questions based on what the person said

MAKING A POSTER

Category	4	3	2	1
Graphics—clarity	Graphics are all in focus, and the content is easily viewed and identified from six feet away	Most graphics are in focus, and the content is easily viewed and identified from six feet away	Most graphics are in focus, and the content is easily viewed and identified from four feet away	Many graphics are not clear or are too small
Graphics—originality	Several of the graphics used on the poster reflect an exceptional degree of student creativity in their creation and/or display	One or two of the graphics used on the poster reflect student creativity in their creation and/or display	The graphics are made by the student, but are based on the designs or ideas of others	No graphics made by the student are included
Graphics—relevance	All graphics are related to the topic and make it easier to understand; all borrowed graphics have a source citation	All graphics are related to the topic, and most make it easier to understand; all borrowed graphics have a source citation	All graphics relate to the topic, and most borrowed graphics have a source citation	Graphics do not relate to the topic, or several borrowed graphics do not have a source citation

Labels	All items of importance on the poster are clearly labeled with labels that can be read from at least three feet away	Almost all items of importance on the poster are clearly labeled with labels that can be read from at least three feet away	Several items of importance on the poster are clearly labeled with labels that can be read from at least three feet away	Labels are too small to view or no important items were labeled
Required elements	The poster includes all required elements as well as additional information	All required elements are included on the poster	All but one of the required elements are included on the poster	Several required elements were missing
Content—accuracy	At least seven accurate facts are displayed on the poster	Five or six accurate facts are displayed on the poster	Three or four accurate facts are displayed on the poster	Fewer than three accurate facts are displayed on the poster
Title	The title can be read from six feet away and is quite creative	The title can be read from six feet away and describes the content well	The title can be read from four feet away and describes the content well	The title is too small and/or does not describe the content of the poster well
Grammar	There are no grammatical mistakes on the poster	There is one grammatical mistake on the poster	There are two grammatical mistakes on the poster	There are more than two grammatical mistakes on the poster

POWERPOINT

Category	4	3	2	1
Buttons and links work correctly	All buttons and links work correctly	Most (90–99 percent) buttons and links work correctly	Many (75–89 percent) of the buttons and links work correctly	Less than 75 percent of the buttons work correctly
Background	The background does not detract from text or other graphics; the choice of background is consistent from card to card	The background does not detract from text or other graphics; the choice of background is consistent from card to card	The background does not detract from text or other graphics	The background makes it difficult to see text or competes with other graphics on the page
Sounds—planning	Careful planning has gone into sounds; all sounds improve the content or feel of the presentation	Some planning has gone into sounds, and most enhance the content or feel of the presentation, but one or two seem to be added for no real reason; none detracts from the overall presentation	Sounds chosen are appropriate for the topic, but some detract from the overall presentation	Sounds are not appropriate for the presentation
Originality	The presentation shows considerable originality and inventiveness; the content and ideas are presented in a unique and interesting way	The presentation shows some originality and inventiveness; the content and ideas are presented in an interesting way	The presentation shows an attempt at originality and inventiveness on one or two cards	The presentation is a rehash of other people's ideas and/or graphics and shows very little attempt at original thought

Category			
Text—font choice and formatting	Font formats (e.g., color, bold, italic) have been carefully planned to enhance readability and content	Font formats have been carefully planned to enhance readability	Font formats have been carefully planned to complement the content; it may be a little hard to read	Font formatting makes it very difficult to read the material
Content—accuracy	All content throughout the presentation is accurate; there are no factual errors	Most of the content is accurate, but there is one piece of information that might be inaccurate	The content is generally accurate, but one piece of information is clearly flawed or inaccurate	Content is typically confusing or contains more than one factual error
Spelling and grammar	The presentation has no misspellings or grammatical errors	The presentation has one or two misspellings, but no grammatical errors	The presentation has one or two grammatical errors, but no misspellings	The presentation has more than two grammatical and/or spelling errors
Sequencing of information	Information is organized in a clear, logical way; it is easy to anticipate the type of material that might be on the next card	Most information is organized in a clear, logical way; one card or item of information seems out of place	Some information is logically sequenced; an occasional card or item of information seems out of place	There is no clear plan for the organization of information
Use of graphics	All graphics are attractive (size and colors) and support the theme/content of the presentation	A few graphics are not attractive, but all support the theme/content of the presentation	All graphics are attractive, but a few do not seem to support the theme/content of the presentation	Several graphics are unattractive and detract from the content of the presentation

LETTER

Category	4	3	2	1
Sentences and paragraphs	Sentences and paragraphs are complete, well-constructed, and of varied structure	All sentences are complete and well-constructed (no fragments, no run-ons); paragraphing is generally done well	Most sentences are complete and well-constructed; paragraphing needs some work	Many sentence fragments or run-on sentences; or paragraphing needs lots of work
Salutation and and closing	The salutation and closing have no errors in capitalization and punctuation	The salutation and closing have one or two errors in capitalization and punctuation	The salutation and closing have three or more errors in capitalization and punctuation	The salutation and/or closing are missing
Grammar and spelling (conventions)	The writer makes no errors in grammar or spelling	The writer makes one or two errors in grammar and/or spelling	The writer makes three or four errors in grammar and/or spelling	The writer makes more than four errors in grammar and/or spelling
Capitalization and punctuation	The writer makes no errors in capitalization and punctuation	The writer makes one or two errors in capitalization and punctuation	The writer makes three or four errors in capitalization and punctuation	The writer makes more than four errors in capitalization and punctuation

Neatness	The letter is typed, clean, not wrinkled, and easy to read, with no distracting error corrections; it was done with pride	The letter is neatly handwritten, clean, not wrinkled, and easy to read, with no distracting error corrections; it was done with care	The letter is typed, but is crumpled or slightly stained and may have one or two distracting error corrections; it was done with some care	The letter is typed, but looks like it has been shoved into a pocket or locker, and it may have several distracting error corrections; it looks like it was done in a hurry or stored improperly
Format	The letter complies with all the requirements for a friendly letter	The letter complies with almost all the requirements for a friendly letter	The letter complies with several of the requirements for a friendly letter	The letter complies with less than 75 percent of the requirements for a friendly letter
Content — accuracy	The letter contains at least five accurate facts about the topic	The letter contains three or four accurate facts about the topic	The letter contains one or two accurate facts about the topic	The letter contains no accurate facts about the topic

MOVIE/SKIT

Category	4	3	2	1
Presentation	The presentation is well-rehearsed with a smooth delivery that holds audience attention	The presentation is rehearsed with a fairly smooth delivery that holds audience attention most of the time	Delivery is not smooth, but the student is able to maintain the interest of the audience most of the time	Delivery is not smooth, and the audience's attention is often lost
Rough draft	The rough draft is brought on the due date; the student shares it with a peer and extensively edits based on peer feedback	The rough draft is brought on the due date, and the student shares it with a peer and the peer makes edits	The student provides feedback and/or edits for a peer, but the student's own rough draft was not ready for editing	The rough draft is not ready for editing, and the student did not participate in reviewing the draft of a peer
Requirements	All requirements are met and exceeded	All requirements are met	One requirement was not completely met	More than one requirement was not completely met
Mechanics	There are no misspellings or grammatical errors	There are three or fewer misspellings and/or mechanical errors	There are four misspellings and/or grammatical errors	There are more than four errors in spelling or grammar

Content	The content covers the topic in depth with details and examples; the student's subject knowledge is excellent	The content includes essential knowledge about the topic; the student's subject knowledge appears to be good	The content includes essential information about the topic, but there are one or two factual errors	The content is minimal, or there are several factual errors
Organization	The content is well organized, using headings or bulleted lists to group related material	Headings or bulleted lists are used to organize the content, but the overall organization of topics appears flawed	The content is logically organized for the most part	There was no clear or logical organizational structure, just lots of facts
Originality	The product shows a large amount of original thought; ideas are creative and inventive	The product shows some original thought; the work shows new ideas and insights	The student uses other people's ideas (giving them credit), but there is little evidence of original thinking	The student uses other people's ideas, but does not give them credit
Workload	The workload is divided and shared equally by all team members	The workload is divided and shared fairly by all team members	The workload was divided, but one person in the group is viewed as not doing his or her fair share of the work	The workload was not divided, or several people in the group are viewed as not doing their fair share of the work

MAKING A COMIC BOOK

Category	4	3	2	1
Originality	The product shows a large amount of original thought; ideas are creative and inventive	The product shows some original thought; the work shows new ideas and insights	The student uses other people's ideas (giving them credit), but there is little evidence of original thinking	The student uses other people's ideas, but does not give them credit
Sentences and paragraphs	Sentences and paragraphs are complete, well constructed, and of varied structure	All sentences are complete and well constructed (no fragments, no run-ons); paragraphing is generally done well	Most sentences are complete and well constructed; paragraphing needs some work	Many sentence fragments or run-on sentences, or paragraphing needs lots of work
Grammar and spelling (conventions)	The writer makes no errors in grammar or spelling	The writer makes one or two errors in grammar and/or spelling	The writer makes three or four errors in grammar and/or spelling	The writer makes more than four errors in grammar and/or spelling
Capitalization and punctuation	The writer makes no errors in capitalization and punctuation	The writer makes one or two errors in capitalization and punctuation	The writer makes three or four errors in capitalization and punctuation	The writer makes more than four errors in capitalization and punctuation

Neatness	The book is typed or neatly handwritten, clean, not wrinkled, and easy to read, with no distracting error corrections; it was done with pride	The book is neatly handwritten, clean, not wrinkled, easy to read, with no distracting error corrections; it was done with care	The book is typed, but is crumpled or slightly stained and may have one or two distracting error corrections; it was done with some care	The book is typed, but looks like it was shoved into a pocket or locker, and it may have several distracting error corrections; it looks like it was done in a hurry or stored improperly
Content— accuracy	At least seven accurate facts are portrayed in the book	Five to six accurate facts are portrayed in the book	Three or four accurate facts are portrayed in the book.	Less than three accurate facts are portrayed in the book.
Significance	All items of importance in the artwork are clearly related to the topic	Almost all items of importance in the artwork are clearly related to the topic	Several items of importance in the art are clearly related to the topic	Items are not related to the topic or are not mentioned
Formatting and editing	The student edited and organized the dialogue in a way that made the information clear and interesting	The student edited and organized the dialogue in a way that made the information clear	The student edited and organized the dialogue, but the information was not as clear or as interesting as it could have been	The student did not edit or organize the dialogue

MAKING A PAINTING/DRAWING

Category	4	3	2	1
Graphics—clarity	The graphics are all in focus, and the content easily viewed and identified from six feet away	Most graphics are in focus, and the content easily viewed and identified from six feet away	Most graphics are in focus, and the content is easily viewed and identified from four feet away	Many graphics are not clear or are too small
Graphics—originality	Several of the graphics used in the artwork reflect an exceptional degree of student creativity in their creation and/or display	One or two of the graphics used in the artwork reflect student creativity in their creation and/or display	The graphics are made by the student, but are based on the designs or ideas of others	No graphics made by the student are included
Significance	All items of importance in the artwork are clearly related to the topic	Almost all items of importance in the artwork are clearly related to the topic	Several items of importance in the artwork are clearly related to the topic	Items are not related to the topic or are not mentioned
Required elements	The artwork includes all required elements, as well as additional information	All required elements are included in the artwork	All but one of the required elements are included in the artwork	Several required elements were missing
Content—accuracy	At least seven accurate facts are portrayed in the artwork	Five to six accurate facts are portrayed in the artwork	Three or four accurate facts are portrayed in the artwork	Fewer than three accurate facts are portrayed in the artwork

SONG

Category	4	3	2	1
Flow and rhythm	All verses sound natural and are easy on the ear when read aloud; each verse is clear and has an obvious emphasis	Almost all verses sound natural and are easy on the ear when read aloud, but one or two are stiff and awkward or difficult to understand	Most verses sound natural and are easy on the ear when read aloud, but several are stiff and awkward or are difficult to understand	The verses are difficult to read aloud because they sound awkward, are distractingly repetitive, or difficult to understand
Sequencing (organization)	Verses are placed in a logical order, and the way they are presented effectively keeps the interest of the listener	Verses are placed in a logical order, but the way they are presented /introduced sometimes makes the song less interesting	Some verses are not in a logical or expected order, and this distracts the listener	Many verses are not in a logical or expected order, and there is little sense that the song is organized
Accuracy of facts (content)	All supporting facts are reported accurately	Almost all supporting facts are reported accurately	Most supporting facts are reported accurately	No facts are reported, or most are inaccurately reported

(continued)

Category	4	3	2	1
Grammar and spelling (conventions)	The writer makes no errors in grammar or spelling that distract the reader from the content	The writer makes one or two errors in grammar or spelling that distract the reader from the content	The writer makes three or four errors in grammar or spelling that distract the reader from the content	The writer makes more than four errors in grammar or spelling that distract the reader from the content
Penmanship (conventions)	The paper is neatly written or typed with no distracting corrections	The paper is neatly written or typed with one or two distracting corrections (e.g., dark cross-outs, bumpy white-out, words written over)	The writing is generally readable, but the reader has to exert quite a bit of effort to figure out some of the words	Many words are unreadable, or there are several distracting corrections

FINGERPRINT SHEET FOR _____

Right Thumb	Right Forefinger	Right Middle Finger	Right Ring Finger	Right Pinkie
Left Thumb	Left Forefinger	Left Middle Finger	Left Ring Finger	Left Pinkie

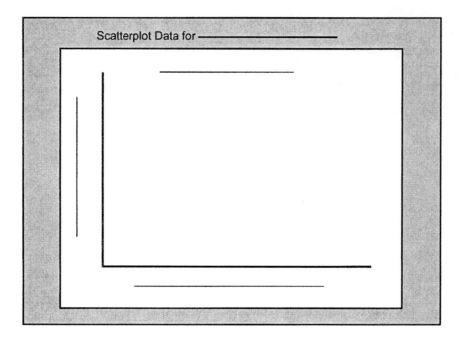

Scatterplot Data for ———————————————

TIC-TAC-TOE CHART: MYSTERY ACTIVITIES

Poster	Painting or Drawing	Song
Comic Book	Written Report	Movie or Skit
PowerPoint	Interview	Letter

Student Name: _____

My choices for the Mystery Activities are (1) the written report, (2)
_____, and (3) _____.

Parent signature_____

Teacher signature_____

GROUP PLAN FORM

Group members: _____

Our plan is to take all the fingerprints and _____

_____

_____

_____

_____ will have the task(s) of _____

_____

_____

_____ will have the task(s) of _____

_____

_____

_____ will have the task(s) of _____

_____

_____

_____ will have the task(s) of _____

_____

_____

Teacher signature of approval: _____

GROUP ROLE SHEET

Artist

Role: The artist will use the tools to create a scale map of the crime scene, aided by the other group members.

Supplier

Role: The supplier will collect all the tools and supplies needed for the artist to draw the scale map. The supplier will also participate in aiding the artist's drawings.

Supervisor

Role: The supervisor will contribute to the making of the scale map by aiding the artist's drawings, as well as keep everyone in the group participating.

Role	Day 1	Day 2	Day 3
Artist			
Supplier			
Supervisor			
(Artist #2)			

Appendix B

Integrated Thematic Unit Examples

AN EXAMPLE OF A THEMATIC
LESSON PLAN—A UNIT ON ANIMALS

Lesson Title: The Best Pet for Me

Day(s): 5

Grade Level: Third

Goal: After the unit, the students will demonstrate in measurable ways an understanding of animals and the proper care they require (behavioral).

Student Materials:

Picture or information about their own pets

Paper, pencils, crayons, markers

Paper/cards to write thank you notes to veterinarian

Internet, library, classroom books/pet folders or magazines to research pets/animals

Construction paper for "Pets" folder and characteristics chart

Tally chart, bar/circle graph forms

Index cards, loose-leaf ring binder for spelling words

"Pet Needs Wheel" form

Butterfly: adding detail graphic organizer form for story web

"Pet Costs" form and pet pictures

Paper half lined, half blank to write illustrated book about their pets.

Letters for making words activity—veterinarian

Teacher Resources:
Books to read to class:

- *Daddy Could I Have an Elephant?* by Jake Wolf
- *The Day Jimmy's Boa Ate the Wash* by Tinka Hakes Noble
- *How Much Is That Doggy in the Window?* by Seth Godin
- *The Stray Dog* or *Socrates* by Mark Simont
- *Dear Mrs. LaRue* by Mark Teague

Indiana third-grade standards
Attached Internet sites
Pet/animal books borrowed from library
Pet folders for each type of pet students are researching—in class
   resource—multiple documents
Local veterinarian to visit class
Video about pets—"Paws, Claws, Feathers, & Fins"
Video about veterinarians—"I Wanna Work with Animals"
Pet store ads and pet costs info from Internet
Overhead of words to "Pet Shop" song adapted from "How Much Is That
   Doggy in the Window?"
Bulletin board to display students' pet pictures and other project work
Letter to parents requesting picture or stuffed animal representing stu-
   dent's pet
Snacks for pet snack party

Objective/Standard(s):

A. Analyze the costs incurred in pet ownership as evidenced by an oral or
   visual presentation.
   Social Studies
      3.1.7 Use a variety of community resources, such as libraries, mu-
         seums, and county historians, to gather information about the lo-
         cal community.
      3.4.8 Illustrate how people compare benefits and costs when mak-
         ing choices and decisions as consumers and producers.
   Language Arts
      3.7.8 Clarify and enhance oral presentations through the use of ap-
         propriate props, including objects, pictures, and charts.

Mathematics

    3.2.1 Add and subtract whole numbers up to one thousand with or without regrouping, using relevant properties of the number system.

    3.2.2 Solve problems involving numeric equations.

    3.5.11 Use play or real money to decide whether there is enough money to make a purchase.

B. Evaluate the characteristics of good household pets as evidenced by children's literary piece on pets, a PowerPoint presentation, or a cognitive map of characteristics.

Science

    3.4.1 Demonstrate that a great variety of living things can be sorted into groups in many ways using various features, such as how they look, where they live, and how they act, to decide which things belong to which group.

    3.5.3 Construct tables and graphs to show how the values of one quantity are related to values of another.

Social Studies

    3.5.5 Use community resources, such as museums, libraries, historic buildings, and other landmarks, to gather cultural information about the community.

Mathematics

    3.1.13 Interpret data displayed in a circle graph, and answer questions about the situation.

    3.3.7 Plot and label whole numbers on a number line up to ten.

Language Arts

    3.2.1 Use titles, tables of contents, chapter headings, a glossary, or an index to locate information in text.

    3.2.2 Ask questions and support answers by connecting prior knowledge with literal information from the text.

    3.2.5 Distinguish the main idea and supporting details in expository (informational) text.

    3.2.6 Locate appropriate and significant information from the text, including problems and solutions.

    3.4.1 Find ideas for writing stories and descriptions in conversations with others, and in books, magazines, school textbooks, or on the Internet.

3.5.2 Write descriptive pieces about people, places, things, or experiences that develop a unified main idea; use details to support the main idea.

3.5.3 Write personal, persuasive, and formal letters, thank-you notes, and invitations that show awareness of the knowledge and interests of the audience and establish a purpose and context; include the date, proper salutation, body, closing, and signature.

3.6.1 Write legibly in cursive, leaving space between letters in a word, between words in a sentence, and between words and the edges of the paper.

3.6.2 Write correctly complete sentences of statement, command, question, or exclamation, with final punctuation: declarative, imperative, interrogative, exclamatory.

3.7.9 Read prose and poetry aloud with fluency, rhythm, and timing, using appropriate changes in the tone of voice to emphasize important passages of the text being read.

3.7.14 Make descriptive presentations that use concrete sensory details to set forth and support unified impressions of people, places, things, or experiences.

Introduction/Overview

Pre-unit request: Send note home to parents requesting a photograph or stuffed animal representing the student's pet(s), which will be returned at end of lesson.

Read book to class—*Daddy Could I Have an Elephant?* by Jake Wolf

Procedures/Activities

DAY 1

1. Engage the class in a discussion on pets.

   • Define—what is a pet? Write definitions and defining characteristics on board or overhead.

   • Have students share picture or stuffed animal representing a pet that they/their families currently own. Display photographs on bulletin board.

- Draw a tally chart on the board/overhead listing the types of pets the students currently have (math). In a separate column, tally the pets each student would like to have. Have students chart information with you. Allow the students to select one to three pets. Record each student's choices to assist in assigning pets. See attached tally charts adapted from "Our Pet Data" at http://ll.terc.edu/Pets.
- Later or next day, have the students draw a circle and/or bar graph from the results of the above tally chart(s) (math).

2. Have students make a folder to keep pet-related work/papers.
   - Use an 18 × 11 piece of construction paper folded in half.
   - Label the front "Pets" with the student's name.
3. Discuss what animals would make good pets and why or why not.
4. Review with students things to consider when selecting a pet. See attached questions adapted from "Care for Animals" at www.avma.org/careforanimals/animatedjourneys/petselection/consider.asp. Provide copy of questions for students to take notes.
5. Show video about pets—"Paws, Claws, Feathers, & Fins." Let students share things from the video.

DAY 2

1. Read book to class—*The Day Jimmy's Boa Ate the Wash* by Trinka Hakes Noble.
2. Have students select their pet or assign a pet from the list the class created from above Day 1 discussion.
3. Provide students time in class to become familiar with their pets. Classroom resources would include a selection of books about pets and a folder for each student specific to their pet. Folders should contain information from the Internet, pictures of the animal, and activities to learn about the pet. Students are borrowing this folder for the entire week for research and to hold all of their specific pet writing papers.
4. Prewriting activity—Pet Needs Wheel—Model for students how to illustrate their pet's basic needs on the Pet Needs Wheel. Needs addressed are shelter, food, water, exercise, and love. Display work on bulletin board.

Alternative prewriting art activity—Using construction paper, fold paper to have four flaps. On the outside square, write the name of the animal/pet and the student's name. On the outside of the flaps, write "Habitat" (food, shelter, space), "Appearance," "Actions," "Favorite Fact about Pet." On the inside of the flaps, list at least three facts/characteristics. On the inside square, under the flaps draw a picture of the pet.

5. Using the overhead, guide students to fill out the butterfly graphic organizer. This will provide them with the questions to research their pets and the foundation for their story map or web. Basic questions students need to research, answer, and later include in their story are
   a. My pet and its name
   b. What it looks like
   c. Where it lives (habitat, shelter, space)
   d. What it eats (food, water)
   e. How it moves and acts
   f. How much it costs (to buy and to care for)
   g. Why it is a good pet for me
   h. My favorite fact about my animal

DAY 3

1. Read book to class—*How Much Is That Doggy in the Window?* by Seth Godin.
2. Using the overhead, read "Pet Shop" song words to students. Assign a group to each section of the song. Have fun with the students singing and doing actions to the song.
3. Using the overhead, model for students transferring information from the butterfly graphic organizer to a beginning-middle-end graphic organizer to prepare them to start writing their pet literary piece.
4. Play some quiet music and have students write the beginning draft of their pet story. Allow time for them to use in-class pet resource information to continue collecting facts and information about their pets.
5. Show video about veterinarians—*I Wanna Work with Animals*.

6. Briefly discuss the video with class. Announce that a veterinarian will be visiting the classroom that afternoon. Have each student write a question on an index card that he or she would like to ask the veterinarian during his or her visit in the classroom.
7. Veterinarian Visit
   • Review classroom rules and visitor rules with students.
   • Welcome the veterinarian and have him or her discuss what animals would make a good pet and the care and costs involved in owning a pet. Make a list on the board or flip chart. Have the students copy the information into their writing journals.
   • Have students write thank-you letters to the veterinarian and illustrate the pet they are researching.

DAY 4

1. Read book to class—*The Stray Dog* or *Socrates*.
2. Making words—lead class in a making-words activity using "veterinarian."
3. Using Pet Store Ads, Costs of Pet Supplies info from www.csmonitor.com and in-class pet resources, have students create a mini collage poster showing their pet, pet supplies and costs, and other costs involved in caring for their pet.

   Another or alternative activity—Assign each student a budget amount that they have to spend on their pet in a year. Using the same pet information resources, use chart examples from www.spca.bc.ca/petcost.htm for students to record "What's Having a Pet Going to Cost?" You could also allow students to work in pairs and take turns paying for pet supplies and veterinarian expenses with play money.
4. Have students continue writing their pet story (beginning-middle-end). Proofread their draft or have another student proofread it. Have students begin revising, adding more details, and rewriting. If there is time, have them write the final draft and begin illustrating their story. Allow more advanced students to use the computer lab to publish their story.

DAY 5

1. Read book to class—*Dear Mrs. LaRue* and discuss with class.

2. Have students complete the writing, revising, rewriting, and illustrating of their pet story.

   Another or alternative activity—Have the students make a "Lost Pet" ad using the information they have already collected about their pet. Display ads on the bulletin board or outside of the room in the hallway or display case.

3. Have students evaluate bar graphs created earlier in week. Working in pairs, have students complete the "Pets—Mathematic Problem Solving" worksheet.

4. Author's chair—once or twice during the day, allow students to read or show their illustrated pet stories to the class.

   Additional (optional) Daily Activities:

   Spelling words—words related to pets

   Use index cards (front/back) to write spelling words, do ABC order, write word-wall words' definitions and sentences for each word. Use loose-leaf ring to hold cards together.

   In writing journal—"What am I?"—Write four sentences about a type of pet on the chalkboard each day. Have students copy information in their journal and then guess what type of pet is described. A fun modification would be to have the students make up "What am I?" cards for other students in the class to guess.

   Pets word search for spelling words and/or for their specific pet.

   Read one to two chapters to class from a pet-related chapter book.

   Daily oral language—Edit one to three sentences about pets each day. Test will be given on last day of week (Friday).

   For specials (art, music, gym, library), request that these teachers tie in pets to their activities this week.

5. Closure:

   Author's chair—finish students' reading or showing their illustrated pet stories to the class.

   Discuss common characteristics between the pets the students researched and reported on. Optional: name groups that the pets/animals with these common characteristics belong to.

   Optional: pet snack party—show a pet bloopers video to class and share snacks (i.e., puppy chow, carrot sticks, and so forth).

Evaluation/Assessment

C. Analyze the costs incurred in pet ownership as evidenced by an oral/visual presentation.

Social Studies

> 3.1.7 Use a variety of community resources, such as libraries, museums, and county historians, to gather information about the local community. *This element will be evidenced by a local veterinarian visit, pet store ads, library books utilized in class to research pets, using the pet folders in class.*
>
> 3.4.8 Illustrate how people compare benefits and costs when making choices and decisions as consumers and producers. *This element will be evidenced by the student's mini pet collage poster and chart of pet costs in a year.*

Language Arts

> 3.7.8 Clarify and enhance oral presentations through the use of appropriate props, including objects, pictures, and charts. *This element will be evidenced by the student's mini pet collage poster.*

Mathematics

> *These elements will be evidenced by the student's mini pet collage poster, chart of pet costs in a year, and activities using play money to pay for pet supplies and services.*
>
> 3.2.1 Add and subtract whole numbers up to one thousand with or without regrouping, using relevant properties of the number system.
>
> 3.3.2 Solve problems involving numeric equations.
>
> 3.5.11 Use play or real money to decide whether there is enough money to make a purchase.

D. Evaluate the characteristics of good household pets as evidenced by children's literary pieces on pets, a PowerPoint presentation, or a cognitive map of characteristics.

Science

> 3.4.1 Demonstrate that a great variety of living things can be sorted into groups in many ways using various features, such as how they look, where they live, and how they act, to decide which things belong to which group. *This element will be evidenced by class discussion on common characteristics of pets.*

3.5.3 Construct tables and graphs to show how the values of one quantity are related to the values of another. *This element will be evidenced by the pets tally charts and bar/circle graphs created from the tally charts.*

Social Studies

3.5.5 Use community resources, such as museums, libraries, historic buildings, and other landmarks, to gather cultural information about the community. *This element will be evidenced by the veterinarian visit, using pet store ads for pet cost information, and using library books.*

Mathematics

3.1.13 Interpret data displayed in a circle graph and answer questions about the situation. *This element will be evidenced by completing the "Pets—Mathematic Problem Solving" worksheet.*

3.3.7 Plot and label whole numbers on a number line up to ten. *This element will be evidenced by completing the pets bar graph.*

Language Arts

3.2.1 Use titles, tables of contents, chapter headings, a glossary, or an index to locate information in text. *This element will be evidence by students using informational pet books in the classroom to research pets.*

3.2.2 Ask questions and support answers by connecting prior knowledge with literal information from the text. *This element will be evidenced by researching pets and writing questions for the veterinarian.*

3.2.5 Distinguish the main idea and supporting details in expository (informational) text. *This element will be evidenced by the completed butterfly graphic organizer and children's literary pieces on pets.*

3.2.6 Locate appropriate and significant information from the text, including problems and solutions. *This element will be evidenced by students using informational pet books in the classroom to research pet.*

3.4.1 Find ideas for writing stories and descriptions in conversations with others, books, magazines, school textbooks, or on the Internet. *This element will be evidenced by participation in classroom discussions and researching pets.*

3.5.2 Write descriptive pieces about people, places, things, or experiences that develop a unified main idea; use details to support the main idea. *This element will be evidenced by children's literary pieces on pets.*

3.5.3 Write personal, persuasive, and formal letters, thank-you notes, and invitations that show awareness of the knowledge and interests of the audience and establish a purpose and context; include the date, proper salutation, body, closing, and signature. *This element will be evidenced by the students' written thank-you notes to the veterinarian.*

3.6.1 Write legibly in cursive, leaving space between letters in a word, between words in a sentence, and between words and the edges of the paper. *This element will be evidenced by the final written draft of the students' literacy pieces on pets.*

3.6.2 Write correctly complete sentences of statement, command, question, or exclamation, with final punctuation: declarative, imperative, interrogative, exclamatory. *This element will be evidenced by editing and correcting pet sentences in daily oral language exercises.*

3.7.9 Read prose and poetry aloud with fluency, rhythm, and timing, using appropriate changes in the tone of voice to emphasize important passages of the text being read. *This element will be evidenced by students reading their illustrated pet story aloud in front of the class.*

3.7.14 Make descriptive presentations that use concrete sensory details to set forth and support unified impressions of people, places, things, or experiences. *This element will be evidenced by the Pets Needs Wheel and the illustrated pet story.*

Rubric

	Beginning 1	Progressing 2	Proficient 3	Advanced 4	Score
Graphs of Classroom Pets	Has half of the information graphed correctly	Has three-quarters of the information graphed correctly	Has all of the information graphed correctly	The graph is complete, neat, and labeled correctly	
Thank-You Letter to Veterinarian	Has a greeting, one to two complete sentences, an ending, and an attempted drawing of pet	Has a greeting, three to four complete sentences, an ending, and a complete drawing of pet	Has a greeting, five or more sentences, and an ending, and it is neat, with a complete drawing of pet	Has a greeting, five or more sentences in paragraph form, an ending, and an enhanced drawing of pet	
Literary Piece on Pets	Has two to three pages with illustrations and basic questions answered about pet	Has four to five pages with illustrations and basic questions answered about pet	Has six to seven pages with illustrations and basic questions answered about pet	Has seven or more pages with illustrations and basic questions answered about pet	
Cognitive Map of Characteristics	Lists one to two characteristics for each type of pet	Lists three to four characteristics for each type of pet	Lists five to six characteristics for each type of pet	Lists six or more characteristics for each type of pet	

CLASSROOM PETS TALLY SHEET

#	Type of Pet	How Many?	
		Currently own	*Would like to own*
1			
2			
3			
4			
5			
6			
7			
8			
9			
10			
11			
12			
13			
14			
15			
16			
17			
18			
19			
20			
Total			

I HAVE A . . .

Name _____　　　Date _____

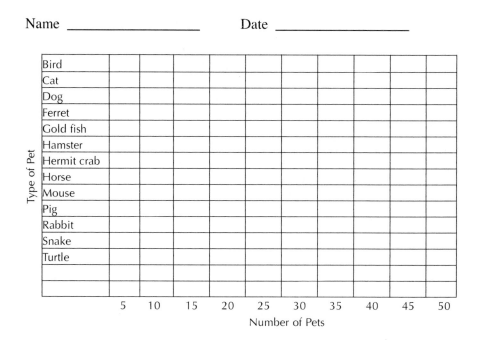

Type of Pet

| | Bird |
| Cat |
| Dog |
| Ferret |
| Gold fish |
| Hamster |
| Hermit crab |
| Horse |
| Mouse |
| Pig |
| Rabbit |
| Snake |
| Turtle |

5　　10　　15　　20　　25　　30　　35　　40　　45　　50

Number of Pets

I WISH I HAD A . . .

Name _____   Date _____

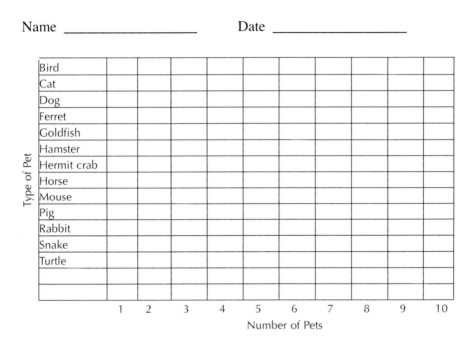

Type of Pet

	Bird										
	Cat										
	Dog										
	Ferret										
	Goldfish										
	Hamster										
	Hermit crab										
	Horse										
	Mouse										
	Pig										
	Rabbit										
	Snake										
	Turtle										

     1   2   3   4   5   6   7   8   9   10

Number of Pets

PETS: MATHEMATIC PROBLEM SOLVING

1. How many dogs does the class have? _____
2. There are _____ more cats than dogs.
3. How many fish does the class own? _____
4. How many animals have feathers? _____
5. How many total pets does the class own? _____
6. Which pet does most of the class own? _____
7. How many different pets are there? _____
8. There are less _____ than _____.
9. How many students do NOT own a pet? _____
10. How many pets are owned by only one person? _____

THINGS TO CONSIDER WHEN SELECTING A PET:

1. Do you have room for a pet?

2. What do you like to do?

3. Where are you during the day?

4. Can you have pets where you live?

5. How much will your pet cost?

6. What tasks will you have to do to take care of your pet?

7. What supplies do you need for your pet?

    • What kind of food will it eat?

    • Does it need water?

    • Where will it sleep?

    • Will it need toys to play with?

8. Is anyone at your home all day to take care of your pet?

9. How do you find out if your pet is healthy?

10. What do you have to do to get your house ready for your pet to come home with you?

PETS: SPELLING/VOCABULARY WORDS

1. Pet: Any tamed animal that is kept as a companion and cared for with love

2. Animals: Living things that are not plants

3. Home: The place where you or your pet lives

4. Cage:

5. Food: What people or animals eat and need to live

6. Water:

7. Care:

8. Money:

9. Groom:

10. Shots:

11. Nose:

12. Tail:

13. Paw:

14. Fur:

15. Owner:

SPELLING: PETS

```
B  S  A  L  O  M  S  S  W  V  A  W  A  P  Z
F  I  T  Y  Z  H  O  E  F  R  G  O  P  S  A
U  H  Q  E  O  M  G  N  U  I  K  E  U  P  C
A  L  G  T  P  A  N  S  E  S  N  M  V  V  M
H  M  S  C  C  E  C  U  F  Y  J  O  E  R  M
R  E  N  W  O  J  C  A  J  B  S  H  S  V  A
R  A  L  H  F  U  X  K  R  L  F  O  O  D  M
R  U  Z  W  A  T  E  R  A  E  B  U  A  P  T
O  P  F  M  S  E  K  M  G  I  J  U  N  B  J
Q  A  O  T  D  O  I  Y  R  A  J  K  O  B  X
J  V  A  U  Z  N  M  H  O  B  O  Z  S  S  H
L  I  V  Q  A  J  Y  F  O  D  G  K  E  W  M
L  L  I  Y  V  X  V  A  M  A  G  D  I  Z  E
I  G  A  X  O  D  R  K  J  I  L  C  E  J  H
S  C  P  W  O  E  U  G  Q  N  I  A  P  C  I
```

ANIMALS	CAGE	CARE
FOOD	FUR	GROOM
HOME	MONEY	NOSE
OWNER	PAW	PETS
SHOTS	TAIL	WATER

PETS: DOL—DAILY ORAL LANGUAGE

1. my cat sammy chased the mose

---

2. how much is that dogy in the window

---

3. a hamster neds food water and a cag

---

4. miss mccartys dog weigs five pounds

---

5. does ms. woods really lik cats

---

6. the sily snake snuck a snck

---

7. first you pik a pet besd for you

---

8. watch out for thate spidder

---

9. wat animal has wings

---

10. the tirtle hide inside his shel

PETS: MATH (GRAPH) VOCABULARY WORDS

1. Tally mark: A mark used to record votes or other items

2. Bar graph: A graph that uses bars to show data

3. Title: Tells what type of data is graphed

4. Scale: The numbers that show the units used on a bar graph

5. Description: Tells what type of data each bar represents

PET NEEDS WHEEL

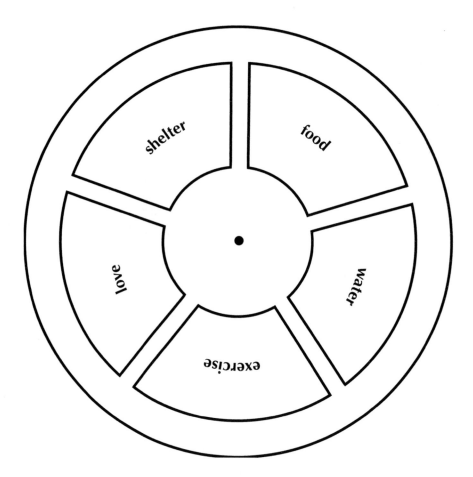

An Example of
Learning via Service

STANLEY HALL ENRICHMENT CENTER
SERVICE-LEARNING PROGRAM:
SERVICE-LEARNING CONTRACT TEMPLATE

Part I: Interests

1. What needs do you see in your community?

   As a volunteer last year at St. Mary's Medical Center, I had noticed that the Alzheimer's Unit had a need for volunteers to assist with their patients. I also have an interest in working with an adult population. Since I have already volunteered for the hospital, I thought it might be a nice way to thank them for allowing me to learn from them in the past.

Part II: Proposed Idea for Project

1. Below, write out a paragraph defining the project that you might be interested in performing. Be sure to include (1) the site of the project, (2) a contact person's name and number, (3) what you propose to do while on site, and (4) how this relates to the course credits you need.

   The project I would like to create is a curriculum that I can use with Alzheimer's patients in their inpatient nursing home program. St. Mary's indicated that the people who live on this unit often have problems with losing thinking abilities and memory. What I would like to do is to create a program that I could run with them two days a week. This program would include memory tasks, hand-eye coordination activities, as well as socialization and group building activities. I would gather the tools to facilitate these groups, including word tiles, memory game cards, link cubes for coordination, and bingo. We will also be building toward doing hands-on equations with the patients. I will also facilitate a current events article time using Stuart Elliot's *Courier Press* articles that are written to nursing home members. During group time they will also be participating in some physical activities to improve stamina.

2. How do you feel that this project will fulfill a community need?

St. Mary's really needs assistance with their patients. By providing them with this support I will be helping them to meet the needs of the patients and giving them supplies that they could not purchase on their own. I plan on writing a grant to obtain the necessary activity supplies.

Part III: Class Credit Required

1. What class credits do you need?

I need credit in English 12-2, economics, and math—Business Math Semester 2.

2. How do you propose that service-learning could help you to obtain these credits?

By writing up my results of the project in my portfolio and facilitating the current events article discussion, I will gain insight into literature and improve my writing abilities. Information on economics will be worked on as I complete a budget and I am working within a grant experience. I also think that I will gain insight into financing and the production of goods, the American labor force (as I understand what happens to workers once they retire), and how government spending affects hospitals. Information on business math will be reviewed as I work on pricing supplies, identifying expenses, creating a budget, and borrowing money.

Part IV: Relationship to State Standards

English 12-2

12.2.1   Analyze both the features and the rhetorical (communication) devices of different types of public documents, such as policy statements, speeches, or debates, and the way in which authors use those features and devices. *This standard will be evidenced through the reflective essay writings and journaling describing my experiences working with the clients.*

12.2.3   Verify and clarify facts presented in several types of expository texts by using a variety of consumer, workplace, public, and historical documents. *This standard will be evidenced through the reflective essay writings I create using information taken from a variety of sources, including information from St. Mary's Medical Center.*

12.2.5   Make reasonable assertions about an author's arguments by using hypothetical situations or elements of the text to defend and clarify interpretations. *This standard will be evidenced through the reflective essay writings I create using information taken from a variety of sources, including information from St. Mary's Medical Center.*

12.4.1   Engage in conversations with peers and the teacher to plan writing, to evaluate how well writing achieves its purposes, and to explain personal reactions to the task. *This standard will be evidenced through the reflective essay writings I create using information taken from a variety of sources, including information from St. Mary's Medical Center, as well as my meetings with Dr. Mike.*

12.4.2   Demonstrate an understanding of the elements of discourse, such as purpose, speaker, audience, and form, when completing narrative, expository, persuasive, or descriptive writing assignments. *This standard will be evidenced through the reflective essay writings I create using information taken from a variety of sources, including information from St. Mary's Medical Center.*

12.4.3   Use point of view, characterization, style, and related elements for specific rhetorical (communication) and aesthetic (artistic) purposes. *This standard will be evidenced through the reflective essay writings I create using information taken from a variety of sources, including information from St. Mary's Medical Center.*

12.4.6   Use language in creative and vivid ways to establish a specific tone. *This standard will be evidenced through the reflective essay writings I create using information taken from a variety of sources, in-cluding information from St. Mary's Medical Center.*

12.4.7 Develop presentations by using clear research questions and cre-ative and critical research strategies, such as field studies, oral histories, interviews, experiments, and Internet sources. *This standard will be ev-idenced through the reflective essay writings I create using information taken from a variety of sources, including information from St. Mary's Medical Center, as well as my meetings with Dr. Mike.*

12.4.8 Use systematic strategies to organize and record information, such as anecdotal scripting or annotated bibliographies. *This standard will be evidenced through the reflective essay writings I create using in-formation taken from a variety of sources, including information from St. Mary's Medical Center.*

12.4.9 Use technology for all aspects of creating, revising, editing, and publishing. *This standard will be evidenced through the reflective essay writings I create using information taken from a variety of sources, in-cluding information from St. Mary's Medical Center.*

12.4.10 Accumulate, review, and evaluate written work to determine its strengths and weaknesses and to set goals as a writer. *This standard will be evidenced through the reflective essay writings I create using infor-mation taken from a variety of sources, including information from St. Mary's Medical Center, as well as my meetings with Dr. Mike.*

12.4.11 Revise, edit, and proofread one's own writing, as well as that of others, using an editing checklist. *This standard will be evidenced through the reflective essay writings I create using information taken from a variety of sources, including information from St. Mary's Med-ical Center, as well as my meetings with Dr. Mike.*

12.4.12 Further develop unique writing style and voice, improve sen-tence variety, and enhance subtlety of meaning and tone in ways that are consistent with the purpose, audience, and form of writing. *This standard will be evidenced through the reflective essay writings I cre-ate using information taken from a variety of sources, including infor-mation from St. Mary's Medical Center, as well as my meetings with Dr. Mike.*

12.5.3 Write reflective compositions that explore the significance of personal experiences, events, conditions, or concerns by using rhetori-cal strategies, including narration, description, exposition, and persuasion. *This standard will be evidenced through the reflective essay writings I create using information taken from a variety of sources, including information from St. Mary's Medical Center, as well as my meetings with Dr. Mike.*

12.5.6   Use varied and extended vocabulary, appropriate for specific forms and topics. *This standard will be evidenced through the reflective essay writings I create using information taken from a variety of sources, including information from St. Mary's Medical Center, as well as my meetings with Dr. Mike.*

12.5.8   Deliver multimedia presentations that combine text, images, and sound, and draw information from many sources, including television broadcasts, videos, films, newspapers, magazines, CD-ROMs, the Internet, and electronic media-generated images. *This standard will be evidenced through the reflective essay writings I create using information taken from a variety of sources, including information from St. Mary's Medical Center, as well as my meetings with Dr. Mike. This standard will also be evidenced as I complete my portfolio of my project.*

12.6.1   Demonstrate control of grammar, diction, paragraph and sentence structure, and understanding of English usage. *This standard will be evidenced through the reflective essay writings and journaling describing my experiences working with the clients.*

12.6.2   Produce writing that shows accurate spelling and correct punctuation and capitalization. *This standard will be evidenced through the reflective essay writings and journaling describing my experiences working with the clients.*

12.6.3   Apply appropriate manuscript conventions in writing including title page presentation, pagination, spacing and margins, and integration of source and support material by citing sources within the text, using direct quotations, and paraphrasing. *This standard will be evidenced through the reflective essay writings and journaling describing my experiences working with the clients.*

12.7.1   Summarize a speaker's purpose and point of view, discuss, and ask questions to draw interpretations of the speaker's content and attitude toward the subject. *This standard will be evidenced through the reflective essay writings I create using information taken from a variety of sources, including information from St. Mary's Medical Center.*

12.7.4   Use logical, ethical, and emotional appeals that enhance a specific tone and purpose. *This standard will be evidenced through the reflective essay writings and journaling describing my experiences working with the clients.*

12.7.16   Deliver reflective presentations that explore the significance of personal experiences, events, conditions, or concerns, using appropriate speech strategies, including narration, description, exposition, and persuasion. *This standard will be evidenced through the reflective essay writings and journaling describing my experiences working with the clients.*

Economics

Chapter 11   "Financing and Producing Goods"
Chapter 13   "The American Labor Force"
Chapter 17   "Government Spends, Collects, and Owes"

Business Math Semester 2

16a   Pricing
19.2   Business expenses
21.3   Borrowing
22.4   Budgeting

Part V: Assessment and Evaluation

1. How do you propose that your service-learning project be evaluated? Be sure to (1) identify three goals for the project and (2) check off the format that the final project is to take.

What goals will be met by this project?

Goal 1: After this project, I will be able to better understand the disease of Alzheimer's, as evidenced by a review in my portfolio of information related to the illness.

Goal 2: After this project, I will be able to better understand what I can do to assist Alzheimer's patients, as evidenced by my completion of group activities to build memory, hand-eye coordination, and socialization skills.

Goal 3: After this project, I will feel more comfortable being with Alzheimer's patients, as evidenced by my ability to work with this population.

☐ Portfolio   ☐ Persuasive Speech to SHEC Peers
☐ Informational Presentation   ☐ Presentation to younger students
   to SHEC Peers   ☐ Alternative format (write below)
☐ Essay

2. How will this project help you to have a greater appreciation for your subject area? How will this project help to teach you more about your area of interest?

By writing up my results of the project in my portfolio and facilitating the current events article discussion, I will gain insight into literature and improve my writing abilities. Information on economics will be worked on as I complete a budget and I am working within a grant experience. I also think that I will gain insight into financing and the production of goods, the American Labor Force (as I understand what happens to workers once they retire), and how government spending affects hospitals. Information on business math will be reviewed as I work on pricing supplies, identifying expenses, creating a budget, and borrowing money.

3. Evaluation—Bloom's Taxonomy: Describe below the area(s) of Bloom's taxonomy that will be met by your project (this should be completed with the assistance of your USI mentor).

• Knowledge—general information about Alzheimer's
• Comprehension—knowledge that can be used to facilitate groups
• Application—use of information on Alzheimer's to establish group activities
• Synthesis—organization of project and creation of portfolio of performance

Part VI: Timeline

This project is to be completed by this date: Spring Break—March 21, 2003. Below, create a timeline with specific dates when (1) you plan to prepare certain parts of your project, (2) you plan to complete certain parts of your project, and (3) you plan to present finished products related to your product/project.

December	Make contact with St. Mary's Medical Center
	Complete paperwork to volunteer
January	Create curriculum for groups
	Begin to organize portfolio
	Start work with groups by end of month
February	Run groups
	Continue work on portfolio
March	Complete groups
	Complete portfolio by March 21, 2003

Part VI: Budget

List below any expenses you might have while performing your project. Identify which items will require reimbursement. If connections are not obvious, please explain the reason for the expense.

See attached budget page.

In order for this project to be approved, you must meet with your USI service-learning mentor, as well as a service-learning coordinator (course teachers, principal) and get approval on the project specifics. Also, this document must be typed up formally and be signed by (1) you, (2) your parent (if you are under the age of eighteen years), (3) your teacher, and (4) principal. NO PROJECT WILL BE CONSIDERED WITHOUT THESE SIGNATURES!!

_____   _____

Student, SHEC   Candidate, USI Department
                                   of Teacher Education

_____   _____

Teacher   Teacher

_____   _____

Service-learning coordinator   Community contact person

_____   _____

Principal   Community contact person

_____

Parent (if student is under the age of eighteen years)

MENTOR/MENTEE APPLICATION
AND INFORMATION SHEET: STANLEY HALL
ENRICHMENT CENTER SERVICE-LEARNING PROGRAM

By submitting this form, you are agreeing to participate in a comprehensive service-learning project. This process pairs a University of Southern Indiana teacher-education candidate with a student at Stanley Hall Enrichment Center. Each person is required to participate in a variety of activities. Specifically, candidates and students will meet each week to review the project, its progress, how the standards are being met, and work to meet course requirements (both the requirements of candidates at USI and the requirements of students at SHEC).

Name _____   Age _____

School _____

Phone _____   E-mail _____

Best time to contact _____

1. Which time would best serve your needs in pairing you with a mentor/mentee?

    Students at SHEC should choose whichever shift they are scheduled to be at Stanley Hall. All students participating in the service-learning experience will be expected to be free at this time on Thursdays to meet with SHEC teachers and Dr. Slavkin to review service-learning projects throughout the semester.

2. Mentees (SHEC student): What credits will you be working on?

    Mentors (USI candidates): What secondary education areas are you comfortable working with?

    _____
    _____
    _____

3. Tell a bit about who you are. _____

_____

_____

_____

4. What are your favorite parts of school? _____

_____

_____

_____

5. What challenges do you face as a student? _____

_____

_____

_____

SERVICE-LEARNING CONFERENCE PROGRESS SHEET: STANLEY HALL ENRICHMENT CENTER SERVICE-LEARNING PROGRAM

Mentor/Mentee _____

Teacher(s) _____

Date of meeting _____

Progress notes _____

_____

_____

_____

_____

Goals for next meeting _____

_____

_____

_____

_____

Expected date for next meeting _____

Strengths this week _____

Pitfalls to work on (issues or concerns) _____

Signatures:

_____   _____

Mentor signature   Mentee signature

_____   _____

Teacher signature   Teacher signature

SERVICE-LEARNING PROJECT LOG

Name _____

Project title _____

Date	Time	Comments

SERVICE-LEARNING QUESTIONNAIRE

Name _____

What projects were you involved with using service-learning?

☐ Indianapolis Conference   ☐ Reality Store
☐ River Watch   ☐ Canned food drive
☐ Deliveries to neighbors   ☐ Day of caring
☐ Campus cleanup   ☐ Blood drive
☐ SLICE class   ☐ Schnucks trip
☐ Early childhood center   ☐ Earth Day activities
☐ Nursing home work   ☐ Other group experience

Were you involved in any individual projects that you worked on with the help of a teacher or Dr. Slavkin?

☐ Yes   ☐ No

If yes, describe here:

_____

_____

_____

Were you involved in any small-group projects that you worked on with the help of a teacher or Dr. Slavkin?

☐ Yes   ☐ No

If yes, describe here:

_____

_____

_____

Have you received any class credits (teachers signed off on assignments) after completing a service-learning activity? If so, for what class and for how many credits/assignments?

Class(es) _____ Credit(s) _____ Assignments _____

References

Academic service-learning. (1997). Lansing, MI: Academic Service-Learning Grants Program—Eastern Michigan University.

Akerson, V. (2001). Teaching science when your principal says "teach language arts." *Science and Children* (April 2001): 42–47.

Alder, M. (2002). Assessment, evaluation, and curriculum redesign. Disney learning partnership workshop, at www.thirteen.org/edonline/concept2class/month7/explor_sub1.html. Accessed August 1, 2003.

Allen, R. (2003). The democratic aims of service-learning. *Educational Leadership* 60(6): 51–54.

Akarakiri, J. B. (1998). Utilization of creativity and innovation by the practice of new product planning in developing countries. *Psychologia: An International Journal* 6(2): 64–80

Amabile, T. M. (1983). *The social psychology of creativity.* New York: Springer Verlag.

———. (1996). Creativity in context: Update to the social psychology of creativity. Boulder, CO: Westview.

———. (1998). How to kill creativity. *Harvard Business Review* 76(5): 76–87.

Apthorp, H. S., DeBassige D'Amato, E., and Richardson, A. (2003). Effective standards-based practices for Native American students: A review of research literature (rev. ed.). Aurora, CO: McRel.

Archambault, F. X., Jr., Westberg, K. L., Brown, S. W., Hallmark, B. W., Zhang, W., and Baer, J. (1994). Divergent thinking is not a general trait: A multi-domain training experiment. *Creativity Research Journal* 7: 35–36.

Baer, J. (1998). The case for domain specificity of creativity. *Creativity Research Journal* 11: 173–77.

Banikowski, A. (1999). Strategies to enhance memory based on brain research. *Focus on Exceptional Children* 32(2): 1–15.

Barbian, J. (2002). A new line of defense. *Training* 39: 38.

Barron, F. (1969). *Creative person and creative process.* New York: Holt.

Barrows, H. S. (1986). A taxonomy of problem-based learning methods. *Medical Education* 20: 481–86.

Bartels, B. (1998). Integrating the disciplines in the elementary grades with problem-based learning. *The Delta Kappa Gamma Bulletin* 64: 9–14.

Baxter, P., and Shavelson, J. (1994). Science performance assessments: Benchmarks and surrogates. *International Journal of Educational Research* 21: 279–99.

Besemer, S. P., and O'Quin, K. (1986). Analyzing creative products: Refinement and test of a judging instrument. *Journal of Creative Behavior* 20: 115–26.

Beyer, L. (1996). Creating democratic classrooms: The struggle to integrate theory and practice. New York: Teachers College Press.

Billing, S. (1999). The impacts of service-learning on youth schools and communities: Research on K–12 school-based service-learning, 1990–1999, at www.Learningindeed.org [retrieved August 5, 2003].

Billing, S. H. (2000a). Research on K–12 school-based service-learning. *Phi Delta Kappan* 81: 658–65.

———. (2000b). Research on K–12 school-based service-learning. The evidence builds. *Phi Delta Kappan* 81(9): 658–64.

Blicbau, A. S., and Steiner, J. M. (1998). Fostering creativity through engineering projects. *European Journal of Engineering Education* 23: 55–65.

Bloland, P. A. (1987). Leisure as a campus resource for fostering student development. *Journal-of-Counseling-and-Development* 65: 291–94.

Bloom, B. S. (1956). Taxonomy of educational objectives: The classification of educational goals: Handbook I, cognitive domain. New York: Longmans, Green.

Bowman, V. E., and Boone, R. K. (1998). Enhancing the experience of community: Creativity in group work. *Journal for Specialists in Group Work* 23: 388–410.

Brandon, J. E., and Majumdar, B. (1997). An introduction and evaluation of problem-based learning in health professions education. *Family and Community Health* 20(1): 1–15.

Brandt, R. (1997). On using knowledge about our brain. *Educational Leadership* 54: 16–20.

———. (2003a). Don't blame the bell curve. *Leadership* 32(3): 18–19.

———. (2003b). Will the real standards-based education please stand up? *Leadership* 32(3): 17–21.

Bridges, E. M., and Hallinger, P. (1991, February). Problem-based learning in medical and managerial education. Paper presented at the Cognition and School Leadership Conference, Nashville, TN.

———. (1997). Using problem-based learning to prepare educational leaders. *Peabody Journal of Education* 72(6): 131–46.

Brower, R. (1999). Dangerous minds: Eminently creative people who spent time in jail. *Creativity Research Journal* 12: 3–13.

Brown, B. L. (1999). Self-efficacy beliefs and career development. *ERIC Digest No. 205*, at www.cete.org/acve/docgen.asp?tbl=digest&ID=89 [retrieved January 16, 2004].

Brown, B. Z. (1998). Service-learning: More than community service. Report No. 198. Columbus, OH: ERIC Clearinghouse on Adult Career and Vocational Education. (ERIC Document Reproduction Service No. ED 421 640).

Bruer, J. T. (1997). Education and the brain: A bridge too far. *Educational Researcher* 26: 4–16.

Bruner, J. (1976). From communication to language—A psychological perspective. *Cognition* 3(3): 255–87.

Burke, P. (1997). Where do the learning theories overlap? *Educational Leadership* 46: 30–31.

Burts, D., Hart, C., Charlesworth, R., DeWolf, D., Ray, J., Manuel, K., and Fleege, P. (1993). Developmental appropriateness of kindergarten programs and academic outcomes in first grade. *Journal of Research in Childhood Education* 8(1): 23–31.

Burts, C. H., Charlesworth, R., and Hart, C. H. (2002). Integrated developmentally appropriate curriculum. In Hart, Burts, and Charlesworth (Eds.) *Integrated curriculum and developmentally appropriate practice: Birth to age eight*. 1st ed. Albany, NY: State University of New York Press.

Butcher, D. A., and Hall, E. (1998). University students learn by helping unmotivated elementary school students: Team Lincoln. *Social Work in Education* 20(3): 191–203.

California Department of Education. (1999). *Service learning: Linking classrooms to communities*. Sacramento, CA: Report of the Superintendent's Service-Learning Task Force.

Cambron-McCabe, N., Lucas, T., Smith, B., Dutton, J., and Kleiner, A. (2000). *Schools that learn*. New York: Doubleday Dell Publishing Group, Inc.

Caprio, M. W. (1994). Easing into constructivism: Connecting meaningful learning with student experience. *Journal of College Science Teaching* 23: 210–12.

Caron, E. (2002). Standards-in-practice: How understanding teachers should guide standards-based reform. *Educational Horizons* 80(2): 72–74.

Carrington, C. H. (1987). Where are we? What is our challenge? And why? *Counseling Psychologist* 15: 271–74.

Case, R. (1991). The mind's staircase: Exploring the conceptual underpinnings of children's thought and knowledge. Hillsdale, NJ: Erlbaum.

Caulfield, J., and Kidd, S. (2000). Brain-based instruction in action. *Leadership* 58(3): 62–65.

Center for the Study of Politics and Government. (1998). *The benefits of service-learning.* Bloomington, IN: Indiana University Press.

Charlesworth, R. (1998). Developmentally appropriate practice is for everyone. *Childhood Education* 74(5) (annual theme issue): 274–82.

———. (2000). *Understanding child development.* 5th ed. Albany: Delmar, Thompson Learning Publishing.

Chessick, R. D. (1998). Creativity in the psychoanalytic process. *Journal of the American Academy of Psychoanalysis* 26: 209–22.

Clark, C. (2002). Unfolding narratives of service-learning: Reflections on teaching, literacy, and positioning in service relationships. *Journal of Adolescent and Adult Literacy* 46(4): 288.

Clarkson, P. (1995). Counseling psychology in Britain: The next decade. *Counseling Psychology Quarterly* 8: 197–204.

Clements, D. H. (1995). Teaching creativity with computers. *Educational Psychology Review* 7: 141–61.

Cole, H. P., and Sarnoff, D. (1980). Creativity and counseling. *Personnel and Guidance Journal* 59: 140–46.

Coletta, A. (1991). *What's best for kids.* Rosemont, NJ: Modern Learning Press.

Corbin, L., and McCarthy, M. (2003). The power of service-learning. *Principal* 82(3): 52–54.

Cowan, W. M. (1979). The development of the brain. *Scientific American* 241(3): 106–17.

Cropley, A. J. (1999a). Creativity and cognition: Producing effective novelty. *Roeper Review* 21: 253–60.

———. (1999b). Definitions of creativity. In M. A. Runco and S. Pritzker (Eds.), *Encyclopedia of creativity*, Vol. 1. San Diego, CA: Academic Press, 511–24.

Cunat, M. (1996). Vision, vitality, and values: Advocating the democratic classroom. In Landon Beyer (Ed.), *Creating democratic classrooms.* New York: Teachers College Press, 127–49.

Cunningham, C. (2003). Engaging the community to support student achievement. Champaign, IL: Eric Digest.

Cunningham, D. (1999). Personal communication regarding educational psychology. For further information, contact D. Cunningham, Indiana University School of Education, 201 North Rose Avenue, Bloomington, Indiana 47405.

Dacey, J. S., and Lennon, K. H. (1998). Understanding creativity: The interplay of biological, psychological and social factors. San Francisco, CA: Jossey-Bass.

Daft, R. L. (1998). *Organization theory and design.* Cincinnati, OH: South-Western College Publishing.

D'Andrea, M. (1995). Addressing the developmental needs of urban, African American youth: A preventive intervention. *Journal of Multicultural Counseling and Development* 23: 57–64.

D'Arcangelo, M. (1998). The brains behind the brain. *Educational Leadership* 56: 20–25.

Daniels, D. H., and Perry, K. E. (Spring 2003). "Learner centered" according to children. *Theory into Practice* 42(2): 102–8.

Davis, C. B. (1989). The use of art therapy and group process with grieving children. *Issues in Comprehensive Pediatric Nursing* 12: 269–80.

Davis, F., and Scott, J. (2001). Service-learning—Through the eyes of a student. *The Agricultural Education Magazine* 74(1): 8–9.

Davis, G. A. (1999). *Creativity is forever.* 4th rev. ed. Dubuque, IA: Kendall/Hunt.

Davis, G. A., and Subkoviak, M. J. (1978). Multidimensional analysis of a personality-based test of creative potential. *Journal of Educational Measurement* 12: 37–43.

Delisle, R. (1997). *How to use problem-based learning in the classroom.* Alexandria, VA: Association for Supervision and Curriculum Development.

Diamond, M. C. (1988). Enriching heredity: The impact of the environment on the anatomy of the brain. New York: Free Press.

Diamond, M. C., and Hopson, J. (1999). *Magic trees of the mind.* New York: Plume.

Dickerson, A. (1998). Service-learning finds its way into schools. *The Atlanta Constitution*, April 11, 1998, p. 7JQ.

Diehle, M., and Stroebe, W. (1986). Productivity loss in brainstorming: Toward the solution of a riddle. *Journal of Personality and Social Psychology* 53: 497–509.

Dodd, A. W., and Konzal, J. L. (2002). *How communities build stronger schools.* New York: Palgrave Macmillan.

Dods, R. F. (1997). An action research study of the effectiveness of problem-based learning in promoting the acquisition and retention of knowledge. *Journal for the Education of the Gifted* 20: 423–37.

Dollinger S. J., Robinson, N. M., and Ross, V. J. (1999). Photographic individuality, breadth of perspective, and creativity. *Journal of Personality* 67: 623–44.

Domino, G. (1970). Identification of potentially creative persons from the Adjective Check List. *Journal of Consulting and Clinical Psychology* 35: 48–51.

Donald, M. (1991). Origins of the modern mind: Three stages in the evolution of culture and cognition. Cambridge, MA: Harvard Press.

Dozier, R. (1992). Codes of evolution: The synaptic language revealing the secrets of matter, life, and thought. New York: Crown.

Duncan, T. K., Kemple, K. M., and Smith, T. M. (Summer 2000). Reinforcement in developmentally appropriate early childhood classrooms. *Childhood Education* 76(4): 194–203.

Dunn, L., Beach, S., and Kontos, S. (1994). Quality of the literacy environment: Day care and children's development. *Journal of Research in Childhood Education* 9(1): 24–34.

Dunn, L., and Kontos, S. (1997). Developmentally appropriate practice: What does research tell us? *ERIC Digest* ED413106, 8–11.

Edelman, G. (1988). Topobiology: An introduction to molecular embryology. New York: Basic Books.

———. (1989). The remembered present: A biological theory of consciousness. New York: Basic Books.

Education Commission of the States. (1999). *Service learning: Every child a citizen.* Education Commission of the States Issue Paper, 1–11.

Emmons, C. L. (1993). Classroom practices used with gifted third and fourth grade students. *Journal for the Education of the Gifted* 16: 103–19.

Engelmann, S. E., and Carnine, D. W. (1982). *Cognitive learning: A direct instruction perspective.* Chicago, IL: Science Research Associates.

Falk, B. (2002). Standards-based reforms: Problems and possibilities. *Phi Delta Kappan* 83(8): 612–21.

Finke, R. A., Ward, T. B., and Smith, S. M. (1992). *Creative cognition: Theory, research, and applications.* Cambridge, MA: MIT Press.

Fisher, K. W., and Rose, S. P. (1998). Growth cycles of brain and mind. *Adolescent Learning* 10: 56–60.

Fishback, S. J. (1998/1999). Learning and the brain. *Adult Learning* 10(2): 18–22.

Flores, B. (Ed.). (2000). Theme cycles. *Primary Voices K–6* 2(1): 11–14.

Fontenot, N. A. (1993). Effects of training in creativity and creative problem finding upon business people. *The Journal of Social Psychology* 133: 11–22.

Fogarty, R. (1999). Architects of the intellects. *Educational Leadership* 57(3): 76–78.

Frede, E., and Barnett, W. (1992). *Developmentally appropriate public school preschool: A study.* Boston, MA: Allyn and Bacon.

Fredericks, L. (2001). *Service learning and standards tool kit.* Washington, D.C.: Department of Education.

Frey, D. H. (1975). The anatomy of an idea: Creativity in counseling. *Personnel and Guidance Journal* 54: 22–27.

Friedland, S. (2003). Developing hearts and minds. *Principal Leadership* 3(8): 70–73.

Friedberg, R. D. (1996). Cognitive-behavioral games and workbooks: Tips for school counselors. *Elementary School Guidance and Counseling* 31: 11–20.

Furco, A. (1996). Service-learning: A balanced approach to experiential education. In Barbara Taylor (Ed.), *Expanding boundaries: Serving and learning.* Washington, D.C.: Corporation for National Service.

Furco, A., and Billig, S. H. (2002). *Service-learning—The essence of pedagogy.* Greenwich, CN: Information Age Publishing.

Furman, A. (1998). Teacher and pupil characteristics in the perception of the creativity of classroom climate. *Journal of Creative Behavior* 32: 258–77.

Gamberg, R. (2003). Learning and loving it: Theme studies in the classroom. Portsmouth, NH: Heinemann.

Gandal, M. (2001). Standards: Here today, here tomorrow. *Educational Leadership* 59(1): 6–13.

Gardner, H. (1993). *Creating minds.* New York: Basic Books.

Gbekobou, K. N. (1984). Counseling African children in the United States. *Elementary School Guidance and Counseling* 18: 225–30.

Gelatt, H. B. (1995). Chaos and compassion. *Counseling and Values* 39: 108–16.

Glenn, S. H., and Brock, M. L. (1998). *7 Strategies for Developing Capable Students.* Rocklin, MA: Prima Publishing.

Goertz, M. E. (2002). Redefining government roles in an era of standards-based reform. *Phi Delta Kappan* 83(1): 62–66.

Godwin, D. (2002). Will they heed the call to service? A different look at the service-learning question. *Educational Horizons* 81(1): 16–17.

Goos, M., and Moni, K. (2001). Modeling professional practice: A collaborative approach to developing criteria and standards-based assessment in pre-service teacher education courses. *Assessment and Evaluation in Higher Education* 26(1): 73.

Gottleib, G. (1974). *Aspects of neurogenesis.* New York: Academic Press.

———. (1976). Conceptions of prenatal development: Behavioral embryology. *Psychological Review* 83: 215–34.

Green, E. (1962). The utilization of creative potential in our society. *Journal of Counseling Psychology* 9: 79–83.

Green, R. R. (1989). Unmotivated youth can succeed. *School Administrator* 46(1): 13–16.

Greenleaf, R. K. (2003). Motion and emotion. *Principal Leadership* 3(9): 14–19.

Guilford, J. P. (1950). Creativity. *American Psychologist* 5: 444–54.

Hadderman, M. (2003). Standards: The policy environment. *Teacher Librarian* 30(4): 63–65.

Hall, R. H. (1999). *Organizations: Structures, processes, and outcomes.* 8th ed. Upper Saddle River, NJ: Prentice Hall.

Halpern, D. F. (1996). *Thought and knowledge: An introduction to critical thinking.* 3rd ed. Mahwah, NJ: Lawrence Erlbaum Associates.

Halsted, A. L., and Schine, J. C. (1994). Service-learning: The promise and the risk. *New England Journal of Public Policy* 10(1): 251–57.

Haupt, J. H., and Ostlund, M. F. (2002). Informing parents, administrators, and teachers about developmentally appropriate practices. In C. H. Burts,

R. Charlesworth, and C. H. Hart (Eds.), *Integrated Curriculum and Developmentally Appropriate Practice: Birth to Age Eight.* 1st ed. (pp. 189–211). Albany, NY: State University of New York Press.

Hebb, D. O. (1949). The organization of behavior: A neuropsychological theory. New York: John Wiley & Sons.

Hennessey, B. A., and Amabile, T. M. (1988). The conditions of creativity. In R. J. Sternberg (Ed.), *The nature of creativity: Contemporary psychological perspectives.* New York: Cambridge University Press, 11–38.

Heppner, M. J., O'Brien, K. M., Hinkelman, J. M., and Humphrey, C. F. (1994). Shifting the paradigm: The use of creativity in career counseling. *Journal of Career Development* 21(2): 77–86.

Heppner, P. P., Fitzgerald, K., and Jones, C. A. (1989). Examining counselors' creative processes in counseling. In J. A. Glover, R. R. Ronning, and C. R. Reynolds (Eds.), *Handbook of creativity. Perspectives on individual differences.* (pp. 259–73). New York: Plenum Press.

Hebert, E. (2001). How does a child understand a standard? *Educational Leadership* 59(1): 71–73.

Herman, J., Aschbacher, P., and Winters, L. (1992). *A practical guide to alternative assessment.* Alexandria, VA: Association for Supervision and Curriculum Development.

Hershman, D. J., and Lieb, J. (1998). *Manic depression and creativity.* Amherst, NY: Prometheus Books.

Hirsh-Pasek, K., Hyson, M, and Rescorla, L. (1990). Academic environments in preschool: Do they pressure or challenge young children? *Early Education and Development* 1: 401–23.

Hoot, J. L., Parmar, R. S., Jujala-Huttunen, E., Cao, Q., and Chacon, A. M. (Spring/Summer 1996). Cross-national perspectives on developmentally appropriate practices for early childhood. *Journal of Research in Childhood Education* 10: 160–69.

Horne, K. (2002). Creating a lifeline for service-learning in a budget storm. *Talk it up: Advocating for service-learning.* 2nd ed. Washington D.C.: National Service-Learning Partnership.

Houts, P. S., Nezu, A. M., Nezu, C. M., and Bucher, J. A. (1996). The prepared family caregiver: A problem-solving approach to family caregiver education. *Patient Education and Counseling* 27: 63–73.

Humphreys, A., Post, T., and Ellis, A. (1981). *Interdisciplinary methods: A thematic approach.* Santa Monica, CA: Goodyear Publishing Company.

Hyson, M., Hirsh-Pasek, K., and Rescorla, L. (1990). The classroom practices inventory: An observation instrument based on NAEYC's guidelines for appropriate practices for 4- and 5-year-old children. *Early Childhood Research Quarterly* 5(4): 475–94.

Indiana's Academic Standards. Indiana Department of Education, at www .indianastandards.org [retrieved August 8, 2003].

Innamorato, G. (1998). Creativity in the development of scientific giftedness: Educational implications. *Roeper Review* 21: 54–59.

Inskip, L. (1998). Service-learning gets a welcome boost from Minnesotans. *Star Tribune*, November 16, 13A.

Isaksen, S. G. (1987). Introduction: An orientation to the frontiers of creativity research. In S. G Isaksen (Ed.), *Frontiers of creativity research*. Buffalo, NY: Bearly Limited, 1–26.

Jacobs, H. (2002). Interdisciplinary learning in your classroom. Disney learning partnership workshop, at www.thirteen.org/edonline/concept2class/ month10/index.html. Accessed August 1, 2003.

Jackson, L. (1998). Connecting communities through service-learning: Linking learning with life. Report No. CE 078 655. South Carolina: Department of Education. (ERIC Document Reproduction Service No. ED 182 465).

Jambunathan, S., Burts, D. C., and Pierce, S. H. (1999). Developmentally appropriate practices as predictors of self-competence among preschoolers. *Journal of Research in Childhood Education* 13(2): 167–74.

Jones, B., Malone, D., and Stallings, D. T. (2002). Perspective transformation: Effects of service-learning tutoring experiences on prospective teachers. *Teacher Education Quarterly* 29(1): 61–81.

Jones, I., and Gullo, D. F. (1999). Differential social and academic effects of developmentally appropriate practices and beliefs. *Journal of Research in Childhood Education* 14(1): 26–35.

Jones, J. M., and Block, C. B. (1984). Black cultural perspectives. *Clinical Psychologist* 37(2): 58–62.

Jurcova, M. (1998). Humor and creativity: Possibilities and problems in studying humor. *Studia Psychologica* 40: 312–16.

Kagan, J. (1985). The emergence of self. *Journal of Child Psychology and Psychiatry and Allied Disciplines* 23(4): 363–81.

Kantrowitz, B., and Wingert, P. (1992). How kids learn. *Young Children* 2(3): 193–202.

Kappel, T. A., and Rubenstein, A. H. (1999). Creativity in design: The contribution of information. *IEEE Transactions on Engineering Management* 46: 132–43.

Kauffman, D., Johnson, S. M., Kardos, S. M., Liu, E., and Peske, H. G. (2002). Lost at sea: New teachers' experiences with curriculum and assessment. *The Teachers College Record* 104(2): 273–300.

Kendall, J., and Marzano, R. (1998). Awash in a sea of standards, at www. mcrel.org/topics/productDetail.asp?topicsID=14andproductID=120 [retrieved August 8, 2003].

Kendall, P. C., Chu, B., Gifford, A., Hayes, C., and Nauta, M. (1998). Breathing life into a manual: Flexibility and creativity with manual-based treatments. *Cognitive and Behavioral Practice* 5: 177–98.

Kielsmeier, J. (2000). A time to serve, A time to learn. Service-learning and the promise of democracy. *Phi Delta Kappan* 81(9): 652–57.

King, B. J., and Pope, B. (1999). Creativity as a factor in psychological assessment and healthy psychological functioning. *Journal of Personality Assessment* 72: 200–7.

King, S. C. (1998). Creativity and problem solving: The challenge for HRD professionals. *Human Resource Development Quarterly* 9: 187–91.

Kinsbourne, M. (1982). Hemispheric specialization and the growth of human understanding. *American Psychologist* 37(4): 411–20.

Klaras, V., and Mowsesian, R. (1970). Releasing creativity in the child: A goal for the creative counselor. *Elementary School Guidance and Counseling* 4: 273–80.

Kluth, P., and Straut, D. (2001). Standards for diverse learners. *Educational Leadership* 59(1): 43–46.

Koblas, Z. (1983). Responsibility and freedom: It works in our school. In M. Hepburn (Ed.), *Democratic Education in Schools and Classrooms.* Washington, D.C.: National Council for the Social Studies, 31–49.

Kochhar, S. (2003). Problem-based learning makes the grade. *Student British Medical Journal* 11: 137.

Koestner, R., Walker, M., and Fichman, L. (1999). Childhood parenting experiences and adult creativity. *Journal of Research in Personality* 33: 92–107.

Kohn, A. (2000). The case against standardized testing: Raising the scores, ruining the schools. Portsmouth, NH: Heinemann.

Kosslyn, S., and Koenig, O. (1992). *The wet mind: The new cognitive neuroscience.* New York: Free Press.

Kostelnik, M. J., Soderman, A. K., and Whiren, A. P. (1993). *Developmentally appropriate programs in early childhood education.* New York: Macmillan Publishing Company.

Kovac, T. (1998). Creativity and prosocial behavior. *Studia Psychologica* 40: 326–30.

Kuffner, T. (1999). *The toddler's busy book.* Minnetonka, MN: Meadowbrook.

Kurtzberg, T. R. (1998). Creative thinking, cognitive aptitude and integrative joint gain: A study of negotiator creativity. *Creativity Research Journal* 11: 283–93.

Laguardia, A., Brink, B., Wheeler, M., Grisham, D., and Peck, C. (2002). From agents to objects: The lived experience of school reform. *Child Study Journal* 32(1): 1–17.

Languis, M. L. (1998). Using knowledge of the brain in educational practice. *NAASP Bulletin* 82: 38–47.

Lankard, B. A. (1996). Acquiring self-knowledge for career development. *ERIC Digest No. 175*, at www.cete.org/acve/docgen.asp?tbl=digests&ID=28 [retrieved January 16, 2004].

Lantieri, L. (1999). Hooked on altruism: Developing social responsibility in unmotivated youth. *Journal of Emotional and Behavioral Problems* 8(2): 83–87.

The latest on how the brain works. (1997). *NEA Today* 15(8): 17–18.

Larrivee, B. (2002). The potential perils of praise in a democratic interactive classroom. *Action in Teacher Education* 23(4): 77–88.

Lawton, E. (1994). Integrating curriculum: A slow but positive process. *Schools in the Middle* 4(2): 27–30.

Learning in Deed. (2003). *Learning in deed.* Ohio: Report from the National Commission on Service-Learning.

Learning through service. (1998). *Sacramento Bee,* B4.

Lee, L. (1997). *Civic literacy, service-learning, and community renewal.* Report No. EDO-JC-97–4. Los Angeles: ERIC Clearinghouse for Community Colleges.

Lehman, H. C. (1953). *Age and achievement.* Princeton, NJ: Princeton University Press.

Lett, W. R. (1987). A conundrum: Counseling and creativity. *Australian Psychologist* 22: 29–41.

Levin, B. R. (Ed.). (2001). *Energizing teacher education and professional development with problem-based learning.* Alexandria, VA: Association for Supervision and Curriculum Development.

Lipson, M., Valencia, S., Wixson, K., and Peters, C. (1993). Integration and thematic teaching: Integration to improve teaching and learning. *Language Arts* 70(4): 252–63.

Livingston, J. A. (1999). Something old and something new: Love, creativity and the enduring relationship. *Bulletin of the Menninger Clinic* 63: 40–52.

Lock, R., and Prigge, D. (2002). Promote brain-based learning and teaching. *Intervention in School and Clinic* 37(4): 237–41.

Lowery, L. (1998). Curriculums reflect brain research. *Educational Leadership* 47: 21–24.

Lubeck, S. (1998). Is developmentally appropriate practice for everyone? *Childhood Education* 74(5) (annual theme issue): 283–92.

Ludwig, A. M. (1996). *The price of greatness: Resolving the creativity and madness controversy.* New York: The Guilford Press.

MacKinnon, D. W. (Ed.). (1961). *The creative person*. Berkeley, CA: University of California Institute of Personality Assessment and Research.

Making the grade: Teacher's attitudes toward academic standards and state testing. (2003). *Education Week,* at www.edweek.org/sreports/qc01/pdfs/qcresearch.pdf. Accessed August 1, 2003.

Malekoff, A. (1987). The preadolescent prerogative: Creative blends of discussion and activity in group treatment. *Social Work with Groups* 10(4): 61–81.

Manning, M., Manning, G., and Long, R. (1994). Theme immersion: Inquiry-based curriculum in elementary and middle schools. Portsmouth, NH: Heinemann.

Marzano, R., and Kendall, J. (1996). A comprehensive guide to designing standards-based districts, schools, and classrooms. *Mid-Continent Regional Education Lab* 293.

Marcon, R. (1992). Differential effects of three preschool models on inner-city 4-year olds. *Early Childhood Research Quarterly* 7(4): 517–30.

———. (1994). Doing the right thing: Linking research and policy reform in the District of Columbia public schools. *Young Children* 50(1): 8–20.

McDermott, C. (1999). *Beyond the silence*. Portsmouth, NH: Heinemann.

McMullen, M. B. (1999). Characteristics of teachers who talk the DAP talk and walk the DAP walk. *Journal of Research in Childhood Education* 13(2): 216–30.

McNergney, R. (1999). Teaching democracy through cases. In Edward Ducharme (Ed.), *Educating for Democracy*. New Jersey: Laverne Erlbaum Association Publishing, 3–13.

Meisels, S. J., Stetson, C., and Marsden, D. B. (2000). *Winning ways to learn: 600 great ideas for children*. New York: Goodard Press, Inc.

Melchior, A. (2001). Evaluating service-learning programs. Center for Youth and Communities. Denver, CO: Brandeis University Press.

Meoli, P. (2001). Family stories night: Celebrating culture and community. *Reading Teacher* 54(8): 746–47.

Mertler, C. A. (2003). *Classroom assessment*. Los Angeles: Pyrczak Publishing.

Meyers, S. (1999). Service-learning in alternative education settings. *Clearing House* 73(2): 114–18.

Moore, K. B. (2000). Assessing children's learning and development. *Scholastic Early Childhood Today* 14(4): 14–15.

Moores, S. (1999). New attitude: Linking kids to the larger community can turn lives around. *Northwest Education* 4(3): 34–39.

Morales, R. (2000). Effects of teacher preparation experiences and students' perceptions related to developmentally and culturally appropriate practices. *Action in Teacher Education* 22(2): 67–75.

Morgan, W. (1998). *Evaluation of school-based service learning in Indiana, 1997–1998.* Report summary prepared for the Indiana Department of Education. Bloomington: Indiana University Press.

Murphy, G. B., Trailer, J. W., and Hill, R. C. (1996). Measuring performance in entrepreneurship research. *Journal of Business Research* 36: 15–23.

Nancrede, S. F. (1998, January 14). Students learn by feeding homeless. *The Indianapolis Star*, B3.

Nave, B. (2000). A lapse in standards: Linking standards-based reform with student achievement. *Phi Delta Kappan* 82(2): 128–32.

Neihart, M. (1998). Creativity, the arts, and madness. *Roeper Review* 21: 47–50.

Neugarten, B. L. (1976). The psychology of aging: An overview. *Catalog of Selected Documents in Psychology* 6(9): 7.

Neuman, S. B., Copple, C., and Bredekamp, S. (2001). Assessing young children's literacy development. *Scholastic Early Childhood Today* 15(4): 12–14.

Newmann, F. M., and Rutter, R. A. (1983). *The effects of high school community service programs on students' social development.* Report No. NIE-G-81-009. Madison, WI: Wisconsin Center for Education Research: National Institute of Education.

———. (1985–1986). A profile of high school community service programs. *Educational Leadership* 43(4): 65–71.

Newmann, F. M., and Wehlage, G. G. (1993, April). Five standards of authentic instruction. *Educational Leadership* 50(7): 8–12.

Ngeow, K., and Kong, Y. (2001). Learning to learn: preparing teachers and students for problem-based learning. *ERIC Digest* (October): 163.

Nix, M. (2001). Service-learning. *The Earth Scientist* 18: 13–14.

Nix, M., and Slavkin, M. L. (2002). The effects of service-learning on at-risk students' self-esteem, self-efficacy, community ownership and curricular ownership. *National Society for Experiential Education Quarterly* 27(4): 1–15.

Noble, E. P., Runco, M. A., and Ozkaragoz, T. Z. (1993). Creativity in alcoholic and nonalcoholic families. *Alcohol* 10: 317–22.

Norlander, T. (1999). Inebriation and inspiration? A review of the research on alcohol and creativity. *Journal of Creative Behavior* 33: 22–44.

Nummela, R., and Caine, G. (1998). How to think about the brain. *Educational Leadership* 47: 25–28.

O'Bannon, F. (1999). Service-learning benefits our schools. *State Education Leader* 17(3): 1–2.

O'Brien, L. M. (1997). Turning my world upside down: How I learned to question developmentally appropriate practice. *Childhood Education* 73: 100–2.

———. (2000). Engaged pedagogy. *Childhood Education* 76(5) (annual theme issue): 283–88.

O'Flanagan, B. (1997). Building purpose through service. *Journal of Emotional and Behavioral Problems* 5(4): 223–25.

Ogbu, J. U., and Simmons, H. D. (1998). Voluntary and involuntary minorities: A cultural-ecological theory of school performance with some implications for education. *Anthropology and Education Quarterly* 29(2): 155–88.

Osborn, A. (1963). Applied imagination: Principles and procedures of creative problem-solving. 3rd ed. New York: Charles Scribner and Sons.

Page, R. (2002). *No child left behind.* Washington, D.C.: U.S. Department of Education.

Parkhurst, H. B. (1999). Confusion, lack of consensus, and the definition of creativity as a construct. *Journal of Creative Behavior* 33: 1–21.

Parikh, A., McReelis, K., and Hodges, B. (2001). Student feedback in problem-based learning: A survey of 103 final-year students across five Ontario medical schools. *Medical Education* 35: 632.

Parnes, S. J. (1962). Can creativity be increased? In S. J. Parnes and H. F. Harding (Eds.), *A source book for creative thinking.* New York: Scribner's Publishing, 185–91.

Parnell, D. (1996). Cerebral context. *Vocational Education Journal* 71(3): 18–22.

Perreault, G. (1997). Citizen leader: A community service option for college students. *NASPA Journal* 34: 147–56.

Perry, B. (2000). How the brain learns best. *Instructor* 110(4): 34–35.

Peterson, P. L. (1989). Teachers' knowledge of students' knowledge and cognitions in mathematics problem solving: Correlational case analyses. *Journal of Educational Psychology* 81(4): 558–69.

Plomin, R. (1990). The role of inheritance in behavior. *Science* 248(4952): 183–88.

Plomin, R., and McClearn, G. E. (1993). *Nature, nurture & psychology.* Washington, DC: American Psychological Association.

Plucker, J. A. (2000). Positive approaches to violence prevention: Peacebuilding in schools and communities. *NASSP Bulletin* 84(614): 1–4.

———. (1998). Beware of simple conclusions: The case for content generality of creativity. *Creativity Research Journal* 11: 179–82.

———. (1999). Reanalyzes of student responses to creativity checklists: Evidence of content generality. *Journal of Creative Behavior* 33: 126–37.

Plucker, J. A., and Beghetto, R. A. (In press). Why not be creative when we enhance creativity? In J. Borland and L. Wright (Eds.), *Current perspectives on giftedness and gifted education.* New York: Teachers College Press.

Plucker, J. A., and Dana, R. Q. (1998a). Alcohol, tobacco, and marijuana use: Relationships to undergraduate students' creative achievement. *Journal of College Student Development* 39: 472–81.

———. (1998b). Creativity of undergraduates with and without family history of alcohol and other drug problems. *Addictive Behaviors* 23: 711–14.

———. (1999). Drugs and creativity. In M. A. Runco and S. Pritzker (Eds.), *Encyclopedia of creativity*. Vol. 1. San Diego, CA: Academic Press, 607–11.

Plucker, J. A., and Runco, M. (1999). Creativity and deviance. In M. A. Runco and S. Pritzker (Eds.), *Encyclopedia of creativity*. Vol. 1. San Diego, CA: Academic Press, 541–45.

Plucker, J. A., and Slavkin, M. L. (2000). The climate of American schools. *NAASP Bulletin* 1: 44–49.

Poduska, K. (1996). To give my students wings. In Landon Beyer (Ed.), *Creating Democratic Classrooms*. New York: Teachers College Press, 106–26.

Powell, D. R. (1994). Parents, pluralism, and the NAEYC statement on developmentally appropriate practice. In B. L. Mallory and R. S. New (Eds.), *Diversity and Developmentally Appropriate Practices*. (pp. 60–67). New York: Teachers College Press.

Prigge, D. (2002). Twenty ways to promote brain-based teaching and learning. *Intervention in School and Clinic* 37(4): 237–41.

Pyryt, M. C. (1999). Effectiveness of training children's divergent thinking: A meta-analytic review. In A. S. Fishkin, B. Cramond, and P. Olszewski-Kubilius (Eds.), *Investigating creativity in youth: Research and methods*. Cresskill, NJ: Hampton Press, 351–65.

Quick, B. N. (1998). Beginning reading and developmentally appropriate practice (DAP): Past, present, and future. *Peabody Journal of Education* 73(3–4): 253–72.

Radz, M. (1983). The school society: Practical suggestions for promoting a democratic school climate. In Mary Hepburn (Ed.), *Democratic Education in Schools and Classrooms*. Washington, D.C.: National Council for the Social Studies, 67–89.

Reardon, M. (1998/1999). The Brain. *Adult Learning* 10(2): 10–17.

Retuned, K. (1999). Systems approach. In M. A. Runco and S. Pritzker (Eds.), *Encyclopedia of creativity*. Vol. 2. San Diego, CA: Academic Press, 605–9.

Reid, L. N., King, K. W., and DeLorme, D. E. (1998). Top-level agency creatives look at advertising creativity then and now. *Journal of Advertising* 27(2): 1–15.

Reis, S. M., and Renzulli, J. S. (1991). The assessment of creative products in programs for gifted and talented students. *Gifted Child Quarterly* 35: 128–34.

Renzulli, J. S. (1994). Schools for talent development: A practical plan for total school improvement. Mansfield Center, CT: Creative Learning Press.

Renzulli, J. S., and Reis, S. M. (1985). *The school wide enrichment model: A comprehensive plan for educational excellence.* Mansfield Center, CT: Creative Learning Press.

Resnick, L. B. (1987). Learning in school and out. *Educational Researcher* 16: 13–20.

Rhoades, R. (2000). Democratic citizenship and service-learning: Advancing the caring self. In M. B. Magdola (Ed.), Teaching to promote intellectual and personal maturity: Incorporating students' worldviews and identities into the learning process. San Francisco: Jossey-Bass Publishers, 37–45.

Ritter, N. (1999). Teaching interdisciplinary thematic units in language arts. *ERIC* Clearinghouse on Reading English and Communication, ED436003. Bloomington, IN.

Robinson, A. G., and Stern, S. (1997). Corporate creativity: How innovation and improvement actually happen. New York: Berrett-Koehler.

Roberts, J. (2002). Beyond learning by doing: The brain-compatible approach. *Journal of Experimental Education* 25(2): 281–85.

Roche, E. (1996). The bumpy ride to the democratic classroom. In Landon Beyer (Ed.), *Creating democratic classrooms.* New York: Teachers College Press, 27–40.

Rosenzweig, M. R., and Bennett, E. L. (1977). *Trends in research on neural mechanisms in processing and storage of information (a report prepared for the National Institute of Education).* Washington, DC: National Institute of Education.

———. (1996). Psychobiology of plasticity: Effects of training and experience on brain and behavior. *Behavioural Brain Research* 78(1): 57–65.

Runco, M. A., and Bahleda, M. D. (1986). Implicit theories of artistic, scientific, and everyday creativity. *Journal of Creative Behavior* 20: 93–98.

Runco, M. A., Johnson, D. J., and Bear, P. K. (1993). Parents' and teachers' implicit theories of children's creativity. *Child Study Journal* 23: 91–113.

Rutter, R. A., and Newmann, F. M. (1989). The potential of community service to enhance civic responsibility. *Social Education* 53(6): 371–74.

Russ, S. (1993). *Affect and creativity: The role of affect and play in the creative process.* Hillsdale, NJ: Erlbaum.

Russ, S. W. (1998). Play, creativity, and adaptive functioning: Implications for play interventions. *Journal of Clinical Child Psychology* 27: 469–80.

Sacks, P. (1999). Standardized minds: The high price of America's testing culture and what we can do to change it. Cambridge, MA: Perseus Books.

Sadler, F. H. (2003). The itinerant special education teacher in the early childhood classroom. *Teaching Exceptional Children* (January/February): 8.

Sandler, L., and Vandgrift, J. A. (1995). From desert to garden: Reconnecting disconnected youth. *Educational Leadership* 52(8): 14–17.

Saunders, J. (2003). Take your kids to the brain gym. *The Times Educational Supplement* (1891): 23.

Savery, J. R., and Duffy, T. M. (1995). Problem-based learning: An instructional model and its constructivist framework. *Educational Technology* 35(5): 31–38.

Scarr, S. Biological and cultural diversity: The legacy of Darwin for development. *Child Development* 64(5): 1333–53.

Scarr, S., and McCartney, K. (1983). How people make their own environments: A theory of genotype (leading to) environment effects. *Child Development* 54(2): 424–35.

Scarr, S., and Weinberg, R. A. (1977). The influence of "family background" on intellectual attainment. *American Sociological Review* 43(5): 674–92.

Schine, J. (1997). School-based service: Recommencing schools, communities, and youth at the margin. *Theory into Practice* 36(3): 170–75.

Schukar, R. (1997). Enhancing the middle school curriculum through service-learning. *Theory into Practice* 36(3): 176–83.

Schlechty, P. C. (2000). Shaking up the schoolhouse: How to support and sustain educational innovation. San Francisco, CA: Wiley Publishers.

Schubert, B. (1993). Literacy—What makes it real: Integrated, thematic teaching. *Social Studies Review* 32(2): 7–16.

Schumer, R., and Belbas, B. (1996). What we know about service-learning. *Education and Urban Society* 28(2): 208–23.

Scott, W. R. (1977). Effectiveness of organizational effectiveness studies: New perspectives on organizational effectiveness. San Francisco, CA: Jossey-Bass Publishers.

Seely, A. E. (1995). *Integrated thematic units.* Westminster, CA: Teacher Created Materials, Inc.

Segers, M., and Dochy, F. (2001). New assessment forms in problem-based learning: The value-added of the students' perspective. *Studies of Higher Education* 26: 307–29.

Shearin Karres, E. V. (2003). *How to empower your child's teacher, and your child, to excellence.* Kansas City, MO: Andrews McMeel Publishing.

Sheldon, K. M. (1995). Creativity and self-determination in personality. *Creativity Research Journal* 8: 23–36.

Shlien, J. M. (1956). Creativity and psychological health. *American Management Association, Personnel Series* (168): 12–21.

Simonton, D. K. (1999). Creativity from a historiometric perspective. In R. J. Sternberg (Ed.), *Handbook of creativity*. New York: Cambridge University Press, 116–33.

Singh, R. P. (1977). Education for creativity. *Indian Psychological Review* 14(2): 67–68.

Slavkin, M. L. (2002). The importance of brain functioning on cognition and teacher practice. *The Journal of Teaching and Learning* 6(1): 21–34.

———. (2003a). Brain science in the classroom. *Principal Leadership* 2(8): 21–28.

———. (2003b). Engaging the heart, hand, brain. *Principal Leadership (High School Ed.)* 3(9): 20–25.

Slavkin, M. L., and Faust, N. (2003). Meeting the requirements of standards-based accountability: Matching curriculum with service-learning to benefit the needs of at-risk students. *The Generator* (Spring): 1–11.

Smith, K. E., and Croom, L. (2000). Multidimensional self-concepts of children and teacher beliefs about developmentally appropriate practices. *Journal of Educational Research* 93(5): 312.

Smith, S. M., Ward, T. B., and Finke, R. A. (Eds.). (1995). *The creative cognition approach.* Cambridge, MA: MIT Press.

Solomon, P., and Geddes, L. (2001). A systematic process for content review in a problem-based learning curriculum. *Medical Teacher* 6: 556–60.

Sorensen, K. (1996). Creating a democratic classroom: Empowering students within and outside school walls. In Landon Beyer (Ed.), *Creating Democratic Classrooms*. New York: Teachers College Press, 87–105.

Sorenson, S. (1991). *Encouraging writing achievement: Writing across the curriculum.* Bloomington, IN: ERIC Clearinghouse on Reading and Communication Skills, ED327879.

Steptoe, A. (Ed.). (1998). *Genius and mind: Studies of creativity and temperament.* New York: Oxford University Press.

Sternberg, R. J. (1985). Implicit theories of intelligence, creativity, and wisdom. *Journal of Personality and Social Psychology* 49: 607–27.

———. (1988). A three-facet model of creativity. In R. J. Sternberg (Ed.), *The nature of creativity.* New York: Cambridge University Press, 125–47.

———. (1999). A propulsion model of types of creative contributions. *Review of General Psychology* 3: 83–100.

Sternberg, R. J., and Lubart, T. I. (1992). Buy low and sell high: An investment approach to creativity. *Current Directions in Psychological Science* 1: 1–5.

———. (1996). Investing in creativity. *American Psychologist* 51: 677–88.

———. (1999). The concept of creativity: Prospects and paradigms. In R. J. Sternberg (Ed.), *Handbook of creativity*. New York: Cambridge University Press, 3–15.

Stevens, G., and Burley, B. (1999). Creativity + business discipline = higher profits faster from new product development. *Journal of Product Innovation Management* 16: 455–68.

Stokes, P. D. (1999). Learned variability levels: Implications for creativity. *Creativity Research Journal* 12(1): 37–45.

Swick, K. J. (2001). Service-learning in teacher education: Building learning communities. *Service-Learning Clearing House* 74(5): 261–65.

Sylwester, R. (1994). What the biology of the brain tells us about learning. *Educational Leadership* 51: 46–52.

———. (1995). *A celebration of neurons: An educator's guide to the human brain.* Alexandria, VA: Association for Supervision and Curriculum Development.

Taylor, B. (2003). *Expanding boundaries: Serving and learning.* Washington, D.C.: Corporation for National Service.

Taylor, C. W. (1988). Various approaches to and definitions of creativity. In R. J. Sternberg (Ed.), *The nature of creativity.* New York: Cambridge University Press, 99–121.

Ted, A. L., and Schine, J. C. (1994). Service-learning: The promise and the risk. *New England Journal of Public Policy* 10(1): 251–57.

Terr, L. C. (1992). Mini-marathon groups: Psychological "first aid" following disasters. *Bulletin of the Menninger Clinic* 56: 76–86.

Tierney, P., Farmer, S. M., and Graen, G. B. (1999). An examination of leadership and employee creativity: The relevance of traits and relationships. *Personnel Psychology* 52: 591–620.

Tomlinson, C. A., and Kalbfleisch, M. L. (1998). Teach me, teach my brain: A call for differentiated classrooms. *Educational Leadership* 47: 52–55.

Toole, J. (2002). The teacher's perspective on adopting service-learning. *Talk it up: Advocating for service-learning.* 1st ed. Washington D.C.: National Service-Learning Partnership.

Torp, L., and Sage, S. (1997). *Problems as possibilities: Problem-based learning for K–12 education.* Alexandria, VA: Association for Supervision and Curriculum Development.

———. (1998). *Problem as possibilities: Problem-based learning for K–12 education.* Alexandria, VA: Association of Supervision and Curriculum Development, 14–15.

———. (2002). *Problems as possibilities: Problem-based learning for K–16 education.* Alexandria, VA: Association for Supervision and Curriculum Development.

Torrance, E. P. (1962). *Guiding creative talent.* Englewood Cliffs, NJ: Prentice-Hall.

———. (1968). A longitudinal examination of the fourth grade slump in creativity. *Gifted Child Quarterly* 12: 195–99.

———. (1972a). Can we teach children to think creatively? *The Journal of Creative Behavior* 6: 114–43.

———. (1972b). Career patterns and peak creative achievements of creative high school students 12 years later. *Gifted Child Quarterly* 16: 75–88

———. (1981). Predicting the creativity of elementary school children (1958–1980)—and the teacher who "made a difference." *Gifted Child Quarterly* 25: 55–62.

———. (1987). Recent trends in teaching children and adults to think creatively. In S. G. Isaksen (Ed.), *Frontiers of creativity research: Beyond the basics.* Buffalo, NY: Bearly Limited, 204–15.

Treffinger, D. J., Isaksen, S. G., and Dorval, B. K. (1996). Creative problem solving: An overview. In M. A. Runco (Ed.), *Problem finding, problem solving, and creativity.* Norwood, NJ: Ablex Publishing Corporation, 223–35.

Turner, L. (2003). Service-learning and student achievement. *Educational Horizons* 81(4): 188–89.

Tuyn, L. K. (1992). Solution-oriented therapy and Rogerian nursing science: An integrated approach. *Archives of Psychiatric Nursing* 6(2): 83–89.

Vars, G., and Beane, J. (2000). *Integrative curriculum in a standards-based world.* Champaign, IL: ERIC Clearinghouse on Elementary and Early Childhood Education, ED441618.

VanSickle, R. (1983). Practicing what we teach: Promoting democratic experiences in the classroom. In M. Hepburn (Ed.), *Democratic Education in Schools and Classrooms.* Washington, D.C.: National Council for the Social Studies, 49–67.

Viney, L. L. (1996). A personal construct model of crisis intervention counseling for adult clients. *Journal of Constructivist Psychology* 9(2): 109–26.

Waddell, C. (1998). Creativity and mental illness: Is there a link? *Canadian Journal of Psychiatry* 43: 166–72.

Wagmeister, J., and Shifrin, B. (2000). Thinking differently, learning differently. *Educational Leadership* 3 (November): 45–48.

Ward, T. B., Smith, S. M., and Vaid, J. (1997). *Creative thought: An investigation of conceptual structures and processes.* Washington, D.C.: American Psychological Association.

Waterman, A. (1997). *Service-learning: applications from the research.* Mahwah, NJ: Lawrence Erlbaum Associates Publishing.

Waterman, R., Akmajian, P., and Kearny, S. (1991). Community-oriented problem-based learning at the University of New Mexico. Albuquerque: University of New Mexico, School of Medicine.

Webb, S. B. (1995). A solution-oriented approach to conflict resolution in a work system. *British Journal of Guidance and Counseling* 23: 409–19.

Weber, E. (1998). Marks of brain-based assessment: A practical checklist. *National Association of Secondary School Principals Bulletin* 82(598): 63–73.

Weeks, D., and James, J. (1995). *Eccentrics: A study of sanity and strangeness.* New York: Villard.

Weiss, R. (2000). Brain-based learning. *Training and Development* 54(7): 20–24.

Westberg, K. L. (1996). The effects of teaching students how to invent. *Journal of Creative Behavior* 30: 249–67.

Westberg, K. L., Archambault, F. X., Jr., Dobyns, S. M., and Salvin, T. J. (1993). The classroom practices observation study. *Journal for the Education of the Gifted* 16: 120–46.

Williams, R. L. (1999). Operational definitions and assessment of higher-order cognitive constructs. *Educational Psychology Review* 11: 411–27.

Williams, W. M., and Yang, L. T. (1999). Organizational creativity. In R. J. Sternberg (Ed.), *Handbook of creativity.* New York: Cambridge University Press, 373–91.

Wolfe, P. (2001). *Brain matters: Translating research into classroom practice.* Alexandria, VA: Association for Supervision and Curriculum Development.

Wolfe, P., and Brandt, R. (1998). What do we know from brain research? *Educational Leadership* 56: 8–13.

Wolfgang, C. H., and Wolfgang, M. E. (1992). *School for Young Children: Developmentally Appropriate Practices.* Needham Heights, MA: Allyn and Bacon.

Wood, D. (2003). Problem-based learning. *British Medical Journal* 326 (February): 328–31.

Woodard, S. L. (1995). Counseling disruptive black elementary school boys. *Journal of Multicultural Counseling and Development* 23: 21–28.

Woolfolk, A. (1998). *Educational psychology.* New York: Allyn and Bacon.

Yamamoto, K. (1965). Research frontier: "Creativity": A blind man's report on the elephant. *Journal of Counseling Psychology* 12: 428.

Young, J. (2002). Mobilizing service-learning students as advocates. *Talk it up: Advocating for service-learning.* 3rd ed. Washington D.C.: National Service-Learning Partnership.

Yurtsever, G. (1998). Ethical beliefs and creativity. *Journal of Social Behavior and Personality* 13: 747–54.

Zelinger, J. (1990). Charting the creative process. *British Journal of Projective Psychology* 35: 78–96.

Zigler, E. F., Finn-Stevenson, M., and Hall, N. W. (2002). *The first three years and beyond.* New Haven, CT: Yale University Press.

Zvacek, S. M. (1999). What's my grade? Assessing learner progress. *Tech Trends* 43(5): 39–43.

Index

About the Author

Michael L. Slavkin is assistant professor of education at the University of Southern Indiana. He has worked as a teacher, counselor, mentor (and parent!) of children in elementary and middle school classrooms for over a decade. His interests in authentic practices and the empowerment of students stem from his intrinsic love of learning and desire to model dynamic teaching practices.